D1104035

WITHDRAWN

Bloom's Shakespeare Through the Ages

Bloom's Shakespeare Through the Ages

TWELFTH NIGHT

Edited and with an introduction by
Harold Bloom
Sterling Professor of the Humanities
Yale University

Volume Editor
Pamela Loos

BLOOM'S
LITERARY CRITICISM
An imprint of Infobase Publishing

Bloom's Shakespeare Through the Ages: Twelfth Night

Copyright © 2008 by Infobase Publishing

Introduction © 2008 by Harold Bloom

Bloom's Literary Criticism
An imprint of Infobase Publishing
132 West 31st Street
New York NY 10001

Library of Congress Cataloging-in-Publication Data
Twelfth night / edited and with an introduction / by Harold Bloom.
    p. cm. — (Bloom's Shakespeare through the ages)
  Includes bibliographical references and index.
  ISBN-13: 978-0-7910-9675-8 (hc : alk. paper) 1. Shakespeare, William, 1564–1616.
Twelfth night. 2. Comedy. I. Bloom, Harold.
  PR2837.T935 2008
  822.3'3—dc22   2007050852

Series design by Erika K. Arroyo
Cover design by Ben Peterson
Cover photo © The Granger Collection, New York

Printed in the United States of America

Bang EJB 10 9 8 7 6 5 4 3 2 1

This book is printed on acid-free paper.

CONTENTS

❧

SERIES INTRODUCTION

Shakespeare Through the Ages presents not the most current of Shakespeare criticism, but the best of Shakespeare criticism, from the seventeenth century to today. In the process, each volume also charts the flow over time of critical discussion of a particular play. Other useful and fascinating collections of historical Shakespearean criticism exist, but no collection that we know of contains such a range of commentary on each of Shakespeare's greatest plays and at the same time emphasizes the greatest critics in our literary tradition: from John Dryden in the seventeenth century, to Samuel Johnson in the eighteenth century, to William Hazlitt and Samuel Coleridge in the nineteenth century, to A.C. Bradley and William Empson in the twentieth century, to the most perceptive critics of our own day. This canon of Shakespearean criticism emphasizes aesthetic rather than political or social analysis.

Some of the pieces included here are full-length essays; others are excerpts designed to present a key point. Much (but not all) of the earliest criticism consists only of brief mentions of specific plays. In addition to the classics of criticism, some pieces of mainly historical importance have been included, often to provide background for important reactions from future critics.

These volumes are intended for students, particularly those just beginning their explorations of Shakespeare. We have therefore also included basic materials designed to provide a solid grounding in each play: a biography of Shakespeare, a synopsis of the play, a list of characters, and an explication of key passages. In addition, each selection of the criticism of a particular century begins with an introductory essay discussing the general nature of that century's commentary and the particular issues and controversies addressed by critics presented in the volume.

Shakespeare was "not of an age, but for all time," but much Shakespeare criticism is decidedly for its own age, of lasting importance only to the scholar who wrote it. Students today read the criticism most readily available to them, which means essays printed in recent books and journals, especially those journals made available on the Internet. Older criticism is too often buried in out-of-print books on forgotten shelves of libraries or in defunct periodicals. Therefore, many students, particularly younger students, have no way of knowing that some of the most profound criticism of Shakespeare's plays was written decades or centuries ago. We hope this series remedies that problem, and more importantly, we hope it infuses students with the enthusiasm of the critics in these volumes for the beauty and power of Shakespeare's plays.

INTRODUCTION BY
HAROLD BLOOM

In spite of my love for *As You Like It*, *Twelfth Night* is for me Shakespeare's masterpiece in relatively unmixed comedy. The maelstrom of the problem plays or dark comedies, *Measure for Measure* in particular, was yet to come, and the so-called Late Romances in fact are tragi-comedies, and include two transcendental masterpieces, *The Winter's Tale* and *The Tempest*. Yet all these are darker works than the madcap *Twelfth Night*, which exhilarates every audience and dazzles me endlessly.

Twelfth Night centers on the torment of Malvolio, who provokes so complex an ambivalence in us that I can conjure up no figure remotely like him in the entire tradition of Western literature. Shakespeare is perhaps never more unfathomable than in his creation of Malvolio, one of the most individual and memorable of all Shakespearean protagonists.

Technically, of course, it is not Malvolio's play but Viola's, and I myself think of it as Feste's play, because he is the most delightful of all Shakespearean fools or clowns. King Charles II wrote "Malvolio" upon the title-page of his copy of *Twelfth Night*, and the Stuart King of the Restoration was an accurate enthusiast for Shakespearean drama. For Charles, as for most of us, Malvolio usurps the play, though at destructive expense to his social self.

Charles Lamb, superb Romantic essayist and Bardolator, saw the tragi-comedy in Malvolio's erotic drive beyond the Pleasure Principle. I go a touch beyond Lamb: Malvolio's disaster is that he is in the wrong play. He would fit splendidly as a figure of outraged virtue in either of Ben Jonson's magnificent comedies: *The Alchemist* and *Volpone*. But Jonson has no persons; only ideograms. Malvolio is a good but limited soul totally dominated by an insane socio-erotic dream: "To be Count Malvolio!"

The increasingly obsessive Malvolio may have begun as a satire upon the fiercely moralizing Ben Jonson, who was at once Shakespeare's closest friend and also his most accomplished rival, at least in comedy. Yet the paradigm of surly Ben rapidly recedes, as Shakespeare's daemonic inventiveness elevates poor Malvolio into what might be termed the sado-comic Sublime. Victimage by socio-erotic daydreaming has never, before or since, been represented so savagely and yet hilariously.

Essentially poor Malvolio is destroyed by his own imagination. That scarcely seems stuff for comedy, and in the abstract would accommodate Hamlet or Macbeth better. Something cuts loose in the Shakespeare of *Twelfth Night*, though I think we have only limited terms for order that could describe the poet's letting go of some portion of his control.

It is difficult to keep in mind that Malvolio is only a minor character, who speaks perhaps a tenth of the play's lines. His depraved will assumes cosmological scope, and touches upon the universal. Who among us does not nurture a Malvolio within herself or himself? Erotic and social fantasies afflict all of us, at every age. If we shudder at Malvolio's social self-immolation it must be because he is the scapegoat for the enigma of our own guilty fictions.

Fortunately, we do not have a Maria to choreograph our debacle. The mystery of *Twelfth Night* may well be Shakespeare's enthusiasm for a practical joke so fearsome that the wretched Malvolio, at play's end, really would be better off dead. Shakespeare the thinker—as gifted as Shakespeare the creator of personality, of language, of wisdom—challenges our ethics and our moral psychology by compelling us to realize that what we enjoy is the guilty pleasure of a solipsism in which we haplessly say: "This cannot happen to me."

Biography of
William Shakespeare
✒

WILLIAM SHAKESPEARE was born in Stratford-on-Avon in April 1564 into a family of some prominence. His father, John Shakespeare, was a glover and merchant of leather goods who earned enough to marry Mary Arden, the daughter of his father's landlord, in 1557. John Shakespeare was a prominent citizen in Stratford, and at one point, he served as an alderman and bailiff.

Shakespeare presumably attended the Stratford grammar school, where he would have received an education in Latin, but he did not go on to either Oxford or Cambridge universities. Little is recorded about Shakespeare's early life; indeed, the first record of his life after his christening is of his marriage to Anne Hathaway in 1582 in the church at Temple Grafton, near Stratford. He would have been required to obtain a special license from the bishop as security that there was no impediment to the marriage. Peter Alexander states in his book *Shakespeare's Life and Art* that marriage at this time in England required neither a church nor a priest or, for that matter, even a document—only a declaration of the contracting parties in the presence of witnesses. Thus, it was customary, though not mandatory, to follow the marriage with a church ceremony.

Little is known about William and Anne Shakespeare's marriage. Their first child, Susanna, was born in May 1583 and twins, Hamnet and Judith, in 1585. Later on, Susanna married Dr. John Hall, but the younger daughter, Judith, remained unmarried. When Hamnet died in Stratford in 1596, the boy was only 11 years old.

We have no record of Shakespeare's activities for the seven years after the birth of his twins, but by 1592 he was in London working as an actor. He was also apparently well known as a playwright, for reference is made of him by his contemporary Robert Greene in *A Groatsworth of Wit*, as "an upstart crow."

Several companies of actors were in London at this time. Shakespeare may have had connection with one or more of them before 1592, but we have no record that tells us definitely. However, we do know of his long association with the most famous and successful troupe, the Lord Chamberlain's Men. (When James I came to the throne in 1603, after Elizabeth's death, the troupe's name changed to the King's Men.) In 1599 the Lord Chamberlain's Men provided the financial backing for the construction of their own theater, the Globe.

The Globe was begun by a carpenter named James Burbage and finished by his two sons, Cuthbert and Robert. To escape the jurisdiction of the Corporation of London, which was composed of conservative Puritans who opposed the theater's "licentiousness," James Burbage built the Globe just outside London, in the Liberty of Holywell, beside Finsbury Fields. This also meant that the Globe was safer from the threats that lurked in London's crowded streets, like plague and other diseases, as well as rioting mobs. When James Burbage died in 1597, his sons completed the Globe's construction. Shakespeare played a vital role, financially and otherwise, in the construction of the theater, which was finally occupied sometime before May 16, 1599.

Shakespeare not only acted with the Globe's company of actors; he was also a shareholder and eventually became the troupe's most important playwright. The company included London's most famous actors, who inspired the creation of some of Shakespeare's best-known characters, such as Hamlet and Lear, as well as his clowns and fools.

In his early years, however, Shakespeare did not confine himself to the theater. He also composed some mythological-erotic poetry, such as *Venus and Adonis* and *The Rape of Lucrece*, both of which were dedicated to the earl of Southampton. Shakespeare was successful enough that in 1597 he was able to purchase his own home in Stratford, which he called New Place. He could even call himself a gentleman, for his father had been granted a coat of arms.

By 1598 Shakespeare had written some of his most famous works, *Romeo and Juliet*, *The Comedy of Errors*, *A Midsummer Night's Dream*, *The Merchant of Venice*, *Two Gentlemen of Verona*, and *Love's Labour's Lost*, as well as his historical plays *Richard II*, *Richard III*, *Henry IV*, and *King John*. Somewhere around the turn of the century, Shakespeare wrote his romantic comedies *As You Like It*, *Twelfth Night*, and *Much Ado About Nothing*, as well as *Henry V*, the last of his history plays in the Prince Hal series. During the next 10 years he wrote his great tragedies, *Hamlet*, *Macbeth*, *Othello*, *King Lear*, and *Antony and Cleopatra*.

At this time, the theater was burgeoning in London; the public took an avid interest in drama, the audiences were large, the plays demonstrated an enormous range of subjects, and playwrights competed for approval. By 1613, however, the rising tide of Puritanism had changed the theater. With the desertion of the theaters by the middle classes, the acting companies were compelled to depend more on the aristocracy, which also meant that they now had to cater to a more sophisticated audience.

Perhaps this change in London's artistic atmosphere contributed to Shakespeare's reasons for leaving London after 1612. His retirement from the theater is sometimes thought to be evidence that his artistic skills were waning. During this time, however, he wrote *The Tempest* and *Henry VIII*. He also wrote the "tragicomedies," *Pericles, Cymbeline*, and *The Winter's Tale*. These were thought to be inspired by Shakespeare's personal problems and have sometimes been considered proof of his greatly diminished abilities.

However, so far as biographical facts indicate, the circumstances of his life at this time do not imply any personal problems. He was in good health and financially secure, and he enjoyed an excellent reputation. Indeed, although he was settled in Stratford at this time, he made frequent visits to London, enjoying and participating in events at the royal court, directing rehearsals, and attending to other business matters.

In addition to his brilliant and enormous contributions to the theater, Shakespeare remained a poetic genius throughout the years, publishing a renowned and critically acclaimed sonnet cycle in 1609 (most of the sonnets were written many years earlier). Shakespeare's contribution to this popular poetic genre are all the more amazing in his break with contemporary notions of subject matter. Shakespeare idealized the beauty of man as an object of praise and devotion (rather than the Petrarchan tradition of the idealized, unattainable woman). In the same spirit of breaking with tradition, Shakespeare also treated themes previously considered off limits—the dark, sexual side of a woman as opposed to the Petrarchan ideal of a chaste and remote love object. He also expanded the sonnet's emotional range, including such emotions as delight, pride, shame, disgust, sadness, and fear.

When Shakespeare died in 1616, no collected edition of his works had ever been published, although some of his plays had been printed in separate unauthorized editions. (Some of these were taken from his manuscripts, some from the actors' prompt books, and others were reconstructed from memory by actors or spectators.) In 1623 two members of the King's Men, John Hemings and Henry Condell, published a collection of all the plays they considered to be authentic, the First Folio.

Included in the First Folio is a poem by Shakespeare's contemporary Ben Jonson, an outstanding playwright and critic in his own right. Jonson paid tribute to Shakespeare's genius, proclaiming his superiority to what previously had been held as the models for literary excellence—the Greek and Latin writers. "Triumph, my Britain, thou hast one to show / To whom all scenes of Europe homage owe. / He was not of an age, but for all time!"

Jonson was the first to state what has been said so many times since. Having captured what is permanent and universal to all human beings at all times, Shakespeare's genius continues to inspire us—and the critical debate about his works never ceases.

SUMMARY OF
TWELFTH NIGHT
❧

Act I

The play opens in Duke Orsino's palace in Illyria, where we see the duke listening to musicians performing. He directs them to continue playing, since, he says, if music is the food of love, then he wants to be completely filled with it. The duke revels in his lovelorn state. About halfway through his speech, however, he calls for the music to stop, saying it is no longer as sweet as it had been, and we wonder what sort of lover he really would be if given the chance. When the duke's attendant Curio asks if he will go for a hunt, Orsino turns even that topic back to his being hopelessly pursued by his own desires. It is here that we discover the object of his love, the countess Olivia.

A few lines later, Valentine, a gentleman who attends the duke, enters and is asked by the duke what news he has from Olivia. Valentine explains that while he was not allowed to speak to the countess, her attendants informed him that Olivia has refused to see anyone for the next seven years, during which time she will be in mourning for her brother. She, like the duke, appears taken with emotion. While most would consider Olivia's plan excessive, the duke finds it laudable and goes off to lie among the flowers, consumed with his own thoughts of love.

Scene 2 takes place along the coast. A young woman named Viola, a sea captain, and sailors are here, having just survived a shipwreck. Viola asks where they are and wonders if her brother, Sebastian, could also have survived the shipwreck. The captain says he might have, since he did see Sebastian, courageous and hopeful, tie himself to a mast that was floating on the water.

The captain recognizes where they are since he was born nearby. He informs Viola of what he knows and tells her about the duke, who is wooing Olivia. The captain fills in some details—namely that Olivia had lost her father about a year earlier and was then cared for by her brother, who himself died soon after. Viola wishes she could be a servant to Olivia, but when the captain explains that Olivia will see no one, Viola decides she will instead disguise herself as a male, work for the duke, and see what happens.

5

In scene 3, we are inside Olivia's house. Sir Toby, Olivia's uncle, and Maria, Olivia's gentlewoman, are speaking. Just as the other characters did in the earlier two scenes, Toby and Maria are discussing Olivia. Toby cannot understand her new plan for mourning her brother. Maria makes no comment on this but instead warns Toby about his own behavior. Specifically, Maria says that Olivia is disturbed by his staying out so late at night. Toby does not want to take Maria seriously, but she will not be deterred and continues to warn him that he should behave reasonably.

Maria also says that she heard Olivia talking about the "foolish knight" Toby has convinced to come and woo the countess. Toby enumerates what he sees as the knight's strong points, yet Maria is not convinced and says that aside from being foolish, the knight is an argumentative coward who goes drinking nightly with Toby. Maria and Toby are interrupted in their conversation when the knight himself, Sir Andrew Aguecheek, arrives. He is readily confused and does not follow as Maria makes fun of him.

After Maria leaves, Andrew admits to Toby that he thinks "he has no more wit than a Christian or an ordinary man." Through this comment, Shakespeare gets a jab in at two groups simultaneously and tells his own audience that they'd better watch out before they look disparagingly upon this character. After all, Christians and ordinary men comprise the audience, too. Andrew announces that he will leave for home the next day, but Toby, eager to keep his moneyed drinking buddy around, encourages him to stay by saying Andrew still has a chance with the countess. Andrew agrees to stay for another month. He remarks on his skill at dancing, Toby encourages him, and they "set about some revels."

Scene 4 returns us to the duke's palace. Here we find Valentine speaking with Viola, who is disguised as a man and calls herself Cesario. Viola, as Cesario, has been serving the duke for only three days, but already the duke is enchanted by "him," Valentine says. The disguised Viola wonders why Valentine is intimating that either the duke will change his feelings toward Cesario, or Cesario will do something to prompt the duke to feel differently toward him. Viola asks if the duke is an inconstant person. Valentine says that he is not, but the commentary puts doubt in our minds, as it has in Viola's.

Duke Orsino and his attendants arrive. We see that the duke has quite a strong relationship with Viola (as Cesario), since he says he's revealed to his new servant even his "secret soul." He tells Cesario that he is to go to Olivia and not leave until he is allowed to see her. Curiously, Orsino speaks of Cesario as having to take "his" step there and as having feet that will not move until "he" is admitted, quite a contrast to the language at the end of the previous scene, in which Andrew and Toby spoke of lighthearted dancing. The duke explains that Cesario is to see Olivia and proclaim the duke's love for her. Despite protest from Viola (as Cesario), the duke says Cesario is well suited for the task, especially in light of "his" womanly traits. The duke gives no hint, though, that he suspects that Cesario could actually be female. Cesario agrees to do his best at the task and remarks in an aside that trouble may ensue because she is actually a female wooing a female.

Scene 5 takes place in Olivia's house. We have heard many talk of Olivia, but we have not yet seen her. As the scene unfolds, Shakespeare holds the audience in suspense about her even longer—for we are in Olivia's house, and characters at the house talk about her, but still she is not onstage. Instead, we see Maria with the clown Feste. We are reminded of Maria's earlier dialogue with Sir Toby, when she warned him that Olivia was angered by his drunkenness. Here Maria asks where the clown has been, since Olivia is mad about his disappearance, too. As in the earlier scene, Maria gets no serious response from the object of her questioning. The clown will not reveal where he's been and seems unconcerned that he is in serious trouble. Maria finally realizes she will get no true response from him, and when he starts to give what she expects is yet another coy answer, she speaks for him, making up her own joke. Feste is impressed and remarks that if Sir Toby were not such a drunkard, and Maria would make a good couple—a hint from Shakespeare about what may happen.

At long last, Olivia enters with her steward Malvolio and other attendants. The clown speaks to her first, a number of lines to put her in a good spirit and get himself out of trouble. Yet his tricks don't work; Olivia only tells the others to take him away. Not to be deterred, the clown twists her words and calls the men to take the lady away, as if this were the order she had just given. Olivia repeats two more times, in between the clown's banter, that he should be gone, yet the clown keeps trying to win her over.

Finally Feste gets her attention when he says he can prove her a fool. She wants to know how, so he asks her a series of questions. He asks why she is mourning and whether she believes her brother is in heaven or hell, and when she answers that she knows he is in heaven, the clown remarks that she is a fool for mourning such a fate. In pointing out her folly, he shows that Olivia is strong enough to take the criticism. Here she could call for her attendants to truly take the clown away, but instead she asks Malvolio what he thinks of Feste. Malvolio gives a strongly negative appraisal, Feste stands up for himself, Olivia urges Malvolio to continue, and Malvolio does, voicing his enmity even more. Olivia chastises Malvolio for being too self-involved and says he needs to see the world as less of a harmful, aggressive force against him.

Maria enters and announces that a young gentleman is at the gate asking to see Olivia. When Maria says Toby is detaining him, Olivia calls him a madman and sends Malvolio off to chase the young man away instead. Toby, half drunk, enters soon after. Olivia asks him about the man at the gate, but Toby has no real answers and leaves. Olivia shows her compassion by sending Feste to look after the inebriated Toby.

Malvolio enters and says the impudent young man at the gate will not leave. Olivia agrees to see him, first getting Maria to her side and covering her face with a veil. Again, Shakespeare has held us in suspense for quite some time before actually having Olivia and Cesario (the disguised Viola) meet. Viola (as Cesario) enters and is determined to know which of the women is the lady of the house. Olivia finally admits it is she, but, it takes some back-and-forth conversation before Olivia can get the supposed young man to reveal his message. Viola (as Cesario) asks that they be alone; Olivia agrees and sends away her attendants. Yet when she finds out that Orsino has sent this messenger, she wants to hear no more.

Viola (as Cesario) then tries another tack. She asks to see Olivia's face, and when Olivia shows it and comments on its attributes, Cesario agrees. Olivia politely says she is not interested in the duke, but Cesario charms her, describing how he would woo her if he loved her. Olivia, impressed, asks Cesario about his own parentage, and when he answers that he's a gentleman, Olivia is happy to hear it. Olivia sends Cesario back to the duke but says he can come again, for she is taken with him. She calls in Malvolio and directs him to chase after Cesario, to give him a ring that she claims he left with her, and to tell him to come again the next day, when she will tell him why she is not the one for the duke.

Act II

Scene 1 brings us back to the coast, where we meet two new characters—Sebastian, Viola's brother, and Antonio, a captain of the ship that was wrecked. The two have just come ashore. Antonio wants to follow wherever Sebastian plans to go, but Sebastian tells him not to, since he feels a dark cloud surrounds him. Sebastian also gives some family background, saying Antonio probably knows him, since his father was Sebastian of Messaline, "whom I know you have heard of." He does not explain why Antonio would have heard of this man, though. We can assume he might have been someone of stature (indicating that if Viola and the duke were to somehow get together by the end of the play, she might not be so far beneath his social status).

Sebastian also talks of his sister, Viola, who he assumes has drowned, and refers to her as a lady of beauty and intelligence. In this scene, then, we see his love for his sister, as well as the love between these two men who have made it ashore. Sebastian says he is going to Duke Orsino's palace and says goodbye to Antonio. Antonio follows him, however, even though he has many enemies at Orsino's.

Scene 2 is another short scene. As ordered by Olivia, Malvolio catches up to Cesario (the disguised Viola). Malvolio tells the supposed young man that he is annoyed that he has had to chase after him, since Malvolio believes what Olivia has told him—that Cesario wouldn't take back the ring that he had brought for Olivia. Malvolio relays Olivia's message that she wants nothing to do with the duke but that Cesario can return to let her know what Orsino thinks of this.

Viola (as Cesario) is surprised, of course, since she left no ring with Olivia. Malvolio throws the ring on the ground and exits, leaving Viola onstage alone. While Malvolio does not seem to wonder why Olivia would want Cesario to return, Viola does, especially in light of Olivia's made-up story about the ring. Viola thinks out loud about how Olivia acted when she visited, in disguise as Cesario. Olivia had looked closely at him/her and could hardly speak in a normal way. Viola realizes Olivia must really be taken with Cesario and says time will have to sort out the complications.

In scene 3, Sir Toby and Sir Andrew are carousing in Olivia's house late at night. They talk about the definition of *late*. After all, Toby points out, once it is after midnight the time is early rather than late. When Feste the clown enters, Toby calls for them all to sing but then decides the clown should sing alone since he is so good at it. The men request a love song. The lyrics of the song say love is about the present and no one should delay in partaking of it, since youth, too, is transitory. The three then join in song, but Maria enters and warns them that Malvolio will be on his way to throw them out.

Indeed, Malvolio enters shortly thereafter and berates them for having no consideration for others. But the men are not to be deterred; they continue to sing, and Toby lashes out at Malvolio for being so seemingly virtuous. Malvolio realizes he has no control over the men and so turns to Maria. He tells her she should not be supplying the men with liquor and that he will let Olivia know about this.

After Malvolio leaves, the men desire revenge, so Maria tells them about a plan she has devised that will work on Malvolio as he is so strait-laced, full of himself, and a flatterer. She explains that she is good at making her handwriting look like Olivia's and that she will write a letter. The men correctly guess that the letter will lead Malvolio to believe that the countess is in love with him. Maria leaves. The men comment on what a good woman she is, and Toby adds that she adores him. This reminds Andrew that the reason he has extended his visit is to further pursue the countess, and yet he seems to not be getting anywhere. Toby reassures him and tells him to send for more money; apparently a lot has been spent already for their carousing.

In scene 4, we are back at the duke's palace. Orsino asks for music to relieve the pain of his unrequited love. He talks to Cesario (the disguised Viola) and tells him that if he ever falls in love, he should think of the duke, who is a true lover. The duke remains obsessed with love and wants others, even in their own lives, to be reminded of his intense love. He asks the supposed young man if he has ever been in love, to which Cesario responds that he has—with someone who has a temperament like the duke's and is about the same age as the duke. Viola (as Cesario) is responding sincerely, since she herself already loves the duke, yet the duke remains convinced of her disguise and does not catch on to the subtext of her comments.

When the duke says that a young man should not be with an older woman, whereas a young woman should be with someone older than herself, Viola (as Cesario) readily agrees. Her loving someone older than herself follows the duke's advice, although he is unaware of it.

The duke's attendant Curio enters with Feste the clown, who can perform the song the duke has requested. Feste sings of a man killed because of his "fair cruel maid"; the narrator of the song requests that no friends attend to his coffin and that his lover never know where his grave is.

After the song, the duke tells Cesario (the disguised Viola) to again let the countess know how much he loves her—not for what she has but for her beauty. Viola (as Cesario) wonders what will happen if the countess still does not want him and asks the duke to imagine the situation if the roles were reversed and there was a woman who intensely loved him while he did not love her. The duke immediately discounts this scenario, saying no woman could love the way he does. Cesario persists and says his father actually had a daughter who loved a man greatly, just as if Cesario were a woman he would love the duke. The duke is intrigued by the story and asks to hear more. Cesario explains that the young woman never revealed her feelings to her lover; Cesario does not know what happened in the end. The duke, who still does not suspect that Cesario is a woman, sends him off again to woo the countess.

In scene 5, Toby, Andrew, and Fabian, one of the countess's servants, are together in Olivia's garden. Maria arrives with the letter that will trick Malvolio. She tells the others to hide, since Malvolio is coming, and she throws the letter into his path. Malvolio, though, does not immediately see the letter but talks to himself about the very possibility that Olivia does truly like him and has a natural attraction to his disposition. As Malvolio speaks, we hear comments from those who are in hiding—mostly reactions of disgust to Malvolio's imagined superiority over the others.

Malvolio imagines aloud what his life would be like married to Olivia. He would dress in his velvet robe, call his many officers, and leave Olivia asleep while taking care of Sir Toby. He would tell Toby he must no longer be a drunkard and ask him why he spends so much time with Andrew. The hiding men are, of course, outraged upon hearing Malvolio mention them specifically.

After all of this, Malvolio sees the letter Maria has written. He picks it up and immediately assumes it is from Olivia, just as Maria had planned. He reads it in sections, giving his reaction after each. The letter writer starts by saying she is in love with someone but only provides certain letters, not the person's whole name. Those hiding in the bushes are gleeful that Malvolio is falling for the trap, and again we hear their thoughts as he ponders over the letter. Malvolio decides that, since all the letters mentioned in the note are in his name, the writer must be referring to him.

Malvolio continues reading the letter. It suggests what the lover should do. Since he is truly a great man, the letter writer says, the lover should act as if he is above others and be hostile. The letter also reminds him of her positive comments about his yellow stockings and cross-gartering. Malvolio is ecstatic. He plans to do all the letter says. Shakespeare throws in another surprise, for the letter is not finished: It says that the lover should smile, and again Malvolio is happy to do so.

Malvolio exits, and the others come out of hiding, gratified that he has so thoroughly fallen for the trick. They are impressed by Maria's craftiness; both Toby and Andrew say they could marry Maria. She enters and they praise her. Maria explains that the countess actually detests yellow stockings, cross-gartering, and, now, smiling, since she is in mourning for her brother. This makes the trick even better; they cannot wait to see how Malvolio appears and behaves the next time he is with the countess.

Act III

The act opens in Olivia's garden, where Viola (as Cesario) approaches Feste. Each character tries to use words to show his wit. For the most part, Feste twists the meaning of Cesario's words. Eventually he bluntly says he does not care for Cesario. Still Cesario speaks with him, until finally he has had enough and tips the clown. Feste says he will alert Olivia that Cesario has arrived. After he exits, Viola (as Cesario) comments on how a good fool like Feste must also be quite wise and observant.

Toby and Andrew appear and greet Cesario and tell him Olivia would like to see him. Although Viola (as Cesario) has shown herself to be a master of words, here she does not understand one of Toby's instructions, just as she was put off balance while speaking to Feste earlier. Similarly, when she arrived at Olivia's for the first time and refused to leave the gate, she had an unsettling exchange with Malvolio, who saw her as petulant. It is as though outsiders are unable to mix well in the world of the countess and her fellow inhabitants.

Olivia arrives with Maria but agrees when Cesario says he and Olivia should be alone. Cesario announces he is there on the duke's behalf, yet Olivia insists she wants to hear nothing of this and then directly refers to her trick of sending Malvolio after Cesario as if the supposed young man had left Olivia a ring. She asks Cesario to respond to this, and Cesario says he pities her. Olivia tries to see this in some positive way; she realizes her pursuit is nearly fruitless, but before Cesario goes, Olivia tells him how intensely passionate she is for him. Even though Cesario says he cannot give his heart to Olivia and that he will not come again on behalf of his master, Olivia still implores the supposed young man to return.

Scene 2 is set inside Olivia's house. Andrew announces to Toby and Fabian that he can stay no longer, since Olivia has never treated him the way he saw her treat Orsino's servant Cesario. Fabian and Toby try to persuade him to stay. Fabian claims Olivia acted as she did because she saw Andrew watching her and wants him to lose his passivity. He either must develop some trick or show his valor in order to win her over. Andrew, aware that he lacks intelligence, says he will have to use his valor since he is not good at tricks. Toby encourages Andrew to write a note to Cesario, challenging him to a duel.

Andrew heads off to do so, and Toby admits to Fabian that he has spent much of Andrew's money. Fabian and Toby both agree that Andrew and Cesario could ever really fight each other, since it is against their natures. Maria enters and tells the men that Malvolio is a laughingstock, dressed just as the phony letter instructed. The three rush off to see how Olivia will respond when she sees him.

In scene 3, we are on the street in Illyria with Antonio and Sebastian. Antonio has gone with Sebastian into town, concerned that Sebastian is a stranger in this place. Sebastian wants to take in the city, but Antonio says he cannot join Sebastian since he was once in a fight with men on Orsino's warships and should try to remain somewhat concealed. Antonio decides to find lodging at an inn, where Sebastian can meet him later. He gives Sebastian his purse, since he knows Sebastian is not wealthy.

Scene 4 opens in Olivia's garden, where Olivia is in a lovesick frenzy in anticipation of Cesario's return. She asks Maria to get Malvolio, since he is serious-minded. Maria, however, says Malvolio is seemingly possessed. Maria warns Olivia to prepare herself for seeing him, building up the suspense for the audience. Olivia says she is as mad as he is and still wants to see him.

Malvolio arrives in full regalia, but Olivia first notices, and questions, his smiling. He says he could be sad if his attire is what she prefers, since the cross-gartering obstructs his blood flow. (Undoubtedly, this scene provokes much laughter from the audience, for Malvolio is pained and ridiculously dressed yet still wildly smiling.) The two women keep asking Malvolio what is wrong with him, and he keeps reciting lines from the letter that he thinks Olivia wrote to him. The comedy intensifies when Olivia asks, "Wilt thou go to bed, Malvolio?" She fears that he is sick, while he takes the question as a sexual proposition. Finally a servant enters and announces that Orsino's gentleman has arrived. Olivia then tells Maria to have others look after Malvolio, for she is concerned that no harm come to him.

Olivia and Maria exit, leaving Malvolio onstage by himself. He surmises that now he must be hostile to those who come to aid him, just as the letter instructed. Toby, Fabian, and Maria all enter and act as if Malvolio is quite unbalanced. Malvolio responds rudely and finally exits. Maria warns Toby and Fabian that they must go after him to be sure the joke is not discovered. Toby devises the plan to have Malvolio bound and locked in a dark room, thinking Olivia will go along with it since she has already seen his seemingly mad behavior.

Andrew arrives with the letter he has written to confront Cesario. Toby reads it, and in between each section Fabian provides positive reinforcement for Andrew. Maria says Cesario is nearly ready to leave, and Toby sends Andrew off to the orchard. Andrew exits and Toby explains that he cannot give the foolish letter to the supposed young gentleman since he will see it as ridiculous. Instead, Toby will challenge Cesario in person and describe Andrew's great valor. Both men will thus be so fearful of each other that just seeing each other will completely petrify them.

Olivia and Viola (as Cesario) enter, while Toby, Fabian, and Maria leave. Olivia and Cesario are still insistent on persuading each other: Olivia wants Cesario to care for her, while Cesario argues for Olivia to open her heart to the duke. At a stalemate, Cesario leaves, and Olivia tells him to come again the next day.

Toby and Fabian enter. Toby tells Cesario that at the end of the orchard a man awaits him who is quite fierce and intent on revenge. Cesario says there must be some mistake since he has done nothing that would anger anyone. Finally Cesario begs Toby to ask the knight what he has done to inspire such a reaction. Toby goes off to do so, and while he is gone, Cesario talks with Fabian, who reiterates how wild a warrior Andrew is. But then Fabian offers to try to make peace with Andrew for Cesario, and the two walk toward Andrew. They exit, and Toby and Andrew enter. Toby now tells Andrew what a skilled swordsman Cesario is. Andrew is so frightened he says he will give the young man his horse if all is called off.

Fabian and Cesario enter. Andrew and Cesario are both pressed by the others until each draws his sword. Just then, Antonio enters and says he will fight for Cesario (the disguised Viola), mistakenly believing that Cesario is Sebastian. Antonio draws his sword and Toby does as well. Before anything can happen, officers enter to arrest Antonio. Before he is taken away, Antonio speaks to Cesario, deeply concerned about how Cesario will fare without Antonio or Antonio's money. Antonio asks Cesario for some of his money, but, of course, Cesario has no idea what he is talking about. Cesario also says he does not know Antonio. The officers want to take Antonio away, but first he explains that he saved this youth and speaks of his disappointment over how the youth now treats him. Antonio calls to the youth, addressing him as Sebastian, and then is taken away.

Having heard the name, Viola (as Cesario) realizes that the man has mistaken him/her for Sebastian, her brother. Viola, realizing her brother may actually be alive, exits. Toby and Fabian remark on what a dishonest coward the young man has turned out to be, and Andrew says he will go after him still. He exits and the other two follow.

Act IV

This act opens in front of Olivia's house, where we find Sebastian and Feste. Feste assumes that Sebastian is actually Cesario (the disguised Viola). Sebastian, of course, does not know Feste or realize that Feste knows a person named Cesario who looks just like Sebastian. Olivia has sent the clown with a message for Cesario to come speak with her, but when Feste addresses Sebastian, Sebastian tries to dismiss him. The clown is surprised by this reaction and wonders what is going on; he states what he knows and what Sebastian does not acknowledge. Sebastian does not say that his name is not Cesario but only tries to chase Feste away. Sebastian even offers Feste money so he will leave him alone.

Toby, Andrew, and Fabian then enter, and all believe Sebastian is Cesario. Andrew, still frustrated from his earlier confrontation with Cesario, hits Sebastian, and Sebastian strikes back and asks if all the people here are mad. Toby grabs Sebastian, and Feste heads off to let Olivia know what is going on. Sebastian breaks free and asks if he must draw his sword, but Toby draws his first. Olivia enters and yells for Toby to hold his sword still. She chastises Toby and sends him off; Andrew and Fabian leave as well.

Olivia tells Sebastian, whom she also believes is Cesario, not to be offended by Toby and Andrew. She invites him inside. Sebastian wonders if he is mad or in a dream, but he goes with Olivia.

The second scene takes place inside Olivia's house. Maria instructs Feste to disguise himself as a curate and then goes to get Toby. Toby and Maria return, and Feste speaks as if he is a curate to Malvolio. Not much earlier, Feste had spoken of things not being what they seem to be; here he says things are what they are, although in actuality he is not who he appears to be, for he is only pretending to be a curate. As Feste insists that Malvolio is mad, Toby praises his craftiness. Malvolio is locked in a dark cell and can only hear Feste. Feste speaks nonsense, trying to make Malvolio feel that he is indeed mad.

Toby says he must leave and tells Maria that the fooling must stop, since he is in so much trouble with Olivia. Toby and Maria leave and Feste speaks, as himself, to Malvolio. Malvolio asks him for paper, ink, and light in order to write a note to Olivia. Feste insists that Malvolio is mad. Since Malvolio still cannot see him, Feste speaks as himself and then as the curate, showing himself to be a real performer as he switches from his own voice to the voice he's assumed for the curate. Feste finally agrees to get the paper, ink, and light, and he leaves.

Scene 3 takes place in Olivia's garden. Sebastian is by himself, trying to comprehend Olivia's behavior toward him. He assures himself that he is not mad. He wonders, also, where Antonio is, since he was supposed to meet him at the inn. He knows Antonio had been there earlier but is unaware that Antonio was taken away by officers. Sebastian knows Antonio had feared getting in trouble in Illyria, yet he fails to grasp that Antonio might indeed have been recognized and arrested. He wishes Antonio were present to help him but does not wonder if perhaps Antonio needs his help as well.

Sebastian is taken with the good luck he seems to have fallen into with Olivia. He wonders if he could be mad or if Olivia could be mad, but then he thinks she must be fine since she seems to ably take care of her home and followers. Olivia arrives with a priest, and since Sebastian seemed so agreeable earlier, she asks if he will go with her to the chapel to be married. He says he will, and they exit.

Act V

This act opens in front of Olivia's house, where Feste and Fabian are speaking. Fabian asks Feste to show him Malvolio's letter, but Feste refuses. In come the duke, Viola (as Cesario), Curio, and lords. Orsino recognizes Feste, who fools with the duke, telling him that his enemies actually are more straightforward and helpful to him than are his friends—further feeding the topsy-turvy atmosphere in Illyria. The duke gives a coin to Feste, who proceeds to ask for more; when the duke says Feste can have more money if he gets Olivia, Feste departs to retrieve her.

Antonio enters with some officers. Cesario (the disguised Viola) says that Antonio is the one who helped him. The duke immediately recognizes Antonio and provides some history. He says that in an intense battle among warships, Antonio proved himself a great fighter, in charge of only a little ship but making great gains. The officer reminds the duke that Antonio took one of their ships and its cargo and went aboard another of their ships, one of which held the duke's nephew, who lost his leg. Cesario explains, however, that Antonio did greatly help him, even though he said some very strange things to him that he did not understand.

Antonio then explains that he helped the now-ungrateful Cesario (whom he thinks is Sebastian) survive a shipwreck and that when he helped defend him, Cesario denied knowing him and denied that Antonio had given him his purse. Cesario and the duke do not understand this story. The duke asks when Antonio arrived, and he replies that he only just arrived but has been in the company of Cesario for the three months prior. Olivia enters with her attendants and is surprised to see Cesario, who she thinks is the man she has just married, still seemingly serving the duke.

This is the first time the duke and Olivia are together onstage. The duke remains intensely emotional, while Olivia again tells him she has no interest in him. He says he could kill her but instead will kill Cesario, even though he greatly cares for him, since he knows Olivia loves Cesario instead. Cesario is ready to be the victim, but Olivia stops the slaughter, calling to her "husband." At this, the others are baffled, but Olivia calls for the priest that married her, and he confirms that Olivia has just been married to this young man.

Sir Andrew enters, calling for a surgeon for Sir Toby. Andrew says Toby has been hurt in the head by Cesario, who also hurt Andrew. Toby enters, out of sorts, and when Andrew offers to help him, he calls him many names. Olivia sends them off to be cared for.

Sebastian enters, apologizes for harming the others, and then notices Antonio and the others staring at him. He sees Viola (as Cesario), and all wonder how there can be two people before them who look exactly alike. After a series of questions, Viola admitts she is, in fact, a woman and each twin is thrilled to realize the other is alive. Orsino reminds Viola of those times she spoke of her love for the duke; he takes Viola's hand and tells her to get her real clothes. Viola says that the captain who knows where her clothes are has been locked up at Malvolio's instigation, offering another example of Malvolio's apparent harshness.

Olivia calls for Malvolio. Feste and Fabian arrive, and Fabian reads Malvolio's letter to Olivia. Again she calls for Malvolio, and while they wait, she tells Orsino to think of her as a sister, since she is married to Sebastian, Viola's brother. She says they should have a celebration, and the duke, happy to hear this, asks Viola to marry him.

Fabian enters with Malvolio. The tone changes as both the duke and Olivia refer to him as a madman and Malvolio accuses Olivia of doing him serious wrong. Malvolio shows Olivia the letter that he thinks she wrote, and she explains that Maria must have written it. Fabian, too, announces his part and Toby's part in the trick on Malvolio. He says that Toby has married Maria. Feste admits his part in the prank as well and says he wanted revenge for Malvolio's speaking harshly about him. Malvolio yells that he will get revenge on all involved and exits. In Shakespeare's time, audiences laughed at Malvolio's plight, but some more modern audiences have felt sorry for him. Olivia says he's "been most notoriously abused." The duke says peace must be made with him. All exit but the clown, who sings of the stages of life. At each section of his song he speaks of wind and rain, yet the piece ends with a promise that the players will always strive to please the audience.

Key Passages in *Twelfth Night*

Act I, i, 25–42

Valentine: So please my lord, I might not be admitted;
But from her handmaid do return this answer:
The element itself, till seven years' heat,
Shall not behold her face at ample view;
But like a cloistress she will veiled walk,
And water once a day her chamber round
With eye-offending brine: all this to season
A brother's dead love, which she would keep fresh
And lasting in her sad remembrance.
Duke: O, she that hath a heart of that fine frame
To pay this debt of love but to a brother,
How will she love when the rich golden shaft
Hath killed the flock of all affections else
That live in her; when liver, brain, and heart,
These sovereign thrones, are all supplied and filled,
Her sweet perfections, with one self king.
Away before me to sweet beds of flow'rs;
Love-thoughts lie rich when canopied with bow'rs.

This passage occurs very early in the play. At this point, we know that Duke Orsino is infatuated with Olivia. Here Valentine returns from a visit to her home, although he was not allowed in to see her. We get some insight about Olivia from what Valentine has learned from her servant. Namely, Olivia is not seeing anyone, and will not for seven years, as part of her mourning for her dead brother. During the seven years, she will cry for her brother once a day in an attempt to "keep fresh" her sadness over losing him and his love for her.

The reader may be struck by the duration of Olivia's mourning, as well as the exacting details she has planned. Why seven years, for instance? Most everyone would call this excessive. And why a plan to cry once a day? If the crying is planned, is it even sincere? Notice, too, that the crying is described as "eye-offending brine," quite a negative description. Her remembrance of her brother is described as "sad," and mention is made not of her dead brother's love but rather of her "brother's dead love." In short, there is nothing positive here; even what is usually positive, love, is described as "dead."

This passage provides background information as well as the duke's reaction, which reveals insight into his personality. Orsino does not react as a typical person would. Rather than finding Olivia's plan disturbing, the duke praises her for it. He sees it as a sign of her great capacity to love and immediately turns his thoughts away from her mourning in order to see Olivia in relation to other lovers she may have. By the duke's logic, if Olivia can mourn to such a degree for her brother, she will have great love for a lover. The duke is thoroughly taken by this idea and goes off to luxuriate in it while surrounded by flowers. We begin to see that he and Olivia may be quite a match for each other—both emotional, both theatrical.

The personality traits of the characters in this opening scene stand out even more in contrast to the next scene, in which Viola first appears. She, too, has lost her brother. She believes he may be dead, yet her concern is with living. While her brother may still be alive, she spends no time figuring out a way to look for him but instead makes plans for what she will do next. When she hears that Olivia's brother has died, she believes it a good idea to get closer to her by working for her. Yet when she finds out that Olivia will see no one, Viola decides instead to disguise herself so she can work for the duke, who, she learns, is still unmarried. While she, too, can be emotional and theatrical, unlike Orsino and Olivia she is active rather than passive and surprisingly full of energy, despite having just survived a shipwreck.

Act II, ii, 16–41

I left no ring with her. What means this lady?
Fortune forbid my outside have not charmed her.
She made good view of me; indeed, so much
That sure methought her eyes had lost her tongue,
For she did speak in starts distractedly.
She loves me sure; the cunning of her passion
Invites me in this churlish messenger.
None of my lord's ring? Why, he sent her none.
I am the man. If it be so, as 'tis,
Poor lady, she were better love a dream.
Disguise, I see thou art a wickedness
Wherein the pregnant enemy does much.

How easy is it for the proper false
In women's waxen hearts to set their forms!
Alas, our frailty is the cause, not we,
For such as we are made of, such we be.
How will this fadge? My master loves her dearly;
And I (poor monster) fond as much on him;
And she (mistaken) seems to dote on me.
What will become of this? As I am man,
My state is desperate for my master's love.
As I am woman (now alas the day!),
What thriftless sighs shall poor Olivia breathe?
O Time, thou must untangle this, not I;
It is too hard a knot for me t' untie.

Viola is alone onstage as she speaks this passage, right after Malvolio has left her. This trick with the ring shows the countess's craftiness, for Olivia has made up a story that Malvolio can believe is true: Viola (disguised as Cesario) could very well have left a ring with her, and Olivia could have decided after Cesario left that she did not want the ring. The story provides a good excuse for Olivia to send Malvolio out after Cesario. The countess knows that Cesario will be surprised by Malvolio's message, and at the same time the countess knows Cesario is smart enough to understand the hidden meaning—namely that Olivia is taken with the supposed young man. Perhaps she does not want to let Malvolio know her true feelings, and/or perhaps she does not want to reveal her feelings directly to Cesario, since he might not feel as strongly for her.

Viola quickly understands that the countess is attracted to "him." She thinks back on their meeting and how the woman looked at "him" and could not even speak clearly, apparently because she had become so enamored. Viola reflects on how this happened and calls her disguise "a wickedness." The disguise seems to get the blame, as if it could act on its own without her. Viola also sees women's frailty as partially to blame. Their hearts can become so readily fixated, a trait that is not in their control but is simply a part of who they are.

Viola wonders what will happen next and thinks about how events have so quickly become complex. Namely, the duke pines for the countess; Viola, though dressed as a man, is just as taken with the duke; and now the countess is enraptured by Viola in disguise (a desire that obviously cannot reach fruition). The situation is quite in disarray, but rather than discard her disguise, Viola says she will wait for time to untangle the confusion.

Of course, we in the audience know that more confusion undoubtedly awaits, since Viola's twin brother, Sebastian, is alive and on his way to the duke's palace. With Viola dressed as a man, it will be easy for the two to be mistaken for each other, especially since, at this point, none of the characters know that both twins did indeed survive the shipwreck.

—⁓— —⁓— —⁓—

Act II, iv, 94–125

Duke: There is no woman's sides
Can bide the beating of so strong a passion
As love doth give my heart; no woman's heart
So big to hold so much; they lack retention.
Alas, their love may be called appetite,
No motion of the liver but the palate,
That suffer surfeit, cloyment, and revolt;
But mine is all as hungry as the sea
And can digest as much. Make no compare
Between that love a woman can bear me
And that I owe Olivia.
Viola: Ay, but I know—
Duke: What dost thou know?
Viola: Too well what love women to men may owe.
In faith, they are as true of heart as we.
My father had a daughter loved a man
As it might be perhaps, were I a woman,
I should your lordship.
Duke: And what's her history?
Viola: A blank, my lord. She never told her love,
But let concealment, like a worm i' th' bud,
Feed on her damask cheek. She pined in thought;
And, with a green and yellow melancholy,
She sat like Patience on a monument,
Smiling at grief. Was not this love indeed?
We men may say more, swear more; but indeed
Our shows are more than will; for still we prove
Much in our vows but little in our love.
Duke: But died thy sister of her love, my boy?
Viola: I am all the daughters of my father's house,
And all the brothers too, and yet I know not.
Sir, shall I to this lady?
Duke: Ay, that's the theme.
To her in haste. Give her this jewel. Say
My love can give no place, bide no denay.

Just before this passage, the duke has told Cesario (Viola in disguise) to go again to woo Olivia for him. Cesario, knowing that the countess does not want the duke, and may become even more taken with Cesario if he visits her again, tries to convince Orsino that his quest may be truly hopeless. Cesario attempts to get him to think of the situation differently. Imagine, he says, if a woman loved the duke as much as the duke loves Olivia. But Orsino does not want to hear this, instead proclaiming that no woman could love as intensely as he loves Olivia. He draws analogies and comparisons, saying his capacity to love her is as great as the sea. Shortly before this conversation, Feste had played a melancholy love song at the duke's request. This, too, encouraged the duke's further musings on unrequited love.

Cesario (Viola) does not give up easily, though, in trying to get Orsino to realize that his perspective is askew. He tells the duke of women who can love the same as men, such as his father's daughter (making reference to herself, then, without the duke realizing it), who loved a man just as, if Cesario were a woman, he might love the duke. The duke, now, is ready to listen and encourages Cesario to tell him what happened. Cesario says this daughter kept her love a secret, describes what that was like, and then asks Orsino if this was not great love—and then goes even further by adding that men, in fact, speak and act like they have greater passion for women than they truly do.

The duke does not say whether he agrees or disagrees with this assessment, but apparently he is convinced of this daughter's emotional capacity, for he asks if the sister died of her love. (This is yet another sign of his dismal perspective and another indication of his passivity when it comes to love, for he does not even ask why the daughter kept her love a secret.) Cesario answers his question in a cryptic manner, yet the duke does not question the supposed young man's description of being "all the daughters" and "all the brothers" in his father's house. Cesario claims he does not know what happened in the end, perhaps because Viola does not know what will happen in her own relationship with the duke.

While Cesario has tried to change the duke's perspective, and indeed has succeeded to a certain degree, still he offers to go to Olivia as the duke has requested. Ironically, the duke tells Cesario to bring Olivia a jewel. Not much earlier, Olivia had pretended to give back to Cesario a ring that was supposedly a gift from the duke.

—◦◦◦— —◦◦◦— —◦◦◦—

Act III, i, 139–166

Olivia: Stay.
I prithee tell me what thou think'st of me.
Viola: That you do think you are not what you are.
Olivia: If I think so, I think the same of you.

Viola: Then think you right. I am not what I am.
Olivia: I would you were as I would have you be.
Viola: Would it be better, madam, than I am?
I wish it might, for now I am your fool.
Olivia: O, what a deal of scorn looks beautiful
In the contempt and anger of his lip.
A murd'rous guilt shows not itself more soon
Than love that would seem hid: love's night is noon.
Cesario, by the roses of the spring,
By maidhood, honor, truth, and everything,
I love thee so that, maugre all thy pride,
Nor wit nor reason can my passion hide.
Do not extort thy reasons from this clause,
For that I woo, thou therefore hast no cause;
But rather reason thus with reason fetter,
Love sought is good, but given unsought is better.
Viola: By innocence I swear, and by my youth,
I have one heart, one bosom, and one truth,
And that no woman has; nor never none
Shall mistress be of it, save I alone.
And so adieu, good madam. Never more
Will I my master's tears to you deplore.
Olivia: Yet come again; for thou perhaps mayst move
That heart which now abhors to like his love.

Here Olivia is with Cesario (Viola in disguise), yet again at a stalemate, since Cesario is only interested in doing the duke's bidding—to woo Olivia for him— while Olivia is only interested in trying to win over Cesario. Cesario is about ready to leave, but Olivia asks him to stay and wishes to know what he thinks of her. Note that, so far, the duke has said he is attracted to Olivia's beauty, and that beauty also came up when Olivia first moved her veil aside for Viola (as Cesario) to see her. In this passage, however, Olivia is not asking about her looks but rather for Cesario's opinion of her overall. In this passage, Viola (as Cesario) speaks cryptically, so that the audience appreciates her meanings, while Olivia, not knowing Viola is disguised, sees the responses differently. Viola (as Cesario) speaks of things not being what they appear to be, while Olivia believes the supposed young man means she is in a state of madness.

Olivia says she wishes Cesario "were as I would have you be," a selfish thought yet one uttered out of frustration since Cesario appears unwilling to budge. Olivia is probably used to men being readily attracted to her and thus does not know how to treat this person, who is different from the others. As a person of high rank, she is also more accustomed to telling people what to do and having them do so (although the antics of Sir Toby are one area in which Olivia has no control). When Olivia voices this desire that Cesario be what she wishes, Cesario calls attention to this selfishness, asking if Olivia getting her wish would truly be better. Cesario says Olivia has made a fool of him, and Olivia, rather than feeling badly about this, toys with him, calling his angry look "beautiful" instead of seeing it as a legitimate response.

Olivia tells Cesario directly how much she loves him. She knows that the situation is unusual in that she is wooing him, yet she tells Cesario that while it may be good for men to go after lovers, when they receive love without even having to go after it, that love is even better.

—◦◦◦— —◦◦◦— —◦◦◦—

Act IV, ii, 24–50

Malvolio: Sir Topas, Sir Topas, good Sir Topas, go to my lady.
Clown: Out, hyperbolical fiend! How vexest thou this man! Talkest thou nothing but of ladies?
Toby: Well said, Master Parson.
Malvolio: Sir Topas, never was man thus wronged. Good Sir Topas, do not think I am mad. They have laid me here in hideous darkness.
Clown: Fie, thou dishonest Satan. I call thee by the most modest terms, for I am one of those gentle ones that will use the devil himself with courtesy. Say'st thou that house is dark?
Malvolio: As hell, Sir Topas.
Clown: Why, it hath bay windows transparent as barricadoes, and the clerestories toward the south north are as lustrous as ebony; and yet complainest thou of obstruction?
Malvolio: I am not mad, Sir Topas. I say to you this house is dark.
Clown: Madman, thou errest. I say there is no darkness but ignorance, in which thou are more puzzled than the Egyptians in their fog.
Malvolio: I say this house is as dark as ignorance, though ignorance were as dark as hell; and I say there was never man thus abused. I am no more mad than you are. Make the trial of it in any constant question.

In this passage, the trick on Malvolio continues. Whereas initially the ruse was to have Malvolio find a fake letter revealing Olivia's longing for him and instructing him in how he should make her even more delighted, the trick now includes locking Malvolio up as if he were mad. Feste the clown here pretends to be a member of the clergy, someone we would expect to be honest and sympathetic as well as good and moral. Most likely Malvolio assumes that, especially since he's led what he thinks is a good life, this curate will help him out of his imprisonment. Instead, the supposed curate is completely against Malvolio.

Malvolio calls out to him in desperation and mentions the lady Olivia, but Feste twists this into something negative, accusing Malvolio of being obsessed with ladies. While Feste distorts Malvolio's meaning here, it is true that Malvolio's attraction to Olivia is part of what has gotten him into trouble in the first place. At various points in the scene, Sir Toby interjects murmurings of encouragement and approval for Feste's performance, although Malvolio does not know Toby is present—yet another subterfuge in the play.

Malvolio explains that he has been wronged, that he is not mad, and that now he is stuck in "hideous darkness." Feste responds by calling him "dishonest Satan." Why Satan? Perhaps because he knows this will disturb Malvolio the most. To further antagonize Malvolio, Feste speaks insanely, for he not only denies that Malvolio is in darkness but also says there are windows that are clear yet obstructed or dark and facing "south north." Feste also says "there is no darkness but ignorance," and Malvolio asserts that the house truly is as dark as ignorance. Malvolio may be thinking of Toby and his cohorts as ignorant, since in his view they do not live a life that is right and good. Feste may be thinking of Malvolio as ignorant, since he was easily fooled by the fake letter. On a larger scale, in the play overall, there are numerous instances of other characters not knowing; most notably, Viola disguises herself and therefore leaves many characters ignorant of who she truly is, while Sebastian allows Olivia to believe he is someone else.

Malvolio also says he is no more mad than Feste. This question of madness comes up in the play in other areas as well, as does the idea of how subjective it is.

LIST OF CHARACTERS IN TWELFTH NIGHT

Duke Orsino is the duke of Illyria. He is more obsessed with the idea of being in love than with the woman he says he loves, Olivia. He is also changeable: He pines for Olivia throughout most of the play yet readily says he will marry Viola when he finds out she is female.

Olivia is a rich countess who insists she will mourn for her brother and see no one for many years. But she readily changes her mind once she meets and falls in love with Viola, who is disguised as the male Cesario. Olivia is patient and shows some concern for others, since she lets her uncle stay with her even though he is burdensome, and she also feels for Malvolio when he is mistreated.

Viola is the twin sister of Sebastian. After surviving a shipwreck, she decides to disguise herself as a male servant, Cesario, so she can work for Duke Orsino, who she's told is still a bachelor. She promptly falls in love with the duke, who does not suspect she is female.

Sebastian is Viola's twin brother. He has also survived the shipwreck but does not know his sister is alive, just as she does not know he is alive. Like his sister, he is willing to go along with other people's mistaken beliefs. In his case, he goes along with marrying Olivia, even though he has never met her and she believes he is the servant Cesario.

Sir Toby Belch is Olivia's uncle, who is staying in Olivia's home and annoying his niece with his drunken horseplay. He convinces Sir Andrew that Olivia really may take him seriously as a suitor. By doing so, Sir Toby keeps Sir Andrew around and can take advantage of his money.

Maria is Olivia's gentlewoman. She enjoys the company of Sir Toby and the clown. She is smart and conniving and makes an elaborate plan to embarrass and distress Malvolio, who acts as though he is better than the others.

Sir Andrew Aguecheek is a wealthy knight who is foolish and slow and therefore easily manipulated. He believes Sir Toby when he tells Andrew that Olivia may take him as her suitor.

Malvolio is Olivia's puritanical steward. He looks down on Sir Toby and his friends for their carousing and tries to retain the quiet that Olivia requests. He easily falls for Maria's trick, which plays on his vulnerabilities. He is yet another man who desires Olivia.

Feste is Olivia's clown. He is a master at wordplay and a keen observer. He has the courage to tell Olivia she is being foolish for wanting to mourn so much for her brother. He aids in torturing Malvolio but also helps free him.

Antonio is a sea captain who helps Sebastian. Upon arriving in Illyria he must remain out of sight because of previous transgressions, but he is willing to stay for Sebastian.

Another **sea captain** helps Viola get ashore and get situated. Later, he is a target of Malvolio's, although the reason is not clear.

Valentine is a gentleman who attends to the duke.

Curio is a gentleman who attends to the duke.

Fabian is a servant to Olivia. He has a grudge against Malvolio and thus is happy to see him made fun of. He also tricks Andrew.

A **priest** marries Olivia and later mistakenly identifies the man who is her husband.

Officers of the law arrive to arrest Antonio.

Sailors arrive onshore with Viola after the shipwreck.

Lords, attendants, and **musicians** wait on Orsino and Olivia.

CRITICISM
THROUGH THE AGES

TWELFTH NIGHT
IN THE SEVENTEENTH CENTURY
❧

It is believed that *Twelfth Night* was first performed for one of the London colleges of law, the Middle Temple, as part of its annual Christmas celebration, a time of great merriment and festivities. The traditional celebration of Twelfth Night, concluding the 12 days of Christmas, occurs on January sixth, also known as the Feast of the Epiphany, which is the day the three kings arrived in Jerusalem to see the newborn Jesus. However, during Shakespeare's time, the holiday of Twelfth Night in England was also known as the Feast of Fools. During this time, the tradition was that fools should rule, kings took on the fools' role of entertaining, and, in general, normal constraints and conventions would not apply. Shakespeare's play *Twelfth Night* fit well into this tradition.

Few comments on the play from the seventeenth century are available today. Two of the most interesting come from diaries. The lawyer John Manningham, for instance, wrote briefly about attending one of the earliest performances. He compared the work to that of a few others, indicating his knowledge of the arts. His comments concentrated on the trick played on Malvolio, which Manningham clearly thought was a clever twist. He explained how Malvolio was duped completely by Maria's note, which she wrote as if it were from Olivia. Manningham's mention of this section of the play showed his focus was on the subplot. Years later, audiences would begin to see Malvolio's part in the play as sympathetic and not purely comical, though, as always, the director's or actor's perspective on the role will strongly affect the viewers' perceptions.

More than 60 years later, another diarist, Samuel Pepys, also wrote that he had seen the play. Like Manningham, he saw the play when he was invited to dinner at someone's home (in this case, a duke's). He praised the acting but found the play "silly." Pepys was also perturbed by the title of the play, believing it was thoroughly unrelated to its plot. Apparently he was a literalist, believing the events of the play should directly tie in with the Twelfth Night celebration. Those who were less literal would see that the title ties in with the *idea* of the Twelfth Night celebration. Pepys also seemed to pay no attention to the play's subtitle, "*or What You Will.*" Later commentators would comment on what they thought was the significance of this part of the title.

1601—John Manningham. From his *Diary*, February 2

John Manningham was a British lawyer. His diary became important for its commentary on religion, society, art, and theater.

At our feast wee had a play called Twelve Night, or what you will, much like the commedy of errores, or Menechmi in Plautus, but most like and neere to that in Italian called *Inganni*. A good practise in it to make the steward beleeve his lady widdowe was in love with him, by counterfayting a letter as from his lady, in generall termes, telling him what shee liked best in him, and prescribing his gesture in smiling, his apparaile, &c., and then when he came to practise making him beleeve they tooke him to be mad.

1663—Samuel Pepys. From *The Diary of Samuel Pepys*

Samuel Pepys (1633–1703), an English naval administrator and member of Parliament, is most famous for his diary, which is considered an invaluable primary source about daily life in the Restoration period.

. . . after dinner to the Duke's house, and there saw *Twelfth Night* acted well, though it be a silly play, and not related at all to the name or day.

TWELFTH NIGHT
IN THE EIGHTEENTH CENTURY
✢

During this century, three notable critics examined the play from somewhat similar perspectives, reflecting a respect for ancient writers and their concerns over what might be called believability.

Charlotte Lennox, in her book on the sources for Shakespeare's plays, wrote of Shakespeare's relationship to the great ancient writers. She stated that, contrary to some critics' beliefs, Shakespeare probably had not read classic works in their original languages of Greek and Roman, nor did he read Italian or Greek; rather, he read such works in translations available in his time. She also criticized Shakespeare for lacking the "exactness and regularity" of the great classical writers.

Lennox examined what she saw as the true source for Shakespeare's *Twelfth Night*, a novel by Bandello, and compared the play to this novel. She pointed out numerous instances in which the events in Bandello's work are more credible in relation to the characters than are the events in Shakespeare's play. She expressed surprise that Shakespeare would borrow so much from Bandello and turn those borrowings into something "unnatural and absurd." As an example, Lennox pointed out that whereas Bandello has logical reasons for placing his characters in a certain locale, Shakespeare does not explain why Sebastian and Viola are on a voyage or where they were planning to go. More significantly, Bandello's novel supplies reasons for why the female character should disguise herself as a man, but Shakespeare's Viola, in contrast, is not only not in love with the duke when the play opens but has never seen him before.

The critic Samuel Johnson also had concerns about credibility in the play. He commented that Olivia's marriage by the play's end is not believable and fails to exhibit a "just picture of life." Overall, though, he deemed the play "elegant and easy" and in its more comical scenes "exquisitely humorous." He found, for instance, Malvolio's soliloquy to be "truly comic." Johnson also touched on the idea of satire. He believed Shakespeare's use of Sir Andrew for satire was inappropriate, since Andrew, while expertly created by Shakespeare, is unintelligent and therefore not someone who should be attacked in this way.

In Johnson's view, Malvolio, in contrast, is a clear target; his pride is what does him in.

Like Lennox and Johnson, the writer Elizabeth Griffith also focused on the believability of the characters. The play's opening, in her view, gives a beautiful description of the allure of music and the essence of love. Yet Griffith found fault in Shakespeare's portrayal of the duke's desire to end his love for Olivia. Griffith thought it was unbelievable that anyone so passionate would want to extinguish that passion, even if he or she were unhappy. Griffith felt, however, that Shakespeare did exhibit a true understanding of humanity when he has Valentine explain how Olivia will grieve and gives the duke's response. Similarly, Griffith found it quite likely that an infatuated person like Olivia would blame the fates for her becoming attracted to the disguised Viola.

Griffith's overarching subject was the morality of Shakespeare's plays. She highlighted, for instance, one of Antonio's speeches that emphasizes the sin of ingratitude. She also touched on disguise as it is used in the play. Antonio explains that one's outward appearance is a manifestation of the internal mind. Griffith wrote that she wished this were completely true.

1753—Charlotte Lennox. "The Fable of *Twelfth-Night, or What You Will," from Shakespear Illustrated, or the Novels and Histories on which the Plays of Shakespear Are Founded*

Charlotte Ramsay Lennox was a novelist, poet, playwright, magazine editor, and translator. Her novels include *The Life of Harriot Stuart, Euphemia*, and *The Female Quixote*. Her *Shakespear Illustrated, or the Novels and Histories on which the Plays of Shakespear Are Founded* is a collection of the works from which Shakespeare derived his plots.

Sebastian and *Viola* his Sister, Twins, and so like each other in Person, that in the same Cloaths they could not be distinguished, embark in a Vessel, (upon what Account, or with what Design we are not informed) which is cast away upon the Coast of *Illyria*.

Viola escapes drowning by the Assistance of the Captain and some of the Mariners, and gets safe to Land; but *Sebastian* her Brother is suspected to have perished.

Viola being informed that the Country where she now is, is *Illyria*, and that it is governed by a Duke, named *Orsino*, who is in Love, but not beloved again by a noble Lady; she expresses a Wish to be received into her Service.

The Captain tells her, the Lady is so afflicted for the Death of her Brother that she will admit of no Solicitations whatever, not even the Duke's; whereupon,

Viola, without further Reflexion, entreats the Captain to provide her with a Disguise, and recommend her as an Eunuch to the Duke, in whose Service she is very desirous to be placed.

The Captain consents, and *Viola*, under the Name of *Caesario*, soon gains the Duke's Favour and Confidence, who sends him to the Countess *Olivia*, the Lady he loves, to solicit her Favour for him.

Viola is by this Time violently in love with the Duke, yet she executes her Commission very faithfully, and pleads strongly for her Master to the Lady; the disconsolate and rigid *Olivia* is presently struck with the Beauty of the young Page, and falls downright in Love with him.

Viola very honestly resists all her Offers; but the Lady will not be repulsed; she sends to entreat he will come to her again; and her Messenger meeting *Sebastian*, who had also escaped drowning, but was ignorant of his Sister's Fate; deceived by the Resemblance, takes him for *Caesario*, and entreats him to come to his Lady.

Sebastian, though much surprized at the Adventure, resolves to follow his Fortune; he is introduced to *Olivia*, who supposing him to be *Caesario*, urges him to marry her; to which *Sebastian*, who is immediately charmed with her Beauty, gladly consents.

The Duke, some Time after, impatient to see *Olivia*, comes to her House, attended by *Caesario*.

Olivia comes out to meet him, and seeing *Caesario*, supposing him to be the Person she had married, reproaches him with Breach of Promise; what that Promise is we are not told.

The Duke complains of her Cruelty; she takes little Notice of him, directing her Looks and Words to *Caesario*; at last the Duke being provoked by her Declaration that she could not love him, tells her he will revenge the Disdain she treats him with upon her Minion his Page, whom he knows she loves.

Caesario professes his Willingness to die by his Commands, and is following the Duke, but stopped by *Olivia*, who bids him remember their late Engagements, and declares he is her Husband; the Duke storms; *Caesario* denies the Charge; and the Priest is called in by *Olivia* to witness that he had married them, which he does.

Caesario persisting in his Denial, many Altercations ensue; at last *Sebastian*, who had been engaged in a Quarrel with *Olivia*'s Uncle, appears; the Company are all astonished at the Resemblance between him and *Caesario*, who is discovered to be *Viola* his Sister:

Olivia acknowledges *Sebastian* for her Husband, and the Duke marries *Viola*. The rest is all Episode, and makes up the greatest as well as the best Part of the Play.

It has hitherto been uncertain whether the Story of *Twelfth-Night*, or *What You Will*, was borrowed from any Novel, or an Invention of *Shakespear*.

Mr. *Langbaine*, in his *Account of the Dramatic Poets and their Writings*, says, that he knows not from whence that Play was taken, but the Resemblance of *Sebastian* to his Sister *Viola* was doubtless first borrowed, not only by *Shakespear*, but all our succeeding Poets, from *Plautus*, who has made Use of it in several Plays, as *Amphitrio, Maenechmi,* &c.

It is really surprising to see the Admirers of *Shakespear* so solicitous to prove he was very conversant with the Ancients; they take all Opportunities to find in his Writings Illusions to them; Imitations of their Thoughts and Expressions; and will not scruple to allow their Favourite to have been guilty of some little Thefts from their Works, provided it will make out his Claim to an Acquaintance with them.

It is very much to be doubted whether or not he understood the *Italian* and *French* Languages, since we find he made Use of Translations from both when he borrowed of their Authors; and still less probable is it that he understood and studied the *Greek* and *Latin* Poets, when he, who was so close a Copyer has never imitated them in their chief Beauties, and seems wholly a Stranger to the Laws of dramatic Poetry, well does the Poet [Milton] say of him,

Shakespear, Fancy's sweetest Child,
Warbles his native Wood-Notes wild.

His true Praise seems to be summ'd up in those two Lines; for wild, though harmonious, his Strains certainly are; and his modern Admirers injure him greatly, by supposing any of those Wood-Notes copied from the Ancients; *Milton*, by calling them native, allows them to have been untaught, and all his own; and in that does Justice to his vast imagination, which is robbed of great Part of its Merit by supposing it to have received any Assistance from the Ancients, whom if he understood, it must be confessed he has profited very little by, since we see not the least Shadow of their Exactness and Regularity in his Works.

Though it should be granted that *Shakespear* took the Hint of *Sebastian* and *Viola*'s Resemblance from the *Maenechmi* and *Amphitrio* of *Plautus*, yet he might have done that without understanding *Latin*, since there were Translations of both those Plays in his Time; and to his own Invention, had that been the Case, might be attributed almost all the perplexing Adventures which the Resemblance of the Brother and Sister gave rise to in the *Twelfth-Night*, and which are very different from those in the *Latin* Author.

But *Shakespear* had a much more ample Supply for the Fable of this Comedy in [Bandello's] Novel, from whence he undoubtedly drew it, and which not only furnished him with the Hint of the Resemblance between *Sebastian* and *Viola*, but also with the greatest Part of the Intrigue of the Play.

Sebastian and *Viola* in the Play are the same with *Paolo* and *Nicuola* in the Novel; both are Twins, and both remarkably like each other.

Viola is parted from her Brother by a Shipwreck, and supposes him to be drowned; *Nicuola* loses her Brother at the sacking of *Rome*, and for a long Time is ignorant whether he is alive or dead.

Viola serves the Duke, with whom she is in love, in the Habit of a Page; *Nicuola*, in the same Disguise, attends *Lattantio*, who had forsaken her for *Catella*.

The Duke sends *Viola* to solicit his Mistress in his Favour; *Lattantio* commissions *Nicuola* to plead for him with *Catella*.

The Duke's Mistress falls in love with *Viola*, supposing her to be a Man; and *Catella*, by the like Mistake, is enamoured of *Nicuola*; and lastly, the two Ladies in the Play, as well as in the Novel, marry their Lovers whom they had waited on in Disguise, and their Brothers wed the Ladies who had been enamoured of them.

Though *Shakspear* has copied the Novelist in all these Particulars, yet he differs from him in others, which very much lessens the Probability of the Story.

Sebastian and *Viola* in the Play are parted by a Shipwreck, and *Viola* is cast upon the Coast of *Illyria*; but we are not told with what Intention this Brother and Sister embarked, or whither their Voyage was bound.

The Poet had Occasion for them in *Illyria*, and there they are at the Service of the Audience; no Matter if introduced with Propriety or not; we must be contented to take them as we find them: Well; *Viola*, after giving some Tears to the Memory of her Brother, whom she fears is drowned, is desirous of being recommended as an Attendant to a Lady with whom the Sovereign of the Country is in love; but being told it would be difficult to procure Admission to her, she all of a sudden takes up an unaccountable Resolution to serve the young Batchelor-Duke in the Habit of a Man; take it in her own Words addressed to the Captain of the wreck'd Vessel:

"Conceal me what I am; and be my Aid
For such Disguise as haply shall become
The Form of my Intent: I'll serve this Duke;
Thou shalt present me as an Eunuch to him;
It may be worth thy Pains; for I can sing;
And speak to him in many Sorts of Music,
That will allow me very worth his Service."

A very natural Scheme this for a beautiful and virtuous young Lady to throw off all at once the Modesty and Reservedness of her Sex, mix among Men, herself disguised like one; and, prest by no Necessity, influenced by no Passion, expose herself to all the dangerous Consequences of so unworthy and shameful a Situation.

We find this Incident managed with much more Decency in the Novel.

Nicuola is violently in love with and beloved by *Lattantio*; and finding that, during a short Absence from him, he became enamoured of *Catella*, upon hearing he had lost his Page and wanted another, she disguises herself like a Boy, and offers her Service to wait upon him with a View of recalling his Affections by this extraordinary Instance of her Tenderness and Fidelity, and of seizing every Opportunity of traversing his new Passion for *Catella*.

This Project, though not altogether prudent and wise, was far from being inconsistent with the Temper and Circumstances of *Nicuola*, stimulated as she was by Love, Jealousy and Despair, to attempt something extraordinary for the Recovery of her Lover.

But what are *Viola*'s Motives for so rash an Enterprize? She is neither in love with or abandoned by the Duke, and cannot reasonably propose to herself any Advantage by thus hazarding her Virtue and Fame: His Person she had never seen; his Affections she was informed were engaged; what then were her Views and Designs by submitting to be his Attendant?

Bandello does not even make *Nicuola* resolve upon such an Expedient till the Design was suggested to her by over-hearing *Lattantio* lament the Loss of his Page and wish for another.

But the Novellist is much more careful to preserve Probability in his Narration than the Poet in his Action: The Wonder is that *Shakespear* should borrow so many Incidents from him, and yet task his Invention to make those Incidents unnatural and absurd.

The Passion of *Olivia*, the Duke's Mistress, for the disguised Lady, is attended with Circumstances that make it appear highly improbable and ridiculous: She is represented as a noble and virtuous Lady, overwhelmed with Grief for the Death of a beloved Brother; her Grief indeed is of a very extraordinary Nature, and inspired her with strange Resolutions according to the Report of *Valentine*, the Duke's Servant, who had been sent by him with a Message to her:

> *Duke.* How now! what News from her?
> *Val.* So please, my Lord, I might not be admitted;
> But from her Hand-maid do return this Answer:
> The Element itself, till seven Years hence,
> Shall not behold her Face at ample View;
> But, like a Cloystress, she will veiled walk,
> And water once a Day her Chamber round
> With eye-offending Brine: All this to season
> A Brother's dead Love, which she would keep fresh
> And lasting in her sad Remembrance.

This sorrowful Lady, however, makes her first Appearance in the Company of a Jester, with whom she is extremely diverted; and notwithstanding her Vow which we are told of in another Place, not to admit the Sight or Company of Men, she permits the Duke's Page to approach her, shews him her Face, and bandies Jests and smart Sentences with all the lively Wit of an airy Coquet.

Then follows her sudden Passion for the supposed Youth, which is as suddenly declared, without any of those Emotions that Bashfulness, Delicacy, and a Desire of preserving the Decorum her Sex and Birth oblige her to observe, must raise in the Mind of a Woman of Honour.

Had *Shakespear*, by mixing so much Levity in the Character of *Olivia*, designed a Satire on the Sex, he would have certainly led us by some Reflexions on the Inconsistency of her Behaviour to have made that Inference; but this is not the Case; for *Olivia* is every where highly extolled for her Virtues.

It is his injudicious Conduct of the Fable that gives so much Impropriety to the Manners of his Persons, at least in this Instance, which is the more surprizing, as the Novel furnished him with one much better contrived, and Characters more suitable to the Action.

Catella acts the same Part in the Novel that *Olivia* does in the Play; but *Catella* is a young gay libertine Girl, whose Birth was but mean, and Education neglected; it was not therefore surprizing that she should so easily fall in Love with a Page, indecently court him, and resolve to marry him, such an inconsiderate Conduct was agreeable to her Character; but in the noble and virtuous Olivia, 'tis unnatural and absurd, and what makes it still more so is, that as *Shakespear* has ordered the Matter, *Olivia* is disgracefully repulsed by this Youth, and yet continues her Suit, whereas *Catella* meets with a ready Compliance from the supposed *Romulo*, who sees his Designs on *Lattantio* likely to succeed by his Mistress's fortunate Passion for him.

Olivia's taking *Sebastian*, the Brother of the disguised *Viola*, for the beautiful Page, and marrying him, is with very little Variation borrowed from *Bandello*; but *Paolo* in the Novel is much more naturally introduced than *Sebastian* in the Play.

Paolo comes to *Esi* to seek for his Father and Sister, but we are not acquainted with Sebastian's Motives for going to *Illyria*; the Poet indeed had Business for him there, and there he lugs him without the least Shadow of a Reason for it, which is left to the Imagination of the Reader to supply.

The Behaviour of *Lattantio* in the Novel is more natural and consistent, than the Duke's in the Play: They both marry the Women that had attended on them disguised, but the Difference of their Stations, Circumstances, and Characters, makes the same Action natural in one, which in the other is absurd and ridiculous.

Lattantio had been in Love with *Nicuola*, but her Absence, joined to the natural Inconstancy of Youth, so wild and inconsiderate as his, transferred his Affections from her to *Catella*; she slights him, and he being informed that his abandoned *Nicuola*, impelled by the Violence of her Passion for him, had disguised herself in Boy's Cloaths, and waited on him as his Page; he repents of his Falsehood, and charmed with her Tenderness and Fidelity makes her his Wife.

This Conduct in *Lattantio* is very natural, but why should the Duke, a sovereign Prince who so passionately adored *Olivia*, all at once take a Resolution to marry *Viola*, a Stranger whom he had never seen in her proper Garb, because she had served him in Disguise; 'tis absurd to suppose he could in a Moment pass from the most extravagant Passion imaginable for Olivia, to one no less extravagant, for a Person, whom till then he had always believed to be a Boy; and 'tis also highly improbable that a great Prince would so suddenly resolve to marry a Girl, who had no other Title to his Favour than an imprudent Passion, which had carried her greatly beyond the Bounds of Decency.

The Duke's Reasons for this extraordinary Action are far from being convincing.

> *Duke* to *Viola*.
> "Your Master quits you; and for your Service done him,
> So much against the Metal of your Sex,
> So far beneath your soft and tender Breeding;
> (And since you call'd me Master for so long)
> Here is my Hand, you shall from this Time be
> Your Master's Mistress."

And as *Viola* at first had not even Love to plead as an Excuse for her indecent Disguise, she is still less worthy of the Fortune she was raised to.

There is a great deal of true Comic Humour in the inferior Characters of this Play, which are entirely of the Poet's Invention; the Mistakes *Antonio* is led into by the Resemblance of *Sebastian* and *Viola*, are no doubt Hints borrowed from the *Amphitrio* and the *Maenechmi* of *Plautus*, for which it is probable he consulted the *French*, or rather the *English* Translations of those Comedies extant in his Time; but these Mistakes, however diverting, take their Rise from a very improbable Circumstance.

Antonio, a Sea Captain, delivers *Sebastian* from the Fury of the Waves; the Youth being obstinately determined to go to the Court, *Antonio*, who in a Sea-fight had done great Mischief to the Duke's Galleys, resolves, out of the Violence of his Friendship, to follow him thither, notwithstanding he knew his Life would be in manifest Danger if he was seen in *Illyria*.

How unaccountably extravagant is this Kindness in a Stranger? what more could a long continued Friendship, confirmed by mutual Obligations have produced? But this Play is full of such Absurdities, which might have been avoided, had the Characters as well as the Action been the same with the Novel.

1765—Samuel Johnson. From "Notes on *Twelfth Night, or What You Will*," from *The Plays of William Shakespear*

Samuel Johnson (1709-1784) is thought by many to be the greatest critic in the English language. He was a poet, critic, prose writer, lexicographer, editor, and celebrated raconteur. His edition of the works of Shakespeare contained some of his famous thoughts on the plays. The following is his general observation on *Twelfth Night*.

The play is in the graver part elegant and easy, and in some of the lighter scenes exquisitely humorous. *Ague-cheek* is drawn with great propriety, but his character is in a great measure that of natural fatuity, and is therefore not the proper prey of a satirist. The soliloquy of *Malvolio* is truly comick; he is betrayed to ridicule merely by his pride. The marriage of *Olivia* and the succeeding perplexity, though well enough contrived to divert on the stage, wants credibility, and fails to produce the proper instruction required in the drama, as it exhibits no just picture of life.

1775—Elizabeth Griffith. "*Twelfth Night: or, What You Will*," from *The Morality of Shakespeare's Drama Illustrated*

Elizabeth Griffith (1720?-1793) was an actress, dramatist, fiction writer, essayist, and translator. She is best known for *A Series of Genuine Letters between Henry and Frances*, a collection of letters published with her husband. She also wrote a critical study of the morality of Shakespeare's plays.

ACT I. SCENE I.

This Play opens with a sweet passage, in which the charms of music, and the nature of love, are beautifully described.

> *Duke.* If music be the food of love, play on;
> Give me excess of it; that, surfeiting,
> The appetite may sicken, and so die.
> That strain again—It had a dying fall—
> O! it came o'er my ear, like the sweet south,
> That breathes upon a bank of violets,

Stealing and giving odour. Enough! no more—
'Tis not so sweet now; as it was before,
O spirit of love, how quick and fresh art thou!
That, notwithstanding thy capacity
Receiveth as the sea, nought enters there,
Of what validity and pitch foe'er,
But falls into abatement and low price,
Even in a minute; so full of shapes in fancy,
That it alone is *hight*[1] fantastical.

As I have hitherto observed upon Shakespeare's critical knowledge in human nature, I hope it will not appear invidious now, if I should here remark upon his deficiency in a passage above—lines second and third. The duke is there made to wish his passion were extinct; which, I believe, the most unhappy lover never yet did. We wish to remove every uneasy sensation it afflicts us with, by any means whatever; sometimes even by death itself; but never by the extinction of the affection.

This is not peculiar to love alone; 'tis the same in all the tender feelings. We wish the object of our grief brought back again to life, but desire not to forget our sorrow. We wish to relieve the subjects of our pity, but would not be deprived of our compassion. Heaven hath so framed us, and Heaven be praised for having endowed and adorned us with such *sweet compunctious visitings of Nature!* 'tis in these features only that we can resemble our Maker. In the more heroic qualities of bravery, and fortitude, can be traced no likeness of the Deity, because superfluous in a perfect state. The subject of love is touched upon again, twice, in the same Scene:

> *Duke.* O, when my eyes did see Olivia first,
> *Methought she purged the air of pestilence;*
> That instant was I turned into a hart,
> And my desires, like fell and cruel hounds,
> E'er since pursue me.[2]

And when Valentine acquaints the Duke with Olivia's vow of sequestering herself from the world, for seven years, to mourn the death of her brother, he cries out in an ecstasy,

> O, she that hath an heart of that fine frame,
> To pay this debt of love but to a brother,
> How will she love, when the rich golden shaft
> Hath killed the flock of all affections else,
> That live in her? When liver, brain, and heart,

Three sovereign thrones, are all supplied and filled
(O sweet perfection!) with one self-same king!

I am happy that this latter passage happens to occur so immediately after my remark above, as it affords me an opportunity of doing justice to Shakespeare, by observing that his inference, from Olivia's grief, to the nature of her heart in love, shews a perfect knowledge in this species of philosophy. The passions are divided into but two classes, the tender and the violent; and any one of either affords an earnest of all others of the same kind.

His distinction, too, of the *three thrones*, the *liver*, *brain*, and *heart*, is admirable. These are truly the seats of the three chief affections of love; the heart for passion, the mind for esteem, and the liver for jealousy; if Horace's anatomy is to be credited.[3]

SCENE XI.

In the last speech of this Act, Olivia speaks in the usual manner of all infatuated persons, who are apt to make the Fates answerable for those follies or vices which they have not sense or virtue enough to extricate themselves from, by their own exertions. For, upon a consciousness of having too weakly betrayed her passion for Viola, appearing under the character of a cavalier, she acquiesces in her indiscretion, by saying,

I do I know not what—and fear to find
Mine eye too great a flatterer for my mind.[4]
Fate, shew thy force, ourselves we do not owe;[5]
What is decreed must be—and this be so!

She repeats the same idle apology for herself, again, in the second Scene of the next Act:

For such as we are made, if such we be,
Alas! our frailty is the cause, not we.

ACT II. SCENE VI.

There are some good rules and reflections here, upon that principal and interesting event of life, our marriage, which are well worth attending to; as the natural consequences of an improper assortment, in that state, have been too strongly marked by the general experience of the world.

Duke, *and* Viola *as a Man.*
Duke. Let still the woman take
An elder than herself, so wears she to him,

So sways she level in her husband's heart,
For, boy, *however we do prize ourselves,*
Our fancies are more giddy and unfirm,
More longing, wavering, sooner lost and won,
Than women's are.
Viola. I think it well, my lord.
Duke. Then let thy love be younger than thyself,
Or thy affection cannot hold the bent;
For women are as roses, whose fair flower,
Being once display'd, doth fall that very hour.
Viola. And so they are—Alas, that they are so—
To die, even when they to perfection grow!

ACT III. SCENE I.

There is a slight stroke thrown out here, against an affected refinement on common speech; which however I shall lay hold of, as one should animadvert upon every species of pedantry, which is an incumbrance to literature, and casts a damp upon all free and liberal conversation.

Clown. My lady is within, Sir; I will *construe* to her whence you came; who you are, and what you would, is out of my *welkin.* I might say *element,* but the word is *overworn.*

SCENE XIV.

There is a most delicate sensibility expressed by a person here, in his reproach to one whom, by a similarity of appearances, he had mistaken for a friend on whom, he had formerly conferred obligations, which he seemed then to have forgotten.

Antonio *and* Viola.
Will you deny me, now?
Is't possible that my deserts to you
Can lack persuasion? *Do not tempt my misery,*
Lest that it make me so unsound a man,
As to upbraid you with those kindnesses
That I have done for you.

To which the innocent and mistaken Viola replies, with a becoming spirit of conscious virtue,

I hate ingratitude more in a man,
Than lying, vainness, babbling, drunkenness,

Or any taint of vice whose strong corruption
Inhabits our frail blood.

There is an ancient adage, which says, that *the sin of ingratitude includes every vice*.[6] It renders us unworthy of all the goods and enjoyments of life, even of our very existence; for we owe them all to favour and benevolence. Religion and virtue are, therefore, but barely the acknowledging a debt, which must ever remain undischarged.

All the moral I have been able to extract from this Piece, concludes in this Scene, with a position which *it were devoutly to be wished* had as much truth in physics, as it has in philosophy: That the outward form is but the visible sign of the Internal mind.

> *Antonio.* Thou hast, Sebastian, done good feature shame—
> In Nature, there's no blemish but the mind:
> None can be called deformed, but the unkind.
> Virtue is beauty; but the beauteous evil
> Are empty trunks, o'erflourished by the Devil.

I shall here give a quotation from a modern dramatic poem of distinguished merit, as the passage relates so immediately to the subject above last mentioned.

> "Beauty and virtue are the same;
> "They differ only in the name.
> "What to the soul is pure and bright,
> "Is beauty in a moral light;
> "And what to sense does charms convey,
> "Is beauty in the natural way.
> "Each from one source its essence draws,
> "And both conform to Nature's laws."
>
> Socrates.

NOTES

1. *Hight*, ycleped, or called, instead of *high*, *Warburton*.
2. A fine allusion to the story of Acteon, and a beautiful exposition of the fable.
3. *Difficili bile tumet jecur.*
4. That my eye has revealed a secret, which my mind should have concealed. *Johnson.*
5. For *own*, or are *masters* of.
6. Ingratum si dixeris, omnia dixeris.

TWELFTH NIGHT
IN THE NINETEENTH CENTURY
🕮

During the nineteenth century, some important commentators wrote about the place of *Twelfth Night* within the progression of Shakespeare's work and within the genre of Western drama in general. Others focused specifically on the play's characters.

William Hazlitt, for instance, in discussing *Twelfth Night*, wrote that Shakespeare's comedies—and especially this one, so "full of sweetness and pleasantry"—are significantly different from other comedies. He considered Shakespeare's characters both natural and true, a result of the playwright's showing them "in the happiest lights" rather than being rendered "contemptible." Hazlitt claimed that the comedies of his own day, in contrast, rely on ridicule and satire. Another commentator, Charles Knight, also found Shakespeare's characters "poetical" and "genuine." The critic Hermann Ulrici, however, viewed almost all of the dramatic characters in *Twelfth Night* as not realistic, but fantastic. As a result, in his view, events occur that are quite out of the ordinary. For example, Ulrici saw love in the play as "a mere freak of the imagination" and certainly not the work's central concern.

Hazlitt put Shakespeare's work in a category with that of Cervantes and Molière. He also noted the play's emphasis on romance and delight. Other critics made similar comments: Symons found the play "delightful," and Georg Brandes noted that while Shakespeare pokes fun at Puritans in the play, he never does it with venom but rather with great humor. G. C. Verplanck remarked that the play was most appropriate for the Twelfth Night season, its characters being not only genuine but full of "spirit and fun."

At the same time, within this one play, according to Hazlitt, Shakespeare shows his gift for creating tragedy as well as comedy. Similarly, F. J. Furnivall remarked that though the play highlights Shakespeare's gift for comedy, "there's the shadow of death and distress across the sunshine." In Brandes's view, Shakespeare's joy for life had peaked, and after this work he would move into melancholy.

As for specific characters in the play, Hazlitt remarked on the strengths of Viola in particular. From his perspective, she is "the great and secret charm" of the play. Indeed, the critic Arthur Symons called Viola a "relief" when compared to the sentimental and self-centered characters in the play, namely the duke and Olivia. Furnivall wrote that Viola is the real heroine in the play, determined and self-sacrificing. Valentine had been unable to get to Olivia on behalf of the duke, but Viola will not be deterred, even though she feels deeply for the duke and wants him for herself. Furnivall also pointed out the difference between Viola's love for the duke and the duke's supposed love for Olivia. He remarked that if the duke's love had been real, nothing would have been able to keep him from wooing Olivia. Brandes had a similar observation: Viola's persistence in wooing Olivia makes her appear superior to the duke, and therefore it is no surprise that Olivia becomes so enchanted with Viola (as Cesario).

Anna Jameson compared the characters in *Twelfth Night* to those in other plays of Shakespeare—Viola to Rosalind and Olivia to Portia. Jameson also pointed out that Olivia should not be condemned for so readily becoming attracted to the disguised Viola. Olivia does have attributes that show her to be admirable, and so we should take her passion with levity. Jameson also asserted that although the duke is overly wrapped up in his own passions, Viola's love for him is understandable, since he is accomplished, has a taste for music, and is tender and poetical. Furnivall also stood up for the duke, writing that Orsino would be a "tender and true" husband.

As for the character of Malvolio, which critics today consider one of the most interesting in the play, nineteenth-century commentators had various responses. Charles Lamb noted that Malvolio is "not essentially ludicrous" but that his morality and manners clash with the norm in the land of Illyria. According to Lamb, Malvolio deserves some respect: "We see no reason why he should not have been brave, honourable, accomplished." This view is reinforced, Lamb pointed out, by the fact that at the play's end the duke wants Malvolio to live peacefully with the others. Charles Knight had a similar reaction to Malvolio. He argued that the audience is meant to pity him, just as Olivia and the duke do at the end of the play. The commentator John Weiss suggested that we should have sympathy for Malvolio since he has to live with the daily stress of Sir Toby being a guest in the household. Weiss saw Malvolio as Shakespeare's device for showing what happens when a virtue becomes a vice.

Not every critic agreed, however. Arthur Symons, for one, wrote that Malvolio should be seen as comic, not tragic, and Georg Brandes pointed out that Malvolio's believing that Olivia could love and desire him serves as a parody of the duke's and Olivia's own follies in love.

1817—William Hazlitt. "*Twelfth Night: or, What You Will*," from *Characters of Shakespear's Plays*

William Hazlitt (1778-1830) was an English essayist and one of the finest Shakespeare critics of the nineteenth century. He also examined the work of poets, dramatists, essayists, and novelists of his own and earlier times. His essays appeared in such volumes as *English Poets*, *English Comic Writers*, and *A View of the English Stage*.

This is justly considered as one of the most delightful of Shakespear's comedies. It is full of sweetness and pleasantry. It is perhaps too good-natured for comedy. It has little satire, and no spleen. It aims at the ludicrous rather than the ridiculous. It makes us laugh at the follies of mankind, not despise them, and still less bear any ill-will towards them. Shakespear's comic genius resembles rather in its power of extracting sweets from weeds or poisons, than in leaving a sting behind it. He gives the most amusing exaggeration of the prevailing foibles of his characters, but in a way that they themselves, instead of being offended at, would almost join in to humour; he rather contrives opportunities for them to shew themselves off in the happiest lights, than renders them contemptible in the perverse construction of the wit or malice of others.—There is a certain stage of society in which people become conscious of their peculiarities and absurdities, affect to disguise what they are, and set up pretensions to what they are not. This gives rise to a corresponding style of comedy, the object of which is to detect the disguises of self-love, and to make reprisals on these preposterous assumptions of vanity, by marking the contrast between the real and the affected character as severely as possible, and denying to those, who would impose on us for what they are not, even the merit which they have. This is the comedy of artificial life, of wit and satire, such as we see it in Congreve, Wycherley, Vanbrugh, etc. To this succeeds a state of society from which the same sort of affectation and pretence are banished by a greater knowledge of the world or by their successful exposure on the stage; and which by neutralising the materials of comic character, both natural and artificial, leaves no comedy at all—but *the sentimental*. Such is our modern comedy. There is a period in the progress of manners anterior to both these, in which the foibles and follies of individuals are of nature's planting, not the growth of art or study; in which they are therefore unconscious of them themselves, or care not who knows them, if they can but have their whim out; and in which, as there is no attempt at imposition, the spectators rather receive pleasure from humouring the inclinations of the persons they laugh at, than wish to give them pain by exposing their absurdity. This may be called the comedy of nature, and it is the comedy which we generally find in Shakespear.—Whether the analysis here given be just or not, the spirit of his comedies is evidently quite distinct from that of the authors above mentioned, as it is in its essence the same with that of Cervantes, and also very frequently of Molière, though he was more systematic in his extravagance than Shakespear. Shakespear's comedy is of a pastoral and poetical cast. Folly is indigenous to the soil, and shoots out with native, happy, unchecked luxuriance. Absurdity has every encouragement afforded it; and nonsense has room to flourish in. Nothing is stunted by the churlish, icy hand of indifference or severity. The poet runs riot in a conceit, and idolises a quibble. His whole object is to turn the meanest or rudest objects to a pleasurable account. The relish which he has of a pun, or of the quaint humour of a low character, does not interfere with the delight with which he describes a beautiful image, or the most refined love. The clown's forced jests do not spoil the sweetness of the character of Viola; the same house is big enough to hold Malvolio, the Countess, Maria, Sir Toby, and Sir Andrew Ague-cheek. For instance, nothing can fall much lower than this last character in intellect or morals: yet how are his weaknesses nursed and dandled by Sir Toby into something 'high fantastical,' when on Sir Andrew's commendation of himself for dancing and fencing, Sir Toby answers—'Wherefore are these things hid? Wherefore have these gifts a curtain before them? Are they like to take dust like mistress Moll's picture? Why dost thou not go to church in a galliard, and come home in a coranto? My very walk should be a jig! I would not so much as make water but in a cinque-pace. What dost thou mean? Is this a world to hide virtues in? I did think by the excellent constitution of thy leg, it was framed under the star of a galliard!'—How Sir Toby, Sir Andrew, and the Clown afterwards *chirp over their cups,* how they 'rouse the night-owl in a catch, able to draw three souls out of one weaver!' What can be better than Sir Toby's unanswerable answer to Malvolio, 'Dost thou think, because thou art virtuous, there shall be no more cakes and ale?'—In a word, the best turn is given to every thing, instead of the worst. There is a constant infusion of the romantic and enthusiastic, in proportion as the characters are natural and sincere: whereas, in the more artificial style of comedy, every thing gives way to ridicule and indifference, there being nothing left but affectation on one side, and incredulity on the other.—Much as we like Shakespear's comedies, we cannot agree with Dr. Johnson that they are better than his tragedies; nor do we like them half so well. If his inclination to comedy sometimes led him to trifle with the seriousness of tragedy, the poetical and impassioned passages are the best parts of his comedies. The great and secret charm of *Twelfth Night* is the character of Viola. Much as we like catches and cakes and ale, there is something that we like better. We have a friendship for Sir Toby; we patronise Sir Andrew; we have an understanding with the Clown, a sneaking kindness for Maria and her rogueries; we feel a regard for Malvolio, and sympathise with his gravity, his smiles, his cross garters, his yellow stockings, and imprisonment in the stocks. But there is something that excites in us a stronger feeling than all this—it is Viola's confession of her love.

> *Duke:* What's her history?
> *Viola: A blank, my lord, she never told her love:*
> She let concealment, like a worm i' th' bud,
> Feed on her damask cheek: she pin'd in thought,
> And with a green and yellow melancholy,
> She sat like Patience on a monument,
> Smiling at grief. *Was not this love indeed?*
> We men may say more, swear more, but indeed,
> Our shews are more than will; for still we prove
> Much in our vows, but little in our love.
> *Duke:* But died thy sister of her love, my boy?
> *Viola:* I am all the daughters of my father's house,
> And all the brothers too;—and yet I know not.

Shakespear alone could describe the effect of his own poetry.

> Oh, it came o'er the ear like the sweet south
> That breathes upon a bank of violets,
> Stealing and giving odour.

What we so much admire here is not the image of Patience on a monument, which has been generally quoted, but the lines before and after it. 'They give a very echo to the seat where love is throned.' How long ago it is since we first learnt to repeat them; and still, still they vibrate on the heart, like the sounds which the passing wind draws from the trembling strings of a harp left on some desert shore! There are other passages of not less impassioned sweetness. Such is Olivia's address to Sebastian, whom she supposes to have already deceived her in a promise of marriage.

> Blame not this haste of mine: if you mean well,
> Now go with me and with this holy man
> Into the chantry by: there before him,
> And underneath that consecrated roof,
> Plight me the full assurance of your faith,
> *That my most jealous and too doubtful soul*
> *May live at peace.*

We have already said something of Shakespear's songs. One of the most beautiful of them occurs in this play, with a preface of his own to it.

"*Duke.* O fellow, come; the song we had last night.
Mark it, Cesario, it is old and plain;
The spinsters and the knitters in the sun,
And the free maids that weave their thread with bones,
Do use to chaunt it: it is silly sooth,
And dallies with the innocence of love,
Like the old age.

SONG
  Come away, come away, death,
And in sad cypress let me be laid;
  Fly away, fly away, breath;
I am slain by a fair cruel maid.
My shroud of white, stuck all with yew,
    O prepare it;
My part of death no one so true
    Did share it.

  Not a flower, not a flower sweet,
On my black coffin let there be strewn;
  Not a friend, not a friend greet
Dry poor corpse, where my bones shall be thrown:
  A thousand thousand sighs to save,
    Lay me, O! where
Sad true-love never find my grave,
    To weep there.

Who after this will say that Shakespear's genius was only fitted for comedy?
Yet after reading other parts of this play, and particularly the garden-scene where
Malvolio picks up the letter, if we were to say that his genius for comedy was
less than his genius for tragedy, it would perhaps only prove that our own taste
in such matters is more saturnine than mercurial.

Enter MARIA.

Sir Toby. Here comes the little villain:—How now, my nettle of India?
Maria. Get ye all three into the box-tree: Malvolio's coming down this
walk: he has been yonder i' the sun, practicing behaviour to his own
shadow this half hour: observe him, for the love of mockery; for I know
this letter will make a contemplative idiot of him. Close, in the name
of jesting! Lie thou there; for here come's the trout that must be caught
with tickling.
  [*They hide themselves. Maria throws down a letter, and Exit.*

Enter MALVOLIO.

Malvolio. 'Tis but fortune; all is fortune. Maria once told me, she did affect me; and I have heard herself come thus near, that, should she fancy, it should be one of my complexion. Besides, she uses me with a more exalted respect than any one else that follows her. What should I think on't?

Sir Toby. Here's an over-weening rogue!

Fabian. O, peace! Contemplation makes a rare turkey-cock of him; how he jets under his advanced plumes!

Sir Andrew. 'Slight, I could so beat the rogue:—

Sir Toby. Peace, I say.

Malvolio. To be count Malvolio;—

Sir Toby. Ah, rogue!

Sir Andrew. Pistol him, pistol him.

Sir Toby. Peace, peace!

Malvolio. There is example for 't; the lady of the Strachy married the yeoman of the wardrobe.

Sir Andrew. Fie on him, Jezebel!

Fabian. O, peace! now he's deeply in; look, how imagination blows him.

Malvolio. Having been three months married to her, sitting in my chair of state,——

Sir Toby. O for a stone bow, to hit him in the eye!

Malvolio. Calling my officers about me, in my branch'd velvet gown; having come from a day-bed, where I have left Olivia sleeping.

Sir Toby. Fire and brimstone!

Fabian. O peace, peace!

Malvolio. And then to have the humour of state: and after a demure travel of regard,——telling them, I know my place, as I would they should do theirs,—to ask for my kinsman Toby.——

Sir Toby. Bolts and shackles!

Fabian. O, peace, peace, peace! now, now.

Malvolio. Seven of my people, with an obedient start, make out for him. I frown the while; and, perchance, wind up my watch, or play with some rich jewel. Toby approaches; curtsies there to me:

Sir Toby. Shall this fellow live?

Fabian. Though our silence be drawn from us with cares, yet peace.

Malvolio. I extend my hand to him thus, quenching my familiar smile with an austere regard to controul:

Sir Toby. And does not Toby take you a blow o'the lips then?

Malvolio. Saying—Cousin Toby, my fortunes having cast me on your niece, give me this prerogative of speech;—

Sir Toby. What, what?

Malvolio. You must amend your drunkenness.
Fabian. Nay, patience, or we break the sinews of our plot.
Malvolio. Besides, you waste the treasure of your time with a foolish
knight—
Sir Andrew. That's me, I warrant you.
Malvolio. One Sir Andrew——
Sir Andrew. I knew, 'twas I; for many do call me fool.
Malvolio. What employment have we here?

[Taking up the letter."

The letter and his comments on it are equally good. If poor Malvolio's treatment
afterwards is a little hard, poetical justice is done in the uneasiness which Olivia
suffers on account of her mistaken attachment to Cesario, as her insensibility
to the violence of the Duke's passion is atoned for by the discovery of Viola's
concealed love of him.

⸺෴⸺ ⸺෴⸺ ⸺෴⸺

1823—Charles Lamb. From
On Some of the Old Actors

Charles Lamb (1775-1834), poet and essayist, is most famous for his
"Elia" essays and his children's book *Tales from Shakespear,* which he
wrote with his sister, Mary Lamb.

Malvolio is not essentially ludicrous. He becomes comic but by accident. He is
cold, austere, repelling; but dignified, consistent, and, for what appears, rather
of an over-stretched morality. (. . .) But his morality and his manners are
misplaced in Illyria. He is opposed to the proper *levities* of the piece, and falls
in the unequal contest. Still his pride, or his gravity, (call it which you will) is
inherent, and native to the man, not mock or affected, which latter only are
the fit objects to excite laughter. His quality is at the best unlovely, but neither
buffoon nor contemptible. His bearing is lofty, a little above his station, but
probably not much above his deserts. We see no reason why he should not
have been brave, honourable, accomplished. His careless committal of the ring
to the ground (which he was commissioned to restore to Cesario), bespeaks a
generosity of birth and feeling. His dialect on all occasions is that of a gentleman,
and a man of education. We must not confound him with the eternal old, low
steward of comedy. He is master of the household to a great Princess; a dignity
probably conferred upon him for other respects than age or length of service.
Olivia, at the first indication of his supposed madness, declares that she 'would

not have him miscarry for half of her dowry.' Does this look as if the character was meant to appear little or insignificant? Once, indeed, she accuses him to his face—of what?—of being 'sick of self-love,'—but with a gentleness and considerateness which could not have been, if she had not thought that this particular infirmity shaded some virtues. His rebuke to the knight, and his sottish revellers, is sensible and spirited; and when we take into consideration the unprotected condition of his mistress, and the strict regard with which her state of real or dissembled mourning would draw the eyes of the world upon her house-affairs, Malvolio might feel the honour of the family in some sort in his keeping; as it appears not that Olivia had any more brothers, or kinsmen, to look to it—for Sir Toby had dropped all such nice respects at the buttery hatch. That Malvolio was meant to be represented as possessing estimable qualities, the expression of the Duke in his anxiety to have him reconciled, almost infers. 'Pursue him, and entreat him to a peace.' Even in his abused state of chains and darkness, a sort of greatness seems never to desert him. He argues highly and well with the supposed Sir Topas, and philosophises gallantly upon his straw.[1] There must have been some shadow of worth about the man; he must have been something more than a mere vapour—a thing of straw, or Jack in office—before Fabian and Maria could have ventured sending him upon a courting-errand to Olivia. There was some consonancy (as he would say) in the undertaking, or the jest would have been too bold even for that house of misrule.

NOTE

1. *Clown.* What is the opinion of Pythagoras concerning wild fowl?
   Mal. That the soul of our grandam might haply inhabit a bird.
   Clown. What thinkest thou of his opinion?
   Mal. I think nobly of the soul, and no way approve of his opinion.
   [Lamb's note. See IV. ii. 48–54]

1833—Anna Jameson. From "Viola," from *Shakspeare's Heroines: Characteristics of Women, Moral, Poetical, & Historical*

Anna Murphy Brownell Jameson (1794-1860), born in Dublin, is best remembered for her character studies of Shakespeare's heroines.

The situation and the character of Viola have been censured for their want of consistency and probability; it is therefore worth while to examine how far this criticism is true. As for her situation in the drama (of which she is properly the heroine), it is shortly this: She is shipwrecked on the coast of Illyria; she is alone and without protection in a strange country. She wishes to enter into the service of the Countess Olivia; but she is assured that this is impossible; "for the lady, having recently lost an only and beloved brother, has abjured the sight of men, has shut herself up in her palace, and will admit no kind of suit." In this perplexity, Viola remembers to have heard her father speak with praise and admiration of Orsino, the Duke of the country; and having ascertained that he is not married, and that therefore his court is not a proper asylum for her in her feminine character, she attires herself in the disguise of a page, as the best protection against uncivil comments, till she can gain some tidings of her brother.

If we carry our thoughts back to a romantic and chivalrous age, there is surely sufficient probability here for all the purposes of poetry. To pursue the thread of Viola's destiny;—she is engaged in the service of the Duke, whom she finds "fancy-sick" for the love of Olivia. We are left to infer (for so it is hinted in the first scene) that this Duke—who, with his accomplishments and his personal attractions, his taste for music, his chivalrous tenderness, and his unrequited love, is really a very fascinating and poetical personage, though a little passionate and fantastic—had already made some impression on Viola's imagination; and, when she comes to play the confidante, and to be loaded with favours and kindness in her assumed character, that she should be touched by a passion made up of pity, admiration, gratitude, and tenderness, does not, I think, in any way detract from the genuine sweetness and delicacy of her character, for "*she never told her love.*"

Now all this, as the critic wisely observes, may not present a very just picture of life; and it may also fail to impart any moral lesson for the especial profit of well-bred young ladies: but is it not in truth and in nature? Did it ever fail to charm or to interest, to seize on the coldest fancy, to touch the most insensible heart?

Viola then is the chosen favourite of the enamoured Duke, and becomes his messenger to Olivia, and the interpreter of this sufferings to that inaccessible beauty. In her character of a youthful page, she attracts the favour of Olivia, and excites the jealousy of her lord. The situation is critical and delicate; but how exquisitely is the character of Viola fitted to her part, carrying her through the ordeal with all the inward and spiritual grace of modesty! What beautiful propriety in the distinction drawn between Rosalind and Viola! The wild sweetness, the frolic humour which sports free and unblamed amid the shades of Ardennes, would ill become Viola, whose playfulness is assumed as part of her disguise as a court page, and is guarded by the strictest delicacy. She has not, like Rosalind, a saucy enjoyment in her own incognito; her disguise does not sit so easily upon her; her heart does not beat freely under it. As in the old ballad, where "Sweet William" is detected weeping in secret over her "man's array,"[1] so in Viola a sweet consciousness of her feminine nature is forever breaking through her masquerade:

> "And on her cheek is ready with a blush
> Modest as morning, when she coldly eyes
> The youthful Phoebus."

She plays her part well, but never forgets, nor allows us to forget, that she is playing a part.

> "*Olivia.* Are you a comedian?
> "*Viola.* No, my profound heart! and yet by the very fangs of malice I swear, I am not that I play!"

And thus she comments on it:

> "Disguise, I see thou art a wickedness,
> Wherein the pregnant enemy does much.
> How easy is it for the proper-false
> In women's waxen hearts to set their forms!
> Alas! our frailty is the cause, not we."

The feminine cowardice of Viola, which will not allow her even to affect a courage becoming her attire,—her horror at the idea of drawing a sword,—is very natural and characteristic; and produces a most humorous effect, even at the very moment it charms and interests us.

Contrasted with the deep, silent, patient love of Viola for the Duke, we have the lady-like wilfulness of Olivia; and her sudden passion, or rather fancy, for the disguised page takes so beautiful a colouring of poetry and sentiment that we do not think her forward. Olivia is like a princess of romance, and has all the privileges of one; she is, like Portia, high-born and high-bred, mistress over her servants—but not, like Portia, "queen o'er herself." She has never in her life been opposed; the first contradiction, therefore, rouses all the woman in her, and turns a caprice into a headlong passion; yet she apologizes for herself:

> "I have said too much unto a heart of stone,
> And laid mine honour too unchary out;
> There's something in me that reproves my fault;
> But such a headstrong potent fault it is,
> That it but mocks reproof!"

And in the midst of her self-abandonment never allows us to contemn, even while we pity her:

"What shall you ask of me that I'll deny,
That honour, sav'd, may upon asking give?"

The distance of rank which separates the Countess from the youthful page—the real sex of Viola—the dignified elegance of Olivia's deportment, except where passion gets the better of her pride—her consistent coldness towards the Duke—the description of that "smooth, discreet, and stable bearing" with which she rules her household—her generous care for her steward Malvolio, in the midst of her own distress,—all these circumstances raise Olivia in our fancy, and render her caprice for the page a source of amusement and interest, not a subject of reproach. *Twelfth Night* is a genuine comedy—a perpetual spring of the gayest and the sweetest fancies. In artificial society men and women are divided into castes and classes, and it is rarely that extremes in character or manners can approximate. To blend into one harmonious picture the utmost grace and refinement of sentiment and the broadest effects of humour, the most poignant wit and the most indulgent benignity, in short, to bring before us in the same scene Viola and Olivia, with Malvolio and Sir Toby, belonged only to Nature and to Shakspeare.

NOTE
1. *Percy's Reliques*, vol. iii. See the ballad of "The Lady turned Serving-man."

1839—Charles Knight.
From *The Pictorial Edition of the Works of Shakspere*

Charles Knight was a publisher of books and magazines, an editor, and an author. Some of his titles include *The Shadows of the Old Booksellers* and *Passages of a Working Life during Half a Century*. The passage below comes from a discussion of Shakespeare's comedies in his edition of Shakespeare's works.

It is scarcely necessary for us to enter into any analysis of the plot of this charming comedy, or attempt any dissection of its characters, for the purpose of opening to the reader new sources of enjoyment. It is impossible, we think, for one of ordinary sensibility to read through the first act without yielding himself up to the genial temper in which the entire play is written. "The sunshine of the breast" spreads its rich purple light over the whole champaign, and penetrates into every thicket and every dingle. From the first line to the last—from the Duke's

"That strain again; it had a dying fall,"

to the Clown's

"With hey, ho, the wind and the rain!"—

there is not a thought or a situation that is not calculated to call forth pleasurable feelings. The love-melancholy of the Duke is a luxurious abandonment to one pervading impression—not a fierce and hopeless contest with one o'er-mastering passion. It delights to lie "canopied with bowers,"—to listen to "old and antique" songs, which dally with its "innocence,"—to be "full of shapes," and "high fantastical." The love of Viola is the sweetest and tenderest emotion that ever informed the heart of the purest and most graceful of beings with a spirit almost divine. Perhaps in the whole range of Shakspere's poetry there is nothing which comes more unbidden into the mind, and always in connection with some image of the ethereal beauty of the utterer, than Viola's "she never told her love." The love of Olivia, wilful as it is, is not in the slightest degree repulsive. With the old stories before him, nothing but the refined delicacy of Shakspere's conception of the female character could have redeemed Olivia from approaching to the anti-feminine. But as it is, we pity her, and we rejoice with her. These are what may be called the serious characters, because they are the vehicles for what we emphatically call the poetry of the play. But the comic characters are to us equally poetical—that is, they appear to us not mere copies of the representatives of temporary or individual follies, but embodyings of the universal comic, as true and as fresh to-day as they were two centuries and a half ago. Malvolio is to our minds as poetical as Don Quixote; and we are by no means sure that Shakspere meant the poor cross-gartered steward *only* to be laughed at, any more than Cervantes did the knight of the rueful countenance. He meant us to pity him, as Olivia and the Duke pitied him; for, in truth, the delusion by which Malvolio was wrecked only passed out of the romantic into the comic through the manifestation of the vanity of the character in reference to his situation. But if we laugh at Malvolio, we are not to laugh ill-naturedly, for the poet has conducted all the mischief against him in a spirit in which there is no real malice at the bottom of the fun. Sir Toby is a most genuine character—one given to strong potations and boisterous merriment; but with a humour about him perfectly irresistible. His *abandon* to the instant opportunity of laughing at and with others is something so thoroughly English that we are not surprised the poet gave him an English name. And like all genuine humorists, Sir Toby must have his butt. What a trio is presented in that glorious scene of the second act, where the two knights and the Clown "make the welkin dance"—the humorist, the fool, and the philosopher!—for Sir Andrew is the fool, and the Clown is the philosopher. We hold the Clown's epilogue song to be the most philosophical clown's song upon record; and a treatise might be written upon its wisdom. It is the history of a life, from the condition of "a little tiny boy," through "man's estate," to decaying age—"when I came into my bed;" and the conclusion is, that what is true of the individual is true of the species, and what was of yesterday was of generations long past away—for

"A great while ago the world begun."

1847—G. C. Verplanck.
From *The Illustrated Shakespeare*

Gulian Crommelin Verplanck (1786–1870), a New York native of Dutch descent, was active in politics, scholarship, and criticism. He was the editor of an edition of Shakespeare's plays and the author of many works. The following comes from his illustrated edition of Shakespeare's works.

We may safely fix the date of this comedy about the year 1600 or 1601, and class it among the later productions of that period of Shakespeare's life when his mind most habitually revelled in humorous delineation, while his luxuriant fancy, turning aside from the sterner and painful passions, shed its gayest tints over innumerable forms of grace and beauty. He seems, by his title of the *Twelfth Night*, to apprise his audience of the general character of this agreeable and varied comedy—a notice intelligible enough at that time, and still not without its significance in a great part of Europe, though quite otherwise among our un-holiday-keeping people on this side of the Atlantic. The *Twelfth Night* (twelfth after Christmas) was, in the olden times, the season of universal festivity—of masques, pageants, feasts, and traditionary sports. This comedy then would not disappoint public expectation, when it was found to contain a delightful combination of the delicate fancy and romantic sentiment of the poetic masque, with a crowd of revelling, laughing, or laugh-creating personages, whose truth all would recognize, and whose spirit and fun no gravity could resist. He gave to these the revelling spirit, and the exaggeration of character necessary for the broadest comic effect, but still kept them from becoming mere buffoon masquers by a truth of portraiture which shows them all to be drawn from real life. Malvolio—the matchless Malvolio—was not only new in his day to comic delineation of any sort, but I believe has never since had his fellow or his copy in any succeeding play, poem, essay, or novel. The gravity, the acquirement, the real talent and accomplishment of the man, all made ludicrous, fantastical, and absurd by his intense vanity, is as true a conception as it is original and droll, and its truth may still be frequently attested by actual comparison with real Malvolios, to be found everywhere, from humble domestic life up to the high places of learning, of the State, and even of the Church. Sir Toby certainly comes out of the same associations where the poet saw Falstaff hold his revels. He is not Sir John, nor a fainter sketch of him, yet with an odd sort of family likeness to him. Dryden and other dramatists have felicitated themselves upon success in grouping together their comic underplots with their more heroic personages. But here all, grave and gay, the lovers, the laughers, and the laughed-at, are made to harmonize in one scene and one common purpose. I cannot help adding—though perhaps it may be a capricious over-refinement—that to my mind this comedy resembles *Macbeth*, in one of the marked characteristics of that great drama; appearing, like it, to have been struck out at a heat, as if the whole plot, its characters and dialogue, had presented themselves at once, in one harmonious group, before the "mind's eye" of the poet, previously to his actually commencing the formal business of writing, and bearing no indication either of an original groundwork of incident, afterwards enriched by the additions of a fuller mind, or of thoughts, situations, and characters accidentally suggested, or growing unexpectedly out of the story, as the author proceeded.

1876—John Weiss.
From *Wit, Humor, and Shakspeare*

The American John Weiss (1818–1879) was active in Transcendentalist circles in New England. The author of many reviews, sermons, and magazine articles, his publications include *Life and Correspondence of Theodore Parker* and *American Religion*.

Malvolio, the steward of Olivia's household, is prized by that lady for his grave and punctilious disposition. He discharges his office carefully and in a tone of some superiority, for his mind is above his estate. At some time in his life he has read cultivated books, knows the theory of Pythagoras concerning the transmigration of the soul, but thinks more nobly of the soul and no way approves that opinion. His gentility, though a little rusted and obsolete, is like a Sunday suit which nobody thinks of rallying. He wears it well, and his mistress cannot afford to treat him exactly as a servant; in fact, she has occasionally dropped good-natured phrases which he has interpreted into a special partiality; for Quixotic conceits can riot about inside of his stiff demeanor. This proneness to fantasy increases the touchiness of a man of reserve. He can never take a joke, and his climate is too inclement to shelter humor. Souls must be at blood-heat, and brains must expand with it like a blossom, before humor will fructify. He wonders how Olivia can tolerate the clown. "I protest," he says, "I take these wise men, that crow so at these set kind of fools, to be no better than the fools' zanies." Olivia hits the difficulty when she replies, "Oh, you are sick of self-love, and taste with a distempered appetite." Perhaps he thinks nobly of the soul because he so profoundly respects his own, and carries it upon stilts over the heads of the servants and Sir Toby and Sir Andrew.

Imagine this saturnine and self-involved man obliged to consort daily with Sir Toby, who brings his hand to the buttery-bar before breakfast, and who hates going to bed "as an unfilled can," unless no more drink is forthcoming; an irascible fellow, too, and all the more tindery because continually dry. He has Sir Andrew Aguecheek for a boon companion, who says of himself that sometimes he has no more wit than a Christian, or than an ordinary man . . . .

But the play does not let Malvolio drop softly on his feet. There is a faint grudge provoked by the ill-tempered quality of his conceit, and Shakspeare indicates this trait of our nature. The Clown, who remembers how the steward used to twit Olivia's contentment at his sallies, and to deprecate it in a lofty way, now mimics his phrases and manner to sting him with a last fluttering dart. Malvolio's pride is already too deeply wounded, for he has indeed been "notoriously abused." There is no relenting in such a man on account of the fun, for that is a crime in the eyes of a Puritan, to be punished for God's sake. His temper acquires sombreness from his belief that total depravity is a good doctrine if you can only live up to it. But when this crime of fun is perpetrated against the anointed self-esteem of the Puritan himself, it is plain he will be revenged on the whole pack of them unless they proceed to make a sop of deference to touch his hurt with, and a pipe out of his own egotism for sounding a truce.

Shakspeare delighted to mark the transition of a virtue to a vice; that elusive moment, as of a point of passage from one species to another, discovered and put into a flash from the light of humor. Malvolio's grave and self-respecting temperament is an excellence. No decent man thinks meanly of himself, and the indecent ones cannot afford the disparagement. The pretence of it is a warning to us to expect mischief, a notice put up, "This is a private way; dangerous passing."

1876—Hermann Ulrici. *"Twelfth Night; or, What You Will,"* from *Shakspeare's Dramatic Art: History and Character of Shakespeare's Plays* (third edition)

Hermann Ulrici (1806–1884) was a German scholar, professor of philosophy, and author of works on Greek poetry and Shakespeare.

The fantastic is expressed not only by giving the *external* form of life a wonderful shape contrary to common reality, but man himself can be fantastic, can think and act fantastically, by yielding completely to his whims, caprices and illusions, or by allowing himself to be led by the play of chance without having any plan or intention of his own. If we bear this in mind we shall readily discover the fantastic colouring in 'What You Will.' The external form of life here described is exactly such as is usually met with in common reality; there is nothing forced or unnatural in the great likeness between the twins, Viola and Sebastian, although it may be a circumstance of rare occurrence. But almost all the dramatic characters are fantastic, and therefore the inner life, in its connection with the outer world, manifests the most wonderful phenomena—strange freaks and equally strange matters of chance, incidents and complications. The fantastic element reveals itself here, on the one hand, in Viola's whimsical freak to play the man, in the Duke's wilful, half capricious love for Olivia, in the latter's capricious and sudden liking for the disguised Viola, and in the final conversion of both, when the Duke marries Viola, and Olivia the latter's brother. It is no less revealed in the mad freak of Sir Andrew Ague-Cheek becoming a suitor to Olivia. On the other hand, we find it also in the complications occasioned by a number of strange accidents; in the accidental deliverance of Sebastian, in his accidental meeting with Viola in Illyria, in the accidental meetings of Olivia, Sir Andrew, Sir Toby, and the rest. The element of intrigue, however, receives its appointed place in the drama by the deliberateness with which Viola, in her disguise, woos Olivia, in order that the latter may be made to repent of her cruelty to the Duke, and still more by the pranks played by Maria, Sir Toby and Fabian, upon the braggart Malvolio and the foolish Sir Andrew.

Accordingly, from the very fundamental plan of the play, it is evident that all the manifold motives and levers at the disposal of the comic poet, are here set in motion. Not only have we freaks and whims, mistakes, folly and perversity, quaint notions and resolves, but we see external accidents also, and well-considered intrigues encountering one another and forming a diversified whole. But the question now is, where is the centre of this whole, the point of unity in the composition, which connects the threads of the confused web of many figures and colours, and unites and arranges the manifold forms, actions and incidents into one harmonious whole? What is the reason that the drama, as such, in spite of the confused play of caprice and accident (which forms its substance) does nevertheless not bear within itself the impress of accident or of a conglomeration of caprices, but that, on the contrary, it makes the impression of an harmonious and well ordered whole? However difficult this question may be to answer in the case of Shakspeare's tragedies, and still more so in his comedies, yet it is nevertheless the main and fundamental question, the decision of which essentially determines the estimate we are to form of his dramas, as of every work of art.

At the first glance it might seem as if in 'What You Will,' the end in view was a comic exhibition of *love*, which of itself can as well form the substance of a comedy as the fundamental theme of a tragedy. However, we have here nothing to do with the real and, in this sense, the significant passion of love. Love here, appears rather as a mere freak of the imagination, a mere glittering kaleidoscope of sentiment, a gay dress in which the soul envelopes itself and which it changes with the various seasons. The Duke's passion for Olivia bursts out into flame as suddenly for Viola, as her heart is kindled with love for him; Olivia's fondness for Viola is quite satisfied with the substitution of the brother, who, on his part, makes no objection about being put in his sister's place, and Malvolio's, and Sir Andrew's affection for Olivia is a mere bubble. Nay, Antonio's very friendship for Sebastian is also somewhat accidental and fantastic in character. Thus the playful capriciousness of love appears only to be the main spring to the merry game of life which is here unrolled before our eyes; it is only a prominent motive for the development of the action, not the nucleus and gravitating point of the whole.

The title of the piece, as I think, points to this even though but in indistinct and indefinite tones. By the choice of this curious title which stands apparently in no relation whatever to its substance, Shakspeare wishes to give us a hint as to his intention, a symbolical intimation as to the manner in which the whole is to be understood—Twelfth Night was the prelude to the merry season of Shrovetide, and was passed amid all kinds of convivial games and jokes. The 'bean king' who was elected by the lot of a bean which was baked in a cake (hence by pure chance) had then to select a 'queen,'[1] and established a burlesque kingdom; his commands had to be punctually obeyed and every one gave free reins to their fun and merriment in this airy kingdom. Games of hazard, also, were exceptionally permitted on this evening, and Tieck justly remarks, that even in the play itself, Sebastian, Viola and Maria (to whom we may also add the Duke and Olivia) win great and important prizes in the lottery of life, and that a blank is drawn by Malvolio alone, who fancies he has the richest prize safe in his own hands. The title also corresponds perfectly with the nature and character of the piece, which—as is easily seen—exhibits life itself as a Twelfth Night, as a merry, fantastic bean-festival. The second title of 'What You Will,' is, in reality, even more significant. It indeed refers to the relation between the public and the play, but not (as has been supposed) in the quite inadmissible sense, that the piece was to give and to represent whatever the spectators wished. This is not the case; the play rather creates what *it* wishes, and the better it is the less can that which it gives be different from what it is: The title is rather intended to signify that that which men all like to see represented is ever the same; namely, a chequered, a varied life, rich in incidents and crossed by misfortunes and complications, one that excites interest and keeps up a state of suspense, but which, nevertheless, does not exceed the bounds of ordinary human life, even though it leads to a happy and harmonious ending through unusual, strange and winding paths. We are, in reality, all as little fond of an existence which passes with nothing unusual, surprising or exciting to the imagination, where everything happens according to well-considered aims and objects, as we are of the reverse, a life governed solely by chance, whim and caprice. We would all prefer the greatest possible equality in the mixture of the usual and the unusual, of accident and intention, of whim and reflection, imagination and reason. It is not merely the experiencing such a life, the very beholding it produces that gaiety, that inward contentment at which we are all aiming. And thus Shakspeare could with justice—especially of this one of his comedies—maintain that it represented 'What You (all) Will.'

Were it necessary, a closer examination of the leading *characters* would still more clearly establish the interpretation which I have given of the title, and thereby of the play itself. I shall content myself with drawing attention to a few points. Viola is in so far the heroine of the piece, as the whole play originates with and is kept in motion by her and her disguise. And yet her character is given in light touches and delicate colours, and is composed of but a few simple elements. It consists, so to say, only in the apparent contradiction between a tender, gentle, sensitive, longing heart, which, being 'deeply skilled in the science of love,' retires in maidenly shyness within itself, and a bold, witty and imaginative mind that whispers to her all kinds of mischievous ideas, which she involuntarily follows from her innate pleasure in romance and in what is fantastic. She thereby falls into situations which cause her anxiety and embarrassment, because, on the other hand, she has not the courage or the practical cleverness possessed by Portia (in the 'Merchant of Venice') whose mind is somewhat akin to her own. To solve harmoniously this apparent contradiction, which places the two elements of the comic—fancy and intrigue—in close juxtaposition, and to form a true and life-like character out of these heterogeneous elements, is a task that Shakspeare leaves to the talent of the actors. In pieces like this and similar ones, he cannot well do otherwise; he has to content himself with giving mere hints of the characters; he has, so to say, but to touch the light pollen of the characterisation; a deeper development and deeper motives would obstruct and retard the rapid, easy, graceful movement of the action.

The other characters, the musical and dreamy Duke, who suns himself in his own love, and spends his time in brooding over his own sorrows;—Olivia, in her girlish self-will, hard to please yet so easy to win over, so serious, strict, and yet so graceful, who is so cold, so shy, so virtuously reserved before she is in love, and so inconsiderate in her desires, so devoted after her love is aroused by contradiction, and has burst forth into a bright flame;—Antonio, with his fantastic friendship for Sebastian, and Sebastian with his healthy, vigorous, youthful nature, taking with one snatch that which the Duke has in vain endeavoured to obtain by entreaties, lamentations and sighs;—the roguish, ingenious Maria, and her clever helper's help Fabian—all these characters are sketched in such fine outlines, the transparent colours and delicate lights and shades of which are so harmoniously blended with one another that, only in this manner, and in no other, could they be the agents of such a light, airy, hazy and yet deeply significant composition. The most carefully worked out contrast is that between the Fool by profession and the involuntary fools, Malvolio, Sir Andrew and Sir Toby. While the latter, in their own conceit and foolishness, unconsciously draw the cap and bells over their own ears, the former, in his self-adopted mental garb of motley colours moves with inimitable adroitness, and pins the lappets of his wit to the back of all the other characters. The meaning of the poem is, so to say, centred in him. He alone, in full consciousness, contemplates life as a merry Twelfth Night, in which everyone has, in fact, only to play his allotted part to the greatest possible amusement of himself and others. He does not wish to be more or less than a fool in the great mad-house of the world; on this account he has an unconquerable aversion to all starched common-sense and calculating plans, to that hollow unmeaning gravity which cannot understand a joke, because it fancies its proudly-adopted dignity thereby injured, and which is never able to rise above the petty, selfish interests of its own dear self; this accounts for his dislike to Malvolio. Again, he alone has respect for his cap and bells, for he is aware that fun and laughter, joke and jest are the seasoning of life, and that there is more depth and sense in humorous folly like his own, than in the sour-mindedness of so-called sensible people, who are in reality devoid of true sense, because the poetry of life, all the higher interests of man which extend beyond common prose, are unintelligible to them.

The chief incidents of the action are spontaneously evolved from the accidental or intentional encounter of these characters. Two groups stand opposed to one another; on the one hand the Duke, Olivia, Viola and her brother, on the other, Sir Toby, Sir Andrew, and Olivia's household. Both of these groups are again linked to each other, and interact with and counteract one another. In the first place the obstinacy of love, and the freak of accident carry on their bantering play with the first group—Viola, who merely wished to trifle with the love of others, becomes very love-sick herself;—the Duke, a slave to the scornful Olivia, is happily released from his chains in order to cure Viola;—Olivia, by way of punishment for her cruelty, falls in love with a girl;—all, in the end, are saved by the matter of chance which is introduced by Sebastian. In the second group Sir

Toby and Sir Andrew are, in the most amusing manner, made the dupes of their own folly and perversity, while Malvolio, in his pride of virtue and puritanical severity, but blinded by conceit, is made the laughing-stock of the intrigues of the Clown, Maria and Fabian. And, in order to increase the complication, Antonio and Sebastian are also drawn into the wide net of accident and error which the dramatic characters have drawn over their own heads. Chance, whim, and caprice, however, again unravel the intricate web, and each, by some good fortune, obtains that which is good for him or herself. The common-place prosaic Malvolio alone, and the equally prosaic Sir Andrew, justly reap mockery and derision as their due; for common prose, which, in truth, is always immoral as well, is invariably wrong in the world of comedy. The ingenuity and grace, the ease and playfulness in the flow of the language of this drama must be self-evident to every reader. Thus here also, characterisation, action (invention), and diction stand in the most perfect harmony with one another. Everything grows forth so organically out of the fundamental plan of the whole, that the composition here is not less masterly than in the case of Shakspeare's best tragedies.

In the same way as this pleasing drama stands midway between the two series of Shakspeare's comedies, so in regard to date also, it belongs to the middle of the poet's career. There is no longer any doubt that it was written about 1600. This opinion is supported by the treatment of the language and the versification, by the tone and character of the whole, more especially however by the view of life represented, and which is not usually met with either in a youth or in a man verging upon old age, but in a man's best and most vigorous years, when the gifted mind has reached the climax of life. But external testimonies, also, confirm the supposition which is based upon the style and character of the whole. The allusion in Ben Jonson's comedy 'Every Man out of his Humour,' which appeared in 1599, and which Tieck refers to 'What You Will,' is indeed unsafe and indefinite. But the reasons given by Malone, Chalmers, Drake, and others—who place it at a much later date (1613–14)—are of no greater value, and in themselves of no weight whatever, compared with the considerations which language and the character of the whole, place in the opposite scale, even were they not refuted by external, historical evidence. These critics supposed the words in Act ii. 5, 'I will not give my part of this sport for a pension of thousands to be paid from the Sophy'—to contain an allusion to the allowance in money, enjoyed in 1612, by Sir Robert Shirley, as Persian ambassador in London; and in Act iii. 1, they found a reference to a drama of Dekker's and Webster's which appeared in 1607. How little such individual passages are to be trusted—which, even where they appear more definite, might easily have been inserted by the poet or the actor upon certain occasions, and subsequently come to be employed in the text—is now proved by a Diary, discovered by Hunter and belonging to a certain Manningham (probably John Manningham) a barrister of the Middle Temple. By this diary it is authentically established that 'What You Will' had been played before the benchers as early as the 2nd of February, 1602, at the feast of Candlemas.[2] Collier thinks that it may have appeared on the boards of Blackfriars shortly before. This, however, is a mere hypothesis which cannot prevent our fixing the date one year earlier. The play of 'What You Will' was first printed in the folio edition of 1623.

Whether Shakspeare borrowed his subject from one of Bandello's novels or from Rich's translation of it (under the title of 'Apollonius and Silla') in 'His Farewell to Militarie Profession' (1581), or from the old Italian comedy *Gl'Inganni* to which Manningham refers, is difficult to decide. It is possible that Manningham confounds the *Inganni* with another Italian comedy, *Gl'Ingannati, commedia degli Academici Intronati di Siena*, which was also founded upon Bandello's novel, and likewise appeared as early as the sixteenth century. The latter, at all events as regards the relative position of the characters, the situations and the course of the action, has more affinity to 'What You Will' than to the *Inganni*. Probably, however, Shakspeare followed Rich's version of Bandello's novel, and the greater resemblance of his work to the comedy of the 'Academician of Siena,' is owing to the latter having likewise closely followed Bandello. And yet Shakspeare might also have become acquainted with the main features of the story from Belleforest's French translation in his *Histoires Tragiques*. J. Klein, in his excellent history of the drama, makes the remark that Rich's 'History of Apollonius and Silla,' which Shakspeare made use of in 'What You Will,' cannot be called a translation of Bandello's novel, for it keeps much closer to Cinthio's novel (the eighth of the 3rd *Decad.*), whereas Bandello's probably followed the earlier comedy of *Gl'Ingannati*. By a careful analysis of the latter comedy, as well as of the one entitled *Gl'Inganni* by Nice Secco (which also comes into consideration here), Klein[3] proves that neither can be regarded as the source of 'What You Will,' but that Shakspeare evidently made use of Rich's narrative and dramatised it in his own fashion.

In what way Shakspeare has made use of the novel, the reader may discover for himself by consulting Echtermeyer, Henschel and Simrock,[4] or Bandello himself (ii. 36). It will be found that in this case, also, the piece, as regards invention, is almost entirely Shakspeare's own.[5]

NOTES

1. Drake, *Life and Times of Shakspeare*, i. 127 f.
2. *Collier's History*, i. 327, and his *Shakespeare*, iii. 317.
3. *Geschichte des Dramas*, vol. iv. p. 749 ff. 801 ff.
4. Simrock, ii. 161, iii. 254 f.
5. Rich's *Apollonius and Silla* has been reprinted by Collier in the second volume of his *Shakespeare's Library*.

1877—F. J. Furnivall. From "Introduction to the Play" from *The Leopold Shakspere*

Frederick James Furnivall (1825-1910) was one of three founders and the second editor of the *Oxford English Dictionary*. He also founded the New Shakspere Society and a number of organizations dedicated to bringing education to the working classes.

[This passage follows the comments upon *As You Like It*, quoted in our edition of that play, page 23 fol. Here, as there, we have retained the author's orthography.]

Still one of the comedies of Shakspere's bright, sweet time. True that we have to change Rosalind's rippling laugh for the drunken catches and bibulous drollery of Sir Toby Belch and his comrade, and Touchstone for the Clown; but the leading note of the play is fun, as if Shakspere had been able to throw off all thought of melancholy, and had devised Malvolio to help his friends "fleet the time carelessly," as they did in the golden world. Still though, as ever in the comedies, except *The Merry Wives*, there's the shadow of death and distress across the sunshine. Olivia's father and brother just dead, Viola and Sebastian just rescued from one death, Viola threatend with another, and Antonio held a pirate and liable to death. And still the lesson is, as in *As You Like It*, "Sweet are the uses of adversity;" out of their trouble all the lovers come into happiness, into wedlock. The play at first sight is far less striking and interesting than *Much Ado* and *As You Like It*. No brilliant Beatrice or Benedick catches the eye, no sad Rosalind leaping into life and joyousness at the touch of assured love.

The self-conceited Malvolio is brought to the front, the drunkards and Clown come next; none of these touch any heart; and it's not till we look past them that we feel the beauty of the characters who stand in half-light behind. Then we become conscious of a quiet harmony of colour and form that makes a picture full of charm, that grows on you as you study it, and becomes one of the possessions of your life. As the two last plays reach backward and forward, so does *Twelfth-Night*: to the earliest *Love's Labours Lost* for the cut at women's painting their faces that we find here; for its men forswearing for three years the company of women, and then of course admitting them and falling in love with the first ones they see, which is the prototype of Olivia abjuring for seven years the company of men, then soon admitting one (as is supposed), falling in love at first sight with him (though he's a woman), and marrying his brother, whom she supposes to be he. For the pair of one family so like as to be mistaken for one another, we go back to the double Antipholus and the double Dromio of Shakspere's second play, *The Comedy of Errors*, which gives us, too, the incidents of both a wife (Antipholus's of Ephesus) and sweetheart

(Dromio's of Syracuse) mistaking another man for her husband and her lover (though here Viola is only a woman disguised). To the same play we go for the refusal or denial of money when trusted to one by another, and for the members of a family sunderd by shipwreck, as we look on to *Pericles* for a somewhat like incident. In the *Errors* we get, too, the saving, though here only of one member of the family, by the binding to a mast. To *The Two Gentlemen of Verona* we go for the parallel to Viola sent disguised as a page by Duke Orsino to woo Olivia for him, to the loving Julia sent by the man she loves (Proteus) to woo Sylvia for him. *Romeo and Juliet* gives us in the lovelorn Romeo repulst by Rosalind, and at once giving her up for Juliet, the match of Duke Orsino resigning the longed-for Olivia, and at the moment taking up Viola. *The Merchant of Venice* gives us another Antonio willing to give his life for his friend Bassanio, just as here in *Twelfth-Night* Antonio[1] faces danger, nay, death, a pirate's due, for his love to his friend Sebastian. And to the same *Merchant* we surely go for recollections of the opening scene here,

"That strain again! it had a dying fall;
O, it came o'er my ear like the sweet sound
That breathes upon a bank of violets,
Stealing and giving odour,"

and for a parallel to the Duke's love of music through the play. *Henry IV* gives us in Falstaff and his followers the company whence Sir Toby Belch and Sir Andrew Aguecheek come, as the Second Part of that play gives us Falstaff playing on Justice Shallow as Sir Toby in *Twelfth-Night* plays on Sir Andrew. Is not also Slender's echoing of Shallow in *Merry Wives* something like Sir Andrew echoing all Sir Toby's sayings here, and fancying himself a man for it? As to the reach forward of the play, I've already alluded to its link with *Pericles*. It is to the *Sonnets* that we turn for a parallel to Viola's pleading with Olivia to marry the Duke, and not forbear to leave a copy of her beauty to the world, and to the *Sonnets* to his mistress for Shakspere's love of music; while to match Viola's entire devotion even to death to the Duke's most unjust will we must look forward, even past the *Sonnets*, to the true and loving Imogen's willingness to die in obedience to her deceived and headstrong husband's iniquitous sentence of death on her (*Cymb.* iii. 4. 65–79). Note, too, that it is with Perdita of *Winter's Tale* that Mrs. Jameson mainly compares Viola, though, as we have seen, Julia in *The Two Gentlemen* is in circumstances nearest her. The interest of this middle time of Shakspere's work is to me great, showing as it does the development of his early powers, the forecast of his later ones. It is at once the fulfilment of the old promise of his genius, and the prophecy of the new.

Viola is the true heroine of the play. She is sad for her brother's supposed death, yet she hopes with the hopefulness of youth and her own escape. She doesn't mope or shut herself up like Olivia, but looks disaster full in the face, and at once takes practical steps for her future life. Sympathy with Olivia's loss draws her first to her; but as she can't enter her service, she resolves to go into the Duke's (Shakspere's women of course take naturally to boys' disguises, because their characters were always acted by boys). She knows the Duke's love of music; she can sing. Her voice, like Cordelia's, was ever soft, gentle, and low, "an excellent thing in woman;" and in the Duke's love-lorn state, Viola is the very person for him. He wants sympathy, and she gives it him; into her gentle breast he pours the sorrows of his secret soul. Her pity for him opens her heart to him; but how bitter-sweet were his confidences to her! Still his happiness, not hers, is what she wants, and she'll win it him, though in doing so she break her heart. Valentine has faild, but she'll not fail: he was urged by duty, she by love. Olivia she *will* see and does see. (Notice the woman's curiosity to see her rival's face and compare it with her own, as Julia does Sylvia's picture after seeing her in *The Two Gentlemen*: both loved ones have, like Chaucer's ladies, "eyes grey as glass.") Then note how in pleading Orsino's cause, through all her words her own love for the Duke speaks, just as in Chaucer's description of his duke's love Blanche, the young poet describes and praises his own love. Note too the difference between the real love that Viola describes and the fancied love the Duke feels. Had his love been like Viola's, no refusal, no rebuff, would have kept him from Olivia's feet. (Contrast Viola's tenderness to Olivia with Rosalind's sharpness to Phoebe.) Then comes the touching scene between Viola and the Duke, where the music makes her speak masterly of love, where Shakspere reveals his own heart's history with his aged wife, and where Viola herself, in answer to the Duke's fancied greatness of his love, gives him such hints of her own far deeper devotion to him that, though she never told her love, no man but one blinded by phantasm could have faild to catch the meaning of her words. But still she will appeal again to his unwilling love Olivia for him. Then comes the last scene. The man she loves, forgetting he's a man, out of spite threatens her with death, and she will take it joyfully for him, whom she then declares she loves more than her life. At last the Duke, seeing that Olivia is impossible to him, turns to his friend and confidante, his half-self, now woman, and challenges the fulfilment of her oft-repeated vows. She denies them not, but confesses she loves him still. She has what she wills, and all is happiness and peace. The Duke has a fanciful nature like Olivia. He is one of your dreamy musical men, and Romeo is his parallel in the earlier time. Still he is a man not to be despised, one of a rich, beautiful, artistic nature, had music in his soul, loved flowers, would make a husband tender and true, and say the prettiest, sweetest things to his wife. Malvolio, the affectioned ass, the sharp-tongued Maria, who'd have all her work to do as my

Lady to keep Sir Toby sober, the clown who sings the capital songs, and all the rest, we must, alas! pass over.

NOTE
1. The second self-sacrificing Antonio is Leonato's brother in *Much Ado*.

—⁓⁓— —⁓⁓— —⁓⁓—

1894—Arthur Symons. "Notes and Introduction to *Twelfth Night; or, What You Will*," from *The Works of William Shakespeare* (The Henry Irving Shakespeare)

The poet Arthur Symons (1865–1945) was also a translator, critic, and literary biographer. He wrote many books and edited seven plays in Henry Irving's edition of Shakespeare, from which the extract below is taken.

The play of *Twelfth Night*, coming midway in the career of Shakespeare, perhaps just between *As You Like It*, the Arcadian comedy, and *All's Well That Ends Well*, a comedy in name, but kept throughout on the very edge of tragedy, draws up into itself the separate threads of wit and humour from the various plays which had preceded it, weaving them all into a single texture. It is in some sort a farewell to mirth, and the mirth is of the finest quality, an incomparable ending. Shakespeare has done greater things, but nothing more delightful. One might fancy that the play had been composed in a time of special comfort and security, when soul and body were in perfect equipoise, and the dice of circumstance had fallen happily. A golden mean, a sweet moderation, reigns throughout. Here and there, in the more serious parts of the dialogue, we have one of Shakespeare's most beautiful touches, as in the divine opening lines, in Viola's story of the sister who "never told her love," and in much of that scene; but in general the fancy is moderated to accord with the mirth, and refrains from sounding a very deep or a very high note. Every element of the play has the subtlest links with its fellow. Tenderness melts into a smile, and the smile broadens imperceptibly into laughter. Without ever absolutely mingling, the two streams of the plot flow side by side, following the same windings, and connected by tributary currents. Was there ever a more transparently self-contradictory theory than that which removes one or two minute textual difficulties by the tremendous impossibility of a double date? No characteristic of the play is more unmistakable than its perfect unity and sure swiftness of composition, the absolute rondure of the O of Giotto, done at a single sweep of the practised arm. It is such a triumph of construction that it is hard, in reading it, to get rid of the feeling that it has been written at one sitting.

The protagonist of the play, the center of our amused interest, is certainly Malvolio, but it is on the fortunes of Viola, in her relations with the Duke and Olivia, that the action really depends. The Duke, the first speaker on the stage, is an egoist, a gentle and refined specimen of the class which has been summed up finally in the monumental character of Sir Willoughby Patterne. He is painted without satire, with the gentle forbearance of the profound and indifferent literary artist; shown, indeed, almost exclusively on his best side, yet, though sadly used as a lover, he awakens no pity, calls up no champion in our hearts. There is nothing base in his nature; he is incapable of any meanness, never harsh or unjust, gracefully prone to the virtues which do not take root in self-denial, to facile kindness, generosity, sympathy; he can inspire a tender love; he can love, though but with a desire of the secondary emotions; but he is self-contemplative, in another sense from Malvolio, one of those who play delicately upon life, whose very sorrows have an elegant melancholy, the sting of a sharp sauce which refreshes the palate cloyed by an insipid dish: a sentimental egoist. See, for a revealing touch of Shakespeare's judgment on him, his shallow words on woman's incapacity for love, so contradictory to what he has said the moment before, an inconsistency so exquisitely characteristic; both said with the same lack of vital sincerity, the same experimental and argumentative touch upon life. See how once only, in the fifth act, he blows out a little frothy bluster, a show of manliness, harsh words but used as goblin tales to frighten children; words whose vacillation in the very act comes out in the "What shall I do?" the pompous declaration, "My thoughts are ripe in mischief," in the side-touches, like an admiring glance aside in the glass at his own most effective attitude,—"a savage jealousy that sometime savours nobly," and the like. When he coolly gives up the finally-lost Olivia, and turns to the love and sympathy he knows are to be found in Viola (as, in after days, Sir Willoughby will turn to his Laetitia), the shallowness of his nature reveals itself in broad daylight.

Olivia is the complement to Orsino, a tragic sentimentalist, with emotions which it pleases her to play on a little consciously, yet capable of feeling, of a pitch beyond the Duke's too loudly-speaking passion. Her cloistral mourning for her brother's death has in it something theatrical, not quite honest, a playing with the emotions. She makes a luxury of her grief, and no doubt it loses its sting. Then, when a new face excites her fancy, the artificial condition into which she has brought herself leaves her an easy prey, by the natural rebound, to a possessing imagination. She becomes violently enamoured, yet honestly enough, of the disguised Viola, and her passion survives the inevitable substitution. Shakespeare has cleansed her from the stains of the old story, as he cleansed the heroine of *Measure for Measure*: the note of wantonness is never struck. She is too like the Duke ever to care for him. She has and she fills her place in the play, but the place is a secondary one, and she is without power over our hearts.

We turn to Viola with relief. She is a true woman, exquisitely gracious in that silent attendance upon a love seeming to have been chosen in vain; yet we can find for her no place in the incomparable company of Shakespeare's very noblest women. She has a touch of the sentimental, and will make a good wife for the Duke; she is without the strength of temperament or dignity of intellect which would scorn a delicately sentimental egoist. She is incapable of the heroism of Helena, of Isabella; she is of softer nature, of slighter build and lowlier spirit than they, while she has none of the overbrimming life, the intense and dazzling vitality, of Rosalind. Her male disguise is almost unapparent; she is covered by it as by a veil; it neither spurs her lips to sauciness, as with Rosalind, nor tames her into infinite dainty fears, as with Imogen; she is here, as she would be always, quiet, secure, retiring yet scarcely timid, with a pleasant playfulness breaking out now and then, the effect, not of high spirits, but of a whimsical sense of her secret when she feels safe in it, coming among women. Without any of the more heroic lineaments of her sex, she has the delicacy and tender truth that we all find so charming: an egoist supremely, when the qualities are his for possessing. She represents the typical female heart offering itself to the man: an ingenuous spectacle, with the dew upon it of early morning. She is permitted to speak the tenderest words in which pathos crowns and suffuses love; and once, under the spell of music, her small voice of low and tender changes rings out with immortal clearness, and for the moment, like the words she says,

It was a very echo to the east
Where love is throned.

Of Malvolio all has been said, and but little shall be said of him here. He is a Don Quixote in the colossal enlargement of his delusions, in the cruel irony of Fate, which twists topsy-turvy, making a mere straw in the wind of him, an eminently sober and serious man of the clearest uprightness, unvisited by a stray glimpse of saving humour. He is a man of self-sufficiency, a noble quality perilously near to self-complacency, and he has passed the bounds without knowing it. His unbending solemnity is his ruin. Nothing presents so fair a butt for the attack of a guerrilla-fighting wit. It is indeed the most generally obnoxious of all tolerable qualities; for it is a living rebuke of our petty levities, and it hints to us of a conscious superior. Even a soldier is not required to be always on drill. A lofty moralist, a starched formalist, like Malvolio, is salt and wormwood in the cakes and ale of gourmand humanity. It is with the nicest art that he is kept from rising sheer out of comedy into a tragic isolation of attitude. He *is* restrained, and we have no heartache in the laughter that seconds the most sprightly of clowns, the sharpest of serving-maids, and the incomparable pair of roysterers, Sir Toby and Sir Andrew.

Shakespeare, like Nature, has a tenderness for man in his cups, and will not let him come to grief. Sir Toby's wit bubbles up from no fountain of wisdom; it is shallow, radically bibulous, a brain-fume blown from a mere ferment of wits. His effect is truly and purely comic; but it is rather from the way in which the playwright points and places him than from his own comic genius—in this how unlike Falstaff, who appears to owe nothing to circumstances, but to escape from and dominate his creator. Sir Toby is the immortal type of the average "funny fellow" and boon-companion of the clubs or the alehouse; you may meet him any day in the street, with his portly build, red plump cheeks, and merry eyes twinkling at the incessant joke of life. His mirth is facile, contagious, continual; it would become wearisome perhaps at too long a dose, but through a single comic scene it is tickling, pervasive, delightful. Sir Andrew is the grindstone on which Sir Toby sharpens his wit. He is an instance of a natural fool becoming truly comic by the subtle handling in which he is not allowed to awaken too keenly either pity or contempt. In life he would awaken both. He is a harmless simpleton, an innocent and unobtrusive bore, "a Slender grown adult in brainlessness;" and he is shown in all his fatuity without a note or touch of really ill-natured sarcasm. Shakespeare's humour plays round him, enveloping him softly; his self-esteem has no shock; unlike Malvolio, he is permitted to remain undeceived to the end. It is to his credit that he is not without glimmerings that he is a fool. The kindness is, that the conviction is not forced upon him from without.

<hr />

1898—Georg Brandes. *"Twelfth Night,"* from *William Shakespeare: A Critical Study*

Georg Brandes (1842–1927) was an important Danish literary critic and critic of Romanticism. He wrote extensively on Shakespeare's plays.

Consummate Spiritual Harmony—*Twelfth Night*—Jibes at Puritanism—the Languishing Characters—Viola's Insinuating Grace—Farewell to Mirth

If the reader would picture to himself Shakespeare's mood during this short space of time at the end of the old century and beginning of the new, let him recall some morning when he has awakened with the sensation of complete physical well-being, not only feeling no definite or indefinite pain or uneasiness, but with a positive consciousness of happy activity in all his organs: when he drew his breath lightly, his head was clear and free, his heart beat peacefully: when the mere act of living was a delight: when the soul dwelt on happy moments in the past and dreamed of joys to come. Recall such a moment, and then conceive it intensified an hundredfold—conceive your memory, imagination, observation, acuteness, and power of expression a hundred times multiplied—and you may divine Shakespeare's prevailing mood in those days, when the brighter and happier sides of his nature were turned to the sun.

There are days when the sun seems to have put on a new and festal splendour, when the air is like a caress to the cheek, and when the glamour of the moonlight seems doubly sweet; days when men appear manlier and wittier, women fairer and more delicate than usual, and when those who are disagreeable and even odious to us appear, not formidable, but ludicrous—so that we feel ourselves exalted above the level of our daily life, emancipated and happy. Such days Shakespeare was now passing through.

It is at this period, too, that he makes sport of his adversaries the Puritans without bitterness, with exquisite humour. Even in *As You Like It* (iii. 2), we find a little allusion to them, where Rosalind says, "O most gentle Jupiter!—what tedious homily of love have you wearied your parishioners withal, and never cried, 'Have patience, good people!'" In his next play, the typical, solemn, and self-righteous Puritan is held up to ridicule in the Don-Quixote-like personage of the moralising and pompous Malvolio, who is launched upon a billowy sea of burlesque situations. Of course the poet goes to work with the greatest circumspection. Sir Toby has made some inquiry about Malvolio, to which Maria answers (ii. 3):—

"*Maria*. Marry, sir, sometimes he is a kind of Puritan.
"*Sir Andrew*. O! if I thought that, I'd beat him like a dog.
"*Sir Toby*. What, for being a Puritan? thy exquisite reason, dear knight?
"*Sir And*. I have no exquisite reason for't, but I have reason good enough.
"*Mar*. The devil a Puritan that he is, or anything constantly but a time-pleaser; an affectioned ass, that cons state without book, and utters it by great swarths."

Not otherwise does Molière expressly insist that Tartuffe is not a clergyman, and Holberg that Jacob von Tyboe is not an officer.

A forged letter, purporting to be written by his noble mistress, is made to fall into Malvolio's hands, in which she begs for his love, and instructs him, as a sign of his affection towards her, always to smile, and to wear cross-gartered yellow stockings. He "smiles his face into more lines than are in the new map [of 1598] with the augmentation of the Indies;" he wears his preposterous garters in the most preposterous fashion. The conspirators pretend to think him mad, and treat him accordingly. The Clown comes to visit him disguised in the cassock of Sir Topas the curate. "Well," says the mock priest (not without intention on the poet's part), when Maria gives him the gown, "I'll put it on, and I will dissemble myself in't; and I would I were the first that ever dissembled in such a gown."

It is to Malvolio, too, that the merry and mellow Sir Toby, amid the applause of the Clown, addresses the taunt:—

> "*Sir Toby*. Dost thou think, because thou art virtuous, there shall be no more cakes and ale?
> "*Clown*. Yes, by Saint Anne; and ginger shall be hot i' the mouth too."

In these words, which were one day to serve as a motto to Byron's *Don Juan*, there lies a gay and daring declaration of rights.

Twelfth Night, or What you Will, must have been written in 1601, for in the above-mentioned diary kept by John Manningham, of the Middle Temple, we find this entry, under the date February 2, 1602: "At our feast wee had a play called Twelve Night, or what you will, much like the commedy of errores, or Menechmi in Plautus, but most like and neere to that in Italian called *Inganni*. A good practise in it to make the steward beleeve his lady widdowe was in love with him," &c. That the play cannot have been written much earlier is proved by the fact that the song, "Farewell, dear heart, since I must needs be gone," which is sung by Sir Toby and the Clown (ii. 3), first appeared in a song-book (*The Booke of Ayres*) published by Robert Jones, London, 1601. Shakespeare has altered its wording very slightly. In all probability *Twelfth Night* was one of the four plays which were performed before the court at Whitehall by the Lord Chamberlain's company at Christmastide, 1601–2, and no doubt it was acted for the first time on the evening from which it takes its name.

Among several Italian plays which bore the name of *Gl'Inganni* there is one by Curzio Gonzaga, published in Venice in 1592, in which a sister dresses herself as her brother and takes the name of Cesare—in Shakespeare, Cesario—and another, published in Venice in 1537, the action of which bears a general resemblance to that of *Twelfth Night*. In this play, too, passing mention is made of one "Malevolti," who may have suggested to Shakespeare the name Malvolio.

The matter of the play is found in a novel of Bandello's, translated in Belleforest's *Histoires Tragiques*; and also in Barnabe Rich's translation of Cinthio's *Hecatomithi*, published in 1581, which Shakespeare appears to have used. The whole comic part of the action, and the characters of Malvolio, Sir Toby, Sir Andrew Aguecheek, and the Clown, are of Shakespeare's own invention.

There occurs in Ben Jonson's *Every Man out of his Humour* a speech which seems very like an allusion to *Twelfth Night*; but as Jonson's play is of earlier date, the speech, if the allusion be not fanciful, must have been inserted later.[1]

As was to be expected, *Twelfth Night* became exceedingly popular. The learned Leonard Digges, the translator of Claudian, enumerating in his verses, "Upon Master William Shakespeare" (1640), the poet's most popular characters, mentions only three from the comedies, and these from *Much Ado* and *Twelfth Night*. He says:—

> "Let but *Beatrice*
> And *Benedicke* be seene, loe in a trice
> The Cockpit, Galleries, Boxes, all are full
> To hear *Malvoglio*, that crosse garter'd Gull."

Twelfth Night is perhaps the most graceful and harmonious comedy Shakespeare ever wrote. It is certainly that in which all the notes the poet strikes, the note of seriousness and of raillery, of passion, of tenderness, and of laughter, blend in the richest and fullest concord. It is like a symphony in which no strain can be dispensed with, or like a picture veiled in a golden haze, into which all the colours resolve themselves. The play does not overflow with wit and gaiety like its predecessor; we feel that Shakespeare's joy of life has culminated and is about to pass over into melancholy; but there is far more unity in it than in *As You Like It*, and it is a great deal more dramatic.

A. W. Schlegel long ago made the penetrating observation that, in the opening speech of the comedy, Shakespeare reminds us how the same word, "fancy," was applied in his day both to love and to fancy in the modern sense of the term; whence the critic argued, not without ingenuity, that love, regarded as an affair of the imagination rather than of the heart, is the fundamental theme running through all the variations of the play. Others have since sought to prove that capricious fantasy is the fundamental trait in the physiognomy of all the characters. Tieck has compared the play to a great iridescent butterfly, fluttering through pure blue air, and soaring in its golden glory from the many-coloured flowers into the sunshine.

Twelfth Night, in Shakespeare's time, brought the Christmas festivities of the upper classes to an end; among the common people they usually lasted until Candlemas. On Twelfth Night all sorts of sports took place. The one who chanced to find a bean baked into a cake was hailed as the Bean King, chose himself a Bean Queen, introduced a reign of unbridled frivolity, and issued whimsical commands, which had to be punctually obeyed. Ulrici has sought to discover in this an indication that the play represents a sort of lottery, in which

Sebastian, the Duke, and Maria chance to win the great prize. The bibulous Sir Toby, however, can scarcely be regarded as a particularly desirable prize for Maria; and the second title of the play, *What you Will*, indicates that Shakespeare did not lay any stress upon the *Twelfth Night*.

This comedy is connected by certain filaments with its predecessor, *As You Like It*. The passion which Viola, in her male attire, awakens in Olivia, reminds us of that with which Rosalind inspires Phebe. But the motive is quite differently handled. While Rosalind gaily and unfeelingly repudiates Phebe's burning love, Viola is full of tender compassion for the lady whom her disguise has led astray. In the admirably worked-up confusion between Viola and her twin brother Sebastian, an effect from the *Comedy of Errors* is repeated; but the different circumstances and method of treatment make this motive also practically new.

With a careful and even affectionate hand, Shakespeare has elaborated each one of the many characters in the play.

The amiable and gentle Duke languishes, sentimental and fancy-sick, in hopeless enamourment. He is devoted to the fair Countess Olivia, who will have nothing to say to him, and whom he none the less besieges with his suit. An ardent lover of music, he turns to it for consolation; and among the songs sung to him by the Clown and others, there occurs the delicate little poem, of wonderful rhythmic beauty, "Come away, come away, death." It exactly expresses the soft and melting mood in which his days pass, lapped in a nerveless melancholy. To the melody abiding in it we may apply the lovely words spoken by Viola of the melody which preludes it:—

"It gives a very echo to the seat
Where love is throned."

In his fruitless passion, the Duke has become nervous and excitable, inclined to violent self-contradictions. In one and the same scene (ii. 4) he first says that man's love is

"More giddy and unfirm,
More longing, wavering, sooner lost and worn"

than woman's; and then, a little further on, he says of his own love—

"There is no woman's sides
Can bide the beating of so strong a passion
As love doth give my heart; no woman's heart
So big to hold so much: they lack retention."

The Countess Olivia forms a pendant to the Duke; she, like him, is full of yearning melancholy. With an ostentatious exaggeration of sisterly love, she has vowed to pass seven whole years veiled like a nun, consecrating her whole life to sorrow for her dead brother. Yet we find in her speeches no trace of this devouring sorrow; she jests with her household, and rules it ably and well, until, at the first sight of the disguised Viola, she flames out into passion, and, careless of the traditional reserve of her sex, takes the most daring steps to win the supposed youth. She is conceived as an unbalanced character, who passes at a bound from exaggerated hatred for all worldly things to total forgetfulness of her never-to-be-forgotten sorrow. Yet she is not comic like Phebe; for Shakespeare has indicated that it is the Sebastian type, foreshadowed in the disguised Viola, which is irresistible to her; and Sebastian, we see, at once requites the love which his sister had to reject. Her utterance of her passion, moreover, is always poetically beautiful.

Yet while she is sighing in vain for Viola, she necessarily appears as though seized with a mild erotic madness, similar to that of the Duke: and the folly of each is parodied in a witty and delightful fashion by Malvolio's entirely ludicrous love for his mistress, and vain confidence that she returns it. Olivia feels and says this herself, where she exclaims (iii. 4)—

"Go call him hither.—I am as mad as he
If sad and merry madness equal be."

Malvolio's figure is drawn in very few strokes, but with incomparable certainty of touch. He is unforgettable in his turkey-like pomposity, and the heartless practical joke which is played off upon him is developed with the richest comic effect. The inimitable love-letter, which Maria indites to him in a handwriting like that of the Countess, brings to light all the lurking vanity in his nature, and makes his self-esteem, which was patent enough before, assume the most extravagant forms. The scene in which he approaches Olivia, and triumphantly quotes the expressions in the letter, "yellow stockings," and "cross-gartered," while every word confirms her in the belief that he is mad, is one of the most effective on the comic stage. Still more irresistible is the scene (iv. 2) in which Malvolio is imprisoned as a madman in a dark room, while the Clown outside now assumes the voice of the Curate, and seeks to exorcise the devil in him, and again, in his own voice, converses with the supposed Curate, sings songs, and promises Malvolio to carry messages for him. We have here a comic *jeu de théâtre* of the first order.

In harmony with the general tone of the play, the Clown is less witty and more musical than Touchstone in *As You Like It*. He is keenly alive to the dignity of his calling: "Foolery, sir, does walk about the orb like the sun: it shines everywhere." He has many delightful sayings, as for example, "Many a good hanging prevents a bad marriage," or the following demonstration (v. 1) that one is the better for one's foes, and the worse for one's friends:—

"Marry, sir, my friends praise me, and make an ass of me; now, my
foes tell me plainly I am an ass: so that by my foes, sir, I profit in the
knowledge of myself, and by my friends I am abused: so that, conclusions
to be as kisses, if your four negatives make your two affirmatives, why
then, the worse for my friends, and the better for my foes."

Shakespeare even departs from his usual practice, and, as though to guard against any misunderstanding on the part of his public, makes Viola expound quite dogmatically that it "craves a kind of wit" to play the fool (iii. 1):—

"He must observe their mood on whom he jests,
The quality of persons, and the time,
And, like the haggard, check at every feather
That comes before his eye. This is a practice
As full of labour as a wise man's art."

The Clown forms a sort of connecting-link between the serious characters and the exclusively comic figures of the play—the pair of knights, Sir Toby Belch and Sir Andrew Aguecheek, who are entirely of Shakespeare's own invention. They are sharply contrasted. Sir Toby, sanguine, red-nosed, burly, a practical joker, always ready for "a hair of the dog that bit him," a figure after the style of Bellman;[2] Sir Andrew, pale as though with the ague, with thin, smooth, straw-coloured hair, a wretched little nincompoop, who values himself on his dancing and fencing, quarrelsome and chicken-hearted, boastful and timid in the same breath, and grotesque in his every movement. He is a mere echo and shadow of the heroes of his admiration, born to be the sport of his associates, their puppet, and their butt; and while he is so brainless as to think it possible he may win the love of the beautiful Olivia, he has at the same time an inward suspicion of his own stupidity which now and then comes in refreshingly: "Methinks sometimes I have no more wit than a Christian or an ordinary man has; but I am a great eater of beef, and, I believe, that does harm to my wit" (i. 3). He does not understand the simplest phrase he hears, and is such a mere reflex and parrot that "I too" is, as it were, the watchword of his existence. Shakespeare has immortalised him once for all in his reply when Sir Toby boasts that Maria adores him (ii. 3), "I was adored once too." Sir Toby sums him up in the phrase:

"For Andrew, if he were opened, and you find so much blood in his
liver as will clog the foot of a flea, I'll eat the rest of the anatomy."

The central character in *Twelfth Night* is Viola, of whom her brother does not say a word too much when, thinking that she has been drowned, he exclaims, "She bore a mind that envy could not but call fair."

Shipwrecked on the coast of Illyria, her first wish is to enter the service of the young Countess; but learning that Olivia is inaccessible, she determines to dress as a page (a eunuch) and approach the young unmarried Duke, of whom she has heard her father speak with warmth. He at once makes the deepest impression upon her heart, but being ignorant of her sex, does not dream of what is passing within her; so that she is perpetually placed in the painful position of being employed as a messenger from the man she loves to another woman. She gives utterance to her love in carefully disguised and touching words (ii. 4):—

"My father had a daughter lov'd a man,
As it might be, perhaps, were I a woman,
I should your lordship.
Duke.   And what's her history?
Vio. A blank, my lord. She never told her love,—
      But let concealment, like a worm i' the bud,
      Feed on her damask cheek: she pin'd in thought
      And, with a green and yellow melancholy,
      She sat like Patience on a monument,
      Smiling at grief."

But the passion which possesses her makes her a more eloquent messenger of love than she designs to be. To Olivia's question as to what she would do if she loved her as her master does, she answers (i. 5):—

"Make me a willow cabin at your gate,
And call upon my soul within the house;
Write loyal cantons of contemned love,
And sing them loud even in the dead of night;
Holla your name to the reverberate hills,
And make the babbling gossip of the air
Cry out, Olivia! O! you should not rest
Between the elements of air and earth,
But you should pity me."

In short, if she were a man, she would display all the energy which the Duke lacks. No wonder that, against her own will, she awakens Olivia's love. She herself, as a woman, is condemned to passivity; her love is wordless, deep, and patient. In spite of her sound understanding, she is a creature of emotion. It is a very characteristic touch when, in the scene (iii. 5) where Antonio, taking her for Sebastian, recalls the services he has rendered, and begs for assistance in his need, she exclaims that there is nothing, not even "lying vainness, babbling drunkenness, or any taint of vice," that she hates so much as ingratitude. However bright her intelligence, her soul from first to last outshines it. Her incognito, which does not bring her joy as it does to Rosalind, but only trouble and sorrow, conceals the most delicate womanliness. She never, like Rosalind or Beatrice, utters an audacious or wanton word. Her heart-winning charm more than makes up for the high spirits and sparkling humour of the earlier heroines. She is healthful and beautiful, like these her somewhat elder sisters; and she has also their humorous eloquence, as she proves in her first scene with Olivia. Yet there rests upon her lovely figure a tinge of melancholy. She is an impersonation of that "farewell to mirth" which an able English critic discerns in this last comedy of Shakespeare's brightest years.[3]

NOTES

1. There is some (ironic) discussion of a possible criticism that might be brought against a playwright: "That the argument of his comedy might have been of some other nature, as of a duke to be in love with a countess, and that countess to be in love with the duke's son, and the son to love the lady's waiting-maid; some such cross wooing, with a clown to their servingman. . . . "

2. See *ante*, p. 219.

3. "It is in some sort a farewell to mirth, and the mirth is of the finest quality, an incomparable ending. Shakespeare has done greater things, but he has never done anything more delightful."—*Arthur Symons.*

TWELFTH NIGHT
IN THE TWENTIETH CENTURY
𝕏

The best commentators of the twentieth century added new perspectives on many aspects of the play. The themes of madness, excess, and disguise became particularly interesting to critics, as did the idea that the play is an attack on Puritanism.

The scholar Morris P. Tilley complained that many past critics did not trouble to look beyond the play's gaiety. In Tilley's view, the play is a "philosophical defence of a moderate indulgence in pleasure," opposed both to excessive self-indulgence and, on the other hand, to the Puritan attack on recreation. Tilley saw Viola and Feste as the embodiment of perfect sanity, for they are able to balance reason and emotion. Malvolio and Olivia, in contrast, like the Puritans, value reason before feeling, while Sir Andrew and Sir Toby pursue only pleasure. Later in the century, the critic Harold Goddard had a similar view. He wrote that the excessive merrymaking and the excessive sentimental love depicted in the play show the dangers of such an infection of excess. Goddard tied this excess to the sea imagery in the play; drowning in the sea is symbolic of drowning in excess.

Leo Salingar pointed out that the play avoids emphasizing one theme only. He saw Shakespeare as exploring the contradictions surrounding love and the play as a validation of the triumph of natural love over both affectation and melancholy. He felt that parts of the play addressed conflicts within the aristocratic society during a period of change in Shakespeare's time.

A later critic, Jan Kott, focused on the theme of disguise. Disguise could bring freedom during Shakespeare's own time, since prevailing customs limited what women and girls were allowed to do; a female disguised as a male would be able to do a number of things she normally could not. Kott also argued that the duke, Olivia, and Viola are "not fully drawn characters." He believed that the "only element that fills them is love" and that they have no selves without it. The critic C. L. Barber also focused on disguise, pointing out that the play, by having Viola disguised as a man, shows both the differences and similarities of the sexes.

Critics continued to explore the tension between the comedy of the play and its more somber aspects. Maurice Hewlett, for example, remarked that whenever the part of Malvolio is played well, "the play becomes a kind of tragedy." G. Wilson Knight, on the other hand, felt that tragedy is not given an outlet in the play; he pointed out that terror in the play often becomes humorous, as in the sword fight with the disguised Viola.

Goddard felt that Shakespeare "hinted at" tragedy in the play. He remarked that just as the play's title made mention of the end of festivities for the Christmas season, so for Shakespeare the play marked the end of *his* festivities, a turning away from comedy toward tragedy. As part of this final step, Shakespeare pilfered extensively from the best of his own past characters and situations.

Malvolio in particular drew the attention of twentieth-century critics. J. B. Priestley saw Malvolio as "outside the real comic tradition." Modern audiences are more sympathetic toward Malvolio than they would have been during Shakespeare's time, Priestley wrote, and Malvolio is full of qualities Shakespeare detested. For William Winter, though, Malvolio is the focus of satire and humor in the play. C. L. Barber wrote that those with sympathy for Malvolio are viewing him from a distorted romantic perspective. He reminded us that Malvolio only wants to be with Olivia so he can acquire the title of count.

Recent critics were also attracted to the character of Feste, the clown. A. C. Bradley pointed out that Feste is different from other Shakespeare fools. We pity him, since he is, though sane and capable, an unloved "relic of the past." He has great insight into character and is mentally superior to those who outrank him. In addition, almost all of the music in the play is produced by Feste. Knight wrote that "Feste embodies the play's essense" and saw music in the play as extremely important, even more important than love—and Feste, of course, is the source of that music. Later in the century, Harold Bloom wrote that Feste is the only sane character in this "unsettling" play, which Bloom called "a highly deliberate outrage." According to Bloom, Feste "knows what most critics of Shakespeare will not learn, which is that *Twelfth Night* does not come to any true resolution, in which anyone has learned anything."

1907—Maurice Hewlett. "Introduction to *Twelfth Night*," from *The Complete Works of William Shakespeare*

Maurice Hewlett (1861–1923) was an essayist, poet, and popular novelist. His most famous novel was *The Forest Lovers*.

In considering with any kind of closeness a play of Shakespeare's, the student is thrown very much upon the probabilities of what he might or might not have got as a base for the work he was about; and when it comes to a question of theory, it is idle and perfectly unnecessary to push the probabilities too far. The enquiry, for instance, rises to the mind after a first reading of "Twelfth Night."

Had Shakespeare any theory of a difference, an essential difference, between a comedy and a tragedy? and many subsequent perusals do but urge it more persistently. Personally, I greatly doubt whether the poet troubled himself with definitions, whether, in fact, he had not something better to do; but if he did, the probabilities surely are that he went no deeper into that particular affair than Dante did once, in his famous letter to Can Grande of Verona. In order, wrote he there, to understand the title of his epic, "one must know that Comoedia is named from kome, *villa*, and ode, which means *cantus*; so that *comoedia* is a sort of *villanus cantus*. It differs from tragedy in this, that tragedy in the commencement is full of admiration and calm, but in the end is stinking and harsh; whence it is named from tragos, which is *hircus*, and ode, as it were *cantus hircinus*, that is, stinking like a goat—as appears in Seneca's tragedies; whereas comedy begins with something harsh, but has a prosperous ending, as is seen in the Comedies of Terence. In like manner the style of tragedy and comedy are different; that of tragedy is heightened and sublime, that of comedy more lax and unpretending, whence," he concludes, "we see why my work is called *Comoedia*." This is very well. "Twelfth Night" does begin—or almost begins—with something harsh: indeed a shipwreck; it ends prosperously with three weddings; in style and texture it is lax and unpretending. The play is assuredly a comedy within the meaning of these requisitions; whether it be so in those qualities which we have now come to think essential to such a piece of art is another matter, and a matter in which, as I began by saying, Shakespeare probably took no interest. But the question is whether we, when we read or behold such a play, do or do not take that interest. Is our laughter, if we have any, over the misfortunes of Malvolio "nothing else but a sudden glory, arising from a sudden conception of some eminency in ourselves by comparison of the infirmity of others"? That was what a learned man, the Philosopher of Malmesbury, living not so long after Shakespeare, thought we ought to find in comedy. If we laugh at Malvolio in his cellar, is that a sudden glory? Can we say that here "the comic mask is ugly and distorted, but does not cause pain?" No doubt but a Jacobean audience could. Can an Edwardian?

More of this presently, and of the curious fate of the play: let me consider for a moment, first, the structure of "Twelfth Night, or What you Will." A twin brother and sister, exactly alike, are in shipwreck; the brother supposed lost, the sister palpably alive. She, for sufficient reasons, disguises herself as a young man and takes service as page with the Duke of Illyria. She falls in love with her master; but he dotes upon a Lady Olivia, who scorns him. The Duke employs his supposed page as ambassador to Donna Olivia, with the result that lady now falls in love with lady; so here we have three persons at the sort of deadlock contrived by Mr. Puff in "The Spanish Armada," and the time seems ripe for the recovery of the lost brother. He duly appears, and contents Olivia; the passionate Duke pairs off with his pretended page; she—and this is important, for everybody is the slave of Viola—is actually the only person on the scene who wins her original desire. So much for the main plot of a comedy, whose scheme, lax and unpretending enough, is rendered still more so by the underplot, relating the buffooneries played upon Olivia's steward, Malvolio, by a set of immortal clowns, as irresponsible, capering, madcap wags as ever delighted this easy world—an underplot, be it added, which its author was at no pains to connect with his main theme; an underplot—and this is extraordinary—which, by the force and bent of Shakespeare's genius for character, has so taken hold of the play that it has usurped the interest, outshone the fantasy, forced the title to abdicate, and (for the last hundred and fifty years at least) turned a comedy into something uncommonly like a tragedy. These are perverse reflections, but they all appear to be true.

It would be curious, and it would be long, to enquire into the sources of those conventions of literature—widely departing from the facts of life—which are dear to us, to which we cling, not because they deceive us, for they do not attempt to deceive us, but partly for the sake of old acquaintance, and partly, no doubt, because we love make-believe and find that the more we have of it to make the better we do it. One of these, which we now call Sir Walter Scott's convention,—the habit of expressing violent emotion in terms of stately and deliberate rhetoric,—is at least as old as Homer. "My post," says Norna of the Fitful Head, "must be high on yon lofty headland, where never stood human foot save mine—or I must sleep at the bottom of the unfathomable ocean, its white billows booming over my senseless corpse. The parricide shall never also be denounced as the impostor." This is what Sir Walter called his "big bow-wow" style, and is certainly very unlike life. But if that is in itself an objection, the answer to it is, Why should we suppose life to be so fine a thing that the poet should never aim at a finer? Is rhetoric inadmissible? Is Turner's palette ruled out? Never in the world, we say, so long as they persuade. Socrates had the root of this matter, and so had Gorgias the rhapsodist, though he did not know it until the sage made it clear. So much for a convention of manner: here in "Twelfth Night" is a convention of matter, in Shakespeare's favourite notion of having a young woman dress like a young man, and of letting her go far into the logical consequences of the adventure. There is no doubt at all but that the Elizabethans considered that highly romantic; and as perversion is strange, and strangeness pleasureable, very likely it is romantic. There is this to be said of it, at any rate, that if we don't like it we shall never like "Twelfth Night," or a great part of Shakespeare's comedy. Once more—Pope Joan apart—we are nowhere near life, and it may then once more become a question whether we are near something better or something a good deal worse. It is very much a matter of taste. If the notion of maid wooing maid please us, stir us pleasurably, all is said; but I may add that the opposite notion, unless treated with an almost impossible tact, would not please us at all. Shakespeare never touched upon that in a play, but Bandello did in a novel, as we shall see; and it seems to have been from Bandello that our poet got his main plot for "Twelfth Night."[1] I don't know how old is this particular romantic device, nor can remember having found it in anything earlier than Boccaccio. There is something not unlike it in one of Lucian's Dialogues, and it probably is, like most notions, of Greek invention.

It is a delicate subject, treated by Shakespeare—in "Twelfth Night" at least—with beautiful, delicate discretion. If I am right in thinking that he took the story from Bandello, one can admire his honesty without reserve; for Bandello—a thick-fingered, heavy-handed prelate—was at no pains to refine away what he thought helpful to a good story. He prefixes the following argument to his tale: *How Nicuola, being in love with Lattanzio, goes to serve him dressed as a page, and after many adventures marries him; and what happened to a brother of hers.*

It should be added to that, for the fact is, that Nicuola and a brother Paolo are twins, and as like as two peas in a pod; and one may be pardoned for thinking that Shakespeare's version would have gained in probability if he had contrived to hint at some such previous inclination of Viola to Orsino as Nicuola had to Lattanzio. But Shakespeare thought otherwise; or wanted his shipwreck; or did not trouble himself in the matter; and Bandello, as might be expected, must needs wreck his own invention by another, and fatal, touch, whereby he asks us to believe that Lattanzio had also been in love with Nicuola before the story opens. This necessitates the extreme absurdity that he has totally forgotten her, and can go so far as to talk to her of his former mistress Nicuola. The incredible postulate is too much; imagination boggles at it, and finds all that depends upon such a shift a weariness. Such as it is, however, the rest of the story is nearly preserved in "Twelfth Night": there is much interwoven love-making. Nicuola, as a page, goes to the embassy to Catella, whom her oblivious Lattanzio now loves; Catella falls in love with her; Paolo arrives and takes his sister's place in Catella's heart; Lattanzio returns to his Nicuola; the bells ring. Instead of the complications of Antonio and Sebastian in our play, Bandello has some not too savoury intrigues of an old Gherardo, who wants to marry Nicuola and mistakes her brother for herself. The novel becomes, indeed, as it proceeds, highly Bandellian, and shows clearly enough in what, to the likes of him, lay the attractiveness of the theme. Shakespeare saves us all that, and gives us instead some of his most delicate love-music. The growth of the emotion in Olivia, from her "Why, what would you?" to her serious, "You might do much," and almost final "What is your parentage?" is surely as subtle a thing as one can find in Shakespeare. Directly we catch the drift of the pondered words, see that they tend to a confession of love, they become charged with significance, a significance which really, in themselves, they do not hold; and it is an instance of the admirable frugality of Shakespeare's literary economy that he contents himself with a bare disclosure of their import, and confidently leaves us to do the rest. What Olivia has said is in truth almost nothing—yet there is no abrupt transition into her swift, following rush of soliloquy, when after she has mused over her questions and Cesario's answers—

> "'What's your parentage?'
> 'Above my fortunes, yet my state is well;
> 'I am a gentleman'"

she breaks out,

>   "I'll be sworn thou art:
> Thy tongue, thy face, thy limbs, actions and spirit,
> Do give thee five-fold blazon. Not too fast: soft! soft!"

The woman is in an ecstasy of love; we accept it as a matter of course; and there's the work of a master. Equally fine, equally delicate and gradual, is the same sort of suggestion of the dawn of Viola's love for Orsino, if we except, as surely we must, her tag at the end of I, iv,—

>   . . . "a barful strife!
> Whoe'er I woo, myself would be his wife."

That was for the ears of the groundlings; and it is one of the puzzles of the play that an audience needing such italics as those before they could grasp at a plot could be made to understand the subtle revealing of Olivia's heart-trouble. Once over that shoal, Viola's story is exquisitely displayed. She is too eloquent one day; she nearly betrays herself—when to her Duke's "How dost thou like this tune?" she thrills her answer,

> "It gives a very echo to the seat
> Where love is thron'd."

Orsino hears: that is indeed to "speak masterly!" Says he:

> "My life upon't, young though thou art, thine eye
> Hath stayed upon some favour that it loves;
> Hath it not, boy?"

She owns to it. What kind of a woman? he asks her. Of his complexion, saith she, of about his years—and so on. Here is wonderful comedy, full of "sudden glory" for us; which deepens, when Feste and his wailing song—

> "Not a flower, not a flower sweet
> On my black coffin let there be strown"—

have departed, into the lovely gravity, the measured words of the girl-page—

> "My father had a daughter loved a man,
> As it might be, perhaps, were I a woman,
> I should your lordship"—

and then music which will never die so long as the English have ears and hearts. This too is comedy, even as "Come away, Death," is comedy; for there is nothing to prevent our sudden glory of laughter ending in a lump in the throat.

All the scenes that follow between these three were never to be surpassed by their poet. There is a dainty perfume about them, a noble discretion, a parsimony beyond words exciting. It is with the introduction of Sebastian that interest threatens to flag: one has had no chance of loving the young man; one would have him get out of the garden and leave us alone with our enchanted trio. As things are, the business ends with unmannerly haste. In IV, i, which is the first meeting of Sebastian with Olivia, he falls in love with her; in IV, iii, he marries her. This will never do! Let be for Sebastian, in whom our only interest is that he is Viola's brother; let be for Bandello, whose Paolo thought Catella a lady of the town, and behaved accordingly; but for Olivia, whose privilege had been to love Viola, to slip so lightly into wedlock with a mere surface image of that lovely person—this, for Viola's lovers, is too much. We feel that we have been tricked into it. It is almost an affront that Shakespeare, having suffered us to linger in a garden of delights, should on a sudden give a smack with his wand. The yew-tree bowers fall down and discover pasteboard; the flowers droop their heads and show us canvas-backing; the moon is a lantern behind a cloth. Or we have been at our dreaming, our make-believe: he tells us there's nothing in it, and hardly feigns an interest in his own magic.

But he has dealt so with us during four acts that a gracious image remains on the mind, too largely gracious even for Malvolio's wrongs to disturb. Seen in reminiscence, "Twelfth Night" appears as one of those lovely things, "wrought of moonbeams and flowing water," which will not bear, and is not meant to bear, examination through a magnifying glass. That way you may enlarge defects, but you dissipate beauties, not enhance them. These romantic figures passing and re-passing over the sward, sighing and longing, bowing, curtseying, in hedged gardens, in a green shade; this Countess love-lorn for a girl, this page adoring his master, these pert, peering maids, and recluse dreamers of states too lofty, and pranked gallants, and "dogs at a catch"—fantasies, things of gossamer: we know that now, but an hour ago could not have dreamed it. Perhaps they are as vain as Ferrarese pictures by Cosimo Tura or Dosso Dossi; they are of the same tender and immature charm. "The earth hath bubbles as the water hath;" this may be of them and needs to make no greater claim.

Lamb has a good saying about "Twelfth Night": "Then a music-piece by Titian—a thousand-pound picture—five figures standing behind a piano, the sixth playing; none of the heads, as M. observed, indicating great men, or affecting it, but so sweetly disposed, all leaning separate ways, but so easy—like a flock of some divine shepherd; the colouring, like the economy of the picture, so sweet and harmonious—as good as Shakespeare's 'Twelfth Night'—almost, that is." So sweetly disposed, so easy, so sweet and harmonious! One may always trust Elia to get the rights of a Shakespeare play.

Now we come to Malvolio and the clowns, upon whose part in the piece there are many things to say; and the first of them is to record the consideration that while, in our day, Shakespeare's tragedy still stands entire and unquestioned, his comedy frequently does not. I explain myself ill, for I mean rather that what Shakespeare shows us to be tragic we think tragic still, but what he found to be comical does not always so appear to us. The Shylock story may be comedy, but we cannot find it comical; Caliban is by no means comical; "Twelfth Night" gives us another case. The contention, if it could seriously be made, that Malvolio is still a comic personage throughout, and his discomfiture a comical episode, is sufficiently answered by the fact that whenever the part is played by a good actor, the play becomes a kind of tragedy. This is not only the experience of those of our generation who may have had the fortune to see Mr. Phelps as Malvolio, it was equally the case with Charles Lamb when Bensley played it. "I confess," he says, "that I never saw the catastrophe of this character while Bensley played it without a kind of tragic interest."[2] The objection that to play it so is to throw the comedy out of balance is beside the point. It must be played so, more or less, nowadays, because so we feel it. Malvolio is too much of a gentleman that such treatment of him should be tolerable to us. Perhaps, as Lamb says, he is too serious, perhaps "his morality and his manners are misplaced in Illyria," perhaps he *is* "opposed to the proper levities of the piece, and falls in the unequal contest." I think all that is quite true. Up to the scene where he is to pick up the letter we have been watching one who seems to be a grave and punctilious gentleman. In that scene Shakespeare shows him indulging in extravagant dreams—before he finds the letter—for which we are unprepared; but from the moment he goes into his cell he resumes his gentle blood, and wins our pity. In Shakespeare's day, it may well be, there was something comical in the notion that a servant should be a gentleman. Gentleness was then a matter of hard and fast category: either you were born a gentleman, or you were a menial. At that rate our times are out of joint; we now agree with Mr. Lang—or *diabolus*—who to the caviller against Dickens's ability to portray a gentleman set up Joe Gargery, and was unanswerable. The comic element in Malvolio is actually more out of our reach than what there may be of it in Shylock, where the Jew is a bogey, acting inhumanly in the beginning that he may be inhumanly treated in the end. Caliban is perhaps more tragic: but Malvolio's sufferings are gratuitous; there is assuredly nothing like them in comedy. We are scandalised, not tickled; we fatally miss our "sudden glory." Hazlitt, who felt the difficulty, as Lamb did, but never confessed it, was driven to a very halting defence. "If poor Malvolio's treatment," says he, "is a little hard, poetical justice is done in the uneasiness which Olivia suffers," etc., etc. Poetical justice![3]

It is worth remarking—it is important to remark—that Malvolio and the plot woven about him took the lead of the main story at once. The famous diary of John Manningham, under date February 2, 1601, has this:—

"At our feast (in Middle Temple Hall) wee had a play called 'Twelve Night, or What you Will,' much like the Commedy of Errores, or Menechmi in Plautus, but most like and neere to that in Italian called *Inganni*. A good practise in it to make the steward beleeve his Lady widdowe was in love with him, by counterfayting a letter as from his Lady in generall termes, telling him what shee liked best in him, and prescribing his gesture in smiling, his apparaile, &c., and then when he came to practice, making him beleeve they tooke him to be mad."[4]

Here it is obvious which part of the play struck the diarist in 1601, and equally obvious that he was diverted by it; in 1628, when it was done at Court, for the Candlemas revels, it was called "Malvolio" outright, and evidently so known in general. Charles I annotated his folio—the second—in his own hand, and against Shakespeare's title, "Twelfth Night," scored "Malvolio" in the margin. All this learning comes from Professor Aldis Wright, who also cites Digges, writing in 1640,

> . . . "lo, in a trice
> The cockpit, galleries, boxes, all are full
> To hear *Malvolio*, that cross-gartered Gull."

A Gull! That was what Shakespeare meant him for, and what we must assume he appeared to be to Caroline audiences. He was not so acceptable to the Restoration play-goer, if Pepys was a type. By Professor Aldis Wright's direction once more we may open the Diary twice. Pepys saw "Twelfth Night" in January, 1663: "but a silly play," he judges it. Perhaps it was a hard winter. Yet six years later, again in January, he again sat it out. "One of the weakest plays that ever I saw on the stage."

The learned consider the underplot to be Shakespeare's invention, and I cannot urge anything to the contrary. Perhaps he knew Bandello's story, from which Webster afterwards took his sombre tragedy, and took it lightly. I think he took everything in "Twelfth Night" lightly, as lightly as he chose the titles. For the titles of the beautiful, flimsy, iridescent, provoking thing are two: the first, from the occasion of its first performance, *Twelfth Night*; the second, *What you Will*. Is it extravagant to say that a deal of Shakespeare's shrouded history is unveiled in this? Is it not plain that he wrote to order, and equally plain that he set little store by his achievement—set little store by Viola? Great Apollo herded cattle for King Admetus, we know. He had his reasons, but need not be supposed to have been proud of the feat. So here, the divine hack, having written for hire a play of no value in his own eyes, gave it a flick of the finger, and let it go. A name for the thing? *What you will.*

NOTES

1. This is my personal belief, though it ought to be said that the experts are not so sure. The Academy of the *Intronati* of Siena produced a play in 1531, first printed to 1537, called *Gl'Ingannati*, which has precisely the same plot as Bandello's tale (published at Lucca in 1554), and is equally like "Twelfth Night." Mr. Lee's supposition that the Sienese play was derived from the novel, is beaten upon that matter of dates: the probabilities point to a common origin for both, but it is not yet clear from which Shakespeare drew his profit: I should have said, myself, that Bandello would have been the more accessible, and I remember that our man quarried from him more than once. This is curious, perhaps, that *Gl'Ingannati*, or rather *Il Sacrificizio*, which is the "induction" to it, contains a character called Malevolti, a well-known Sienese family name—the name, in fact, of the historian of the city. Mr. Morton Luce suggests that Olivia's steward may be scented here; but Malvolio has nothing else in common with Malevolti except that first syllable of his name, and against the vantage of that I can set the fact that in Bandello's story the phrase *Mala Voglia* occurs on nearly every page—so much so as to become an eyesore and offence. It is impossible to read the tale and not be conscious of this "damn'd iteration;" and Mala Voglia is much nearer Malvolio than Malevolti is. The question of origin has only an academic interest, except in the case of the Malvolio underplot—and here the learned fail me.

2. All that Lamb says of Malvolio, and of Bensley, is much to the point. It is in "On some of the old Actors" (ed. Lucas, Vol. II, pp. 280 *seq.*). See especially p. 282—"Bensley threw over the part an air of Spanish loftiness" . . . —Elia at his highest. He does not forget either that Malvolio had an exemplar in Antonio, steward to the Duchess of Malfy, whom that unhappy lady wedded, to her undoing. That play also, be it noted, came from Bandello.

3. If Campbell, as I am told is the case, really considered Malvolio "an exquisitely vulgar coxcomb," why, then, Campbell's memory must pay the shot.

4. Let not the unwary be deceived by the *Inganni*, here referred to, into thinking he has a proof that Shakespeare must have used *Gl'Ingannati*. There were many

plays called *Gl'Inganni* or *L'Inganno*. The word meant *cheat, deception*, and it is probable that Manningham used it generically, to describe a class of play. *Inganno* is a cheat, *ingannare* to cheat, *ingannati*, the cheated.

—◆◆◆—　—◆◆◆—　—◆◆◆—

1914—Morris P. Tilley. "The Organic Unity of *Twelfth Night*," from *PMLA*

Morris P. Tilley was a professor at the University of Michigan. His best-known work was *A Dictionary of the Proverbs in England in the Sixteenth and Seventeenth Centuries*.

There is no agreement among Shakespearian critics with regard to the organic unity of *Twelfth Night*. Dr. Furnivall in one place believes that "the leading note of the play is fun."[1] In another place he says less aptly that "the lesson is, sweet are the uses of adversity."[2] Morton Luce records his "impression that the perfect unity of *Twelfth Night* lies in the wise good humor that pervades the play."[3] Schlegel is representative of a group of critics who believe that "love regarded as an affair of the imagination rather than of the heart, is the fundamental theme running through all the variations of the play."[4] Most commentators, however, have agreed that the leading thought of this play may be discovered in its title; that the words *Twelfth Night, or What You Will*, are themselves the key-note of the play; that Shakespeare's first thought was to provide a comedy suitable for the festival. No one of these critics has thought that an organic idea has been more than incidental in this creation of pure mirth. So purely comic are its scenes, and so entirely sufficient are all of its incidents, that critics have not gone behind its gay life to look for an underlying moral law.

But such a moral law does exist as the fundamental idea of the play. *Twelfth Night* is a philosophical defence of a moderate indulgence in pleasure, in opposition on the one hand to an extreme hostility to pleasure and on the other hand to an extreme self-indulgence. Of the two extremes, the course of life that would banish all indulgence is emphasized as the more objectionable. In contrast to both, wise moderation is held up as the course to follow.

In opposing the extreme of excessive austerity Shakespeare is taking up cudgels for the stage in its struggle against the puritans; for the dramatists and the puritans fell out about the question of pleasure and pastime. The puritans in Shakespeare's day were permitting less and less of pleasure in their own lives, and in the lives of those about them. In this endeavor they were turning away from "stage-plays" as one of the chief purveyors to the people's pleasure. So little recreation, indeed, did they allow in their own life of discipline that their enemies accused them of banishing all recreation.

Stephen Gosson in his *Apology of the School of Abuse*,[5] contended that the puritans did not banish recreation. However, recreation meant one thing to the dramatists and another and entirely different thing to the puritans. Puritans allowed as recreation, "food, sleep, change of labour, music, conference with holy men, reading Fox, the Bible, and doing problems."[6] To the puritans it was strictly re-creation, "signifying to refresh either the body or the mind . . . when wearied, or spent in the employment of men's lawful callings, to the end that men re-created and refreshed, may cheerfully return to their lawful callings again, and therein serve God faithfully."[7] To the man of the renaissance, with his love of imaginative freedom and of pagan latitude, this definition of a recreation leading to asceticism was entirely repellent.

The puritan's aversion to pleasure did not cease with his withdrawing of himself from pastimes and plays. He strove to make it impossible for others to enjoy what he thought a sin. It was not enough that, being virtuous, he did not care for cakes and ale, and ginger hot in the mouth; he was determined that others enjoying these things of the flesh should join him in giving them up, if not of their own free will, then by force of legislation or of arms. As a result the puritans stood out prominently and disagreeably in the mind of the average man of the street in Shakespeare's day, for their hostile attitude towards pleasure, and their zeal in trying to force their opinion upon others.

To the dramatist the name of puritan was, therefore, anathema; and he savagely attacked him in his most effective way. On every stage he held him up to scorn as a man who merely affected holiness. This he gave out to be the real puritan. In these attacks he presented the puritan condemning all pastimes, not that the puritan might grow strong by righteous living, but that he might enjoy the good opinion of others for a piety which in reality he did not possess. In short the dramatist made the puritan out to be a religious hypocrite: to the world a strict observer of religious forms, but at heart a self-seeker.

William Prynne in 1633, reviewing the dramatist's hostility to his fellow puritans, said rightly that in their plays puritans were represented as either "hypocrites, fools, or furious mad-ones." Such indeed might be a general description of the puritans that Jonson, Marston, and Chapman give us in their plays. Zeal-of-the-Land Busy in *Bartholomew Fair* and Deacon Ananias in *The Alchemist* well correspond to Prynne's description of the dramatist's attack upon the puritan.

The puritan as he appears in the plays of the Elizabethan dramatists meets no mercy. He is created for the purpose of derision. After he has been given an opportunity to display his churlish parts in denouncing vices, he is quickly revealed the hypocrite in word and deed, while the degree of his back-sliding is proportioned to his earlier pretence of virtue. As a result his disgrace at the end of the play is as satisfying to his enemies as it is humiliating to himself.

Shakespeare's method of attacking the puritans, however, is far less obvious than that of his fellow dramatists. By some he has even been thought to pass over with indifference the dispute of the theatre with the puritans. His infrequent mention of puritans lends appearance to this view, as does the fact that in his dramas we find only infrequent, and then only obscured, satire of puritan costume, speech, and manner. However, he does take part in the dispute, but in his distinctive way. *Measure for Measure* is characteristic of Shakespeare's method of attacking the enemy of the stage. In it he elevates his criticism of the religious reformers of the day from the level of personal satire and abuse to a higher plane of philosophical discussion. Angelo in this play is a scathing denunciation of a hypocrite who in his abuse of power falls from heights of severe virtue to gross sin.

In *Twelfth Night* certain factors have obscured the organic unity that is behind the spontaneous and satisfying mirth of the play. The fact that Shakespeare's art is romantic and not realistic, has hidden the underlying purpose of the play behind its story of love at cross purposes. Another fact that contributes to make our understanding of the play less complete is our removal from the thought of the day for which the play was written. There is no doubt that in this as in Shakespeare's other plays there is a large body of ideas, facts, and sentiments which the author could presuppose on the part of his audience, but which we have to reconstruct with the assistance of notes and comments, so far as we are able to reconstruct them at all. The theme of *Twelfth Night*, closely related as I believe that it is to the actual thought of the day, required less explanation at that time than it requires now. Malvolio's dress, his starched gait, his close cut hair, his nasal intonation of voice, told the Elizabethan audience what has frequently been doubted by critics since that time, that Malvolio was none other than a puritan.

The organic idea quickening and giving life to *Twelfth Night* was born of the strife of Shakespeare's day. Written at a time when the renaissance and the reformation had come in England to the parting of the ways, *Twelfth Night* bears testimony of the influence of these contending currents of freedom and of restraint. Society was at variance with itself; and in the excitement of political and religious strife, extremes of every kind were championed. The puritan party was rallying to the defense of an extreme virtue; and against them were arrayed all the elements of society that held either other ideals or no ideals at all. It was no time for dispassionate judgment to assert itself. A judicious Hooker was at this time as rare as he was influential. Well-balanced natures that could at the same time feel deeply and judge rightly were conspicuously infrequent.

There was in the controversial puritan writing of the time as in the writing of their opponents, especially at the beginning of the dispute, the attempt to insist upon moderation in everything in life. In and out of the drama is heard the plea for moderation, measure, a mean in all things; it is pointed out repeatedly that nature tolerates nothing in extreme degree. At first both puritans and their enemies allowed the use, but disallowed the abuse. The middle ground of things that were "indifferent," however, grew smaller to the puritans as the years advanced; and forms and ceremonies, recreations and diversions, that at one time were allowed, were gradually added to the list of forbidden things. The moderate middle ground upon which the man of the renaissance could meet and enjoy the reformed protestant became finally too small to stand upon; and the sweet uses of philosophy and of reasonableness gave way to party strife and prejudice.

The well balanced life, although an ideal that in theory hovered before the eyes of both dramatists and puritans, gave way in the heat of persecution and of hatred to passion; and as a result the followers of the reformation found an ever-increasing gulf forming between themselves and the men of the new learning. "Tell many of these men of the Scripture," says an ardent follower of the reformation, in speaking of the true sons of the renaissance, "they will scoff and turn it into a jest. Rebuke them for breaking the Sabbath day, they will say, you are a man of the Sabbath, you are very precise, you will allow us nothing, you will have nothing but the word of God; you will permit us no recreation, but have men like asses, who never rest but when they are eating."[8]

The correction of the abuse alone did not satisfy the cry for reform, but because this or that practice was not found mentioned in Holy Scripture, it should, therefore, the reformer maintained, be taken away. The determination of the puritans to follow every action of Christ's (and no other's) as nearly as they were able ("omnis Christi actio nostra est instructio"),[9] left no common standing ground upon which the pleasure seeker of the theatre and the sterner abstainer from pleasure could meet. The lack of balance, of moderation, on the part of the reformers, caused the friends of the arts to plead in vain that because of the abuse, the use should not be denied. "But what!" Sir Philip Sidney exclaims in defending poetry against its defamers, "Shall the abuse of a thing, make the right use odious?"[10]

Shakespeare, one of the sanest men that ever lived, viewed the struggles about him with a calmness that refused to allow him to become a partisan on either side. When the reformers were sweeping aside all pastime, and their opponents in reaction were sinking to new follies in their opposition, Shakspeare composed *Twelfth Night* in praise of the much-needed, well-balanced nature, to extol that happy union of judgment and of feeling which is the basis of a higher sanity. He does this so deftly, with so little intrusion of his purpose in other than the most perfect dramatic form, that we of another time, removed from the strife of the puritan age, enjoy the result without realizing the purpose behind the finished production. Only the figure of Malvolio stands out in his hostility to all forms of amusement, to remind us that he is Shakespeare's contribution to the portraits of those enemies of art and of life in its fullest development, which aroused the Elizabethan dramatists to energetic and continued opposition.

The problem of life as Shakespeare saw it, and reveals it to us in this play, is basic; far greater than that of any group or sect of persons. It is the conflict in human nature between the reason and the emotions; and he suggests to us in the perfect sanity of Viola and of Feste that the solution lies not in the exclusion of the one or the other, but in the union of the two. In two groups of characters in the play he presents to us the evil results of following, to the exclusion of the other, either reason or emotion. In the self-conceited Malvolio and the strict Olivia he gives us representatives of those reformers of his day who, ignoring the moderate, gravitate to an extreme course of life in which reason is exalted to the exclusion of the emotions. Similarly, in Sir Andrew and Sir Toby, the other extreme from a well-ordered life is represented, one in which pleasure and folly make up the whole existence of man.

Edmund Spenser, in the second canto of the second book of the *Fairie Queene*, which is devoted to the virtue of temperance, gives us in allegorical narrative form what Shakespeare is giving us in *Twelfth Night* in dramatic form. There we are shown "the face of golden Mean," whom "her sisters, two extremities, strive to banish clean." These three sisters correspond to the three divisions that may be made of the important characters of *Twelfth Night*. Of the three sisters, Medina, or Golden Mean, is opposed on the one hand to Elissa, melancholy and unfriendly to good cheer; and on the other hand to the young Perissa, "full of disport still laughing, loosly light."

> Betwixt them both the fair Medina sate,
> With sober grace and goodly carriage;
> With equal measure she did moderate
> The strong extremities of their outrage.
> The forward pair she ever would assuage
> When they would strive due reason to exceed.

Malvolio and Olivia in *Twelfth Night* may be said to correspond to Elissa who "with bent lowering brows, as she would threat, she scould and fround with froward countenance." Similarly Andrew Aguecheek and Orsino correspond to Perissa, the other sister, in whom is embodied the opposite extreme:

> No measure in her mood, no rule of right,
> But poured out in pleasure and delight;
> In wine and meats she flowed above the bank,
> And in excess exceeded her own might.

In Feste and Viola, we have the golden mean of the play. The description of Medina by Spenser might well describe Viola:

> Ne in her speech, ne in her havior,
> was lightness seen or looser vanity,
> But gracious womanhood and gravity,
> Above the reason of her youthly years.

There is general agreement among critics with regard to the excellence and the sanity of the characters of Viola and Feste. To them Shakespeare has given self-control and a penetration that guide them in their course of life, without exposing them to the extreme either of folly or of austerity. They represent the golden mean of temperance, in whom reason and emotion are at poise.

The affection that Shakespeare has for Viola, who with Feste shares the distinction of standing between the "lighter people" and "the prudent ones," is clear. It is she to whom Shakespeare gives his own thoughts when she defends Feste's fooling, condemned by both Malvolio and Olivia:

> This fellow is wise enough to play the fool,
> And to do that well, craves a kind of wit;
> He must observe their mood upon whom he jests,
> The quality of person and the time:
> . . . .
>   This is a practice
> As full of labour as a wise man's art:
>
>   III, 1.

In another place Viola shows a sense of proportion in rating sins, that we neither expect nor find in Malvolio or Olivia.

> I hate ingratitude more in a man
> Than lying, vainess, babling, drunkeness,
> Or any taint of vice, whose strong corruption
> Inhabits our frail blood.
>
>   III, 4.

But this ability to see and to think clearly, and to control her affections when necessary, was Viola's part in Shakespeare's plan of the play. As a further result of her well-balanced character, the plan of the play rewards her with the husband of her choice, while Orsino and Olivia are defeated in the aims of their affections.

Similarly Feste in the sub-plot does not meet disappointment as do Andrew and Malvolio, but remains the happy son of mirth, to whom Shakespeare has given in goodly measure his own penetration into the motives of others.

In the persons of Orsino and Sir Andrew we have characters that are accepted as examples, in different degrees, of ungoverned natures. Orsino has surrendered himself entirely to his passion for Olivia, that will "bide no denay." No check of reason holds him back from his extravagance of love; and when count is taken at the end, his suit for the hand of Olivia is no more successful than that of the witless Sir Andrew, who has wasted his time in "fencing, dancing, and bear-baiting." So far as they are shown to us they have acted without reference to the guidance of reason; and are the products of their surrender to their unchecked inclinations.

With Sir Andrew may be included Sir Toby, Maria, and Fabian, as representatives of the extreme of mirth and frivolity. Andrew is in the fore-rank of these "lighter people." He is closely followed, however, by Sir Toby, who will not hear of a song of "good-life," but clamors for a "love-song," which has as its theme the present enjoyment of life—

For in delay there lies no plenty,
Present mirth has present laughter,
What's to come is still unsure.

II, 3.

On the same occasion it is Sir Andrew who gives utterance to his belief that life consists not of the four elements, but rather of eating and drinking; and for this sentiment he is proclaimed by Sir Toby, to the accompaniment of a call for wine, no less than a scholar.

The character of Olivia is open to no misunderstanding. She is the most impulsive of the whole impulsive group; nor do we feel the smallest surprise when her exaggerated grief gives sudden place to exaggerated passion. With regard to grouping her with Malvolio, however, it is important to dwell upon her determination to spend seven years in mourning. Her actions and words ally her with "her sad and civil steward," who suits so well with her fortunes. Her nature and his agree in looking upon life with severity. Her austere attitude is natural to her, so that it is not solely because of the recent death of her brother that she hath abjured the company and the sight of men. Until her distracting frenzy for Cesario seizes upon her, she not only rules pleasure out of her own life but regulates the life of her household with severity. The reproofs that she administers to Feste and to Cesario, upon her first visit, reveal her a stern governess of her household. "She has no folly," as the Clown says of her. Her whole endeavor is concentrated upon a rule of reform that will either separate

Sir Toby and the other members of her household from their disorders, or else dismiss them from her house.

It is to this model of virtue that comes the distracting frenzy of falling in love with Viola disguised as a messenger from Orsino. Her self-discipline does not save her from the folly of loving Viola madly in spite of her resolution not to admit the suit of man. She is conscious of her revolt from her standard of reason and refers to it several times:

> There is something in me that reproves my fault
> But such a headstrong potent fault it is,
> That it but mocks reproof.
>
> III, 4.

> I love thee so, that maugre all thy pride,
> Nor wit nor reason can my passion hide.
>
> III, 1.

Olivia is only one of a number of examples that Shakespeare gives us in his plays, to show the futility of the aims of those who would be wiser than nature; and seek, in ruling out of life the emotions, to exalt the single standard of reason to supreme importance.

Malvolio shares with Olivia the distinction of representing the extreme of austerity, and is similarly brought to see his error. The placing of Olivia and Malvolio in the centre of the plot interest, points to Shakespeare's intention in this play of emphasizing the inability of the puritans to rule out of life pleasure and pastime.

Those critics who have found Malvolio's punishment[11] both coarse and excessive have failed to conceive Malvolio as the hypocrite that Shakespeare intended him to be. This was the Elizabethan dramatist's usual denunciation of the puritans who ordered their life after Malvolio's principles. It is Maria, Olivia's handmaid, who reveals him to us. She knows from frequent observation both what he is and what he is not. He is not as he seems, a genuinely pious man. It is only sometimes that he is a kind of a puritan. His puritanism is a pose that he adopts to advance himself at this time when with his mistress puritanical mannerisms are in favor. He affects it all. The show of wisdom and of gravity that he puts on, he learns from books. He is not what he appears, a grave and sedate man of virtue, acting from the conviction of his inner spirit, zealous in the truth, and therefore not suffering any vice to go unreprehended in Olivia's house. At heart he is very different, as Maria tells us, from that which he appears to be. He is not humble in spirit; but proud and arrogant to those below him. He is the best persuaded of himself, so crammed, as he thinks, with excellences, that it is his ground of faith that all who look upon him love him.

A complete antithesis exists between his ground of faith and that of the true Christian of the day, who, wishing to make more sincere his expression of love to God and man, had given to him, in derision at first, the name of puritan. Maria's exposition of Malvolio's ground of faith as self-love marks him off in spirit from the part he acts, and classes him as a hypocrite.

The inconsistencies in Malvolio's character that Mr. Archer and other critics[12] have noted and have attributed to Shakespeare's incomplete mastery in the delineation of Olivia's steward, are not defects, but the natural inconsistencies that would arise in such a conflict between the real Malvolio and the part that he is acting.

It is probable that to the audience of his day, Malvolio appeared as a designing steward, who hoped to win his lady's favor by playing the puritan in her household. Feste had a shrewd suspicion of his motive when he wished him a "speedy infirmity for the better increasing his folly." Maria also saw through him. She based her plot of the letter on this weakness. Finally we hear Malvolio confessing in secret that his thoughts are upon the days when he shall be Count Malvolio by reason of marriage to his lady. If we keep this motive of his in mind, and measure his desire to please Olivia accordingly, there will arise no doubt in our mind as to whether his punishment is excessive.

In the presence of Olivia and of others he may feign a humbleness, but there is no genuine humility in Malvolio's make-up. When alone, in thinking of the favor his mistress shows him, "contemplation makes a rare turkey-cock of him" and "he jets under his advanced plumes." And later he shows his inner self by believing the passages of impossible grossness in the letter with their appeal to his enormous self-conceit. Besides being encouraged in the letter to make love to Olivia, he is urged to cast his humble slough, and appear fresh, to be opposite with a kinsman, surly with servants. He is commanded to let his tongue tang with arguments of state and to put himself into the trick of singularity.

No order could be more welcome to Malvolio, whose thoughts are constantly on "state" and on the acquiring of power. "This is open," he exclaims with delight upon receiving the command, "I will be proud, I will read politick authors, I will baffle Sir Toby, I will wash off gross acquaintance, I will be point devise the very man. I will be strange, stout, in yellow stockings and cross-gartered, even with the swiftness of putting on." And he is "strange" and "stout" when he comes to Olivia in yellow stockings. With ridiculous boldness in his lady's presence, he answers Maria with, "Shall nightingales answer daws?" And later, when given over to the care of Sir Toby, he is both surly with servants and opposite with a kinsman. Here it is that he revels according to his nature in disdain and arrogance, "Go hang yourselves all, you are idle, shallow things; I am not of your element; you shall know more hereafter."

If further proof were needed to mark off Malvolio and Olivia as of "the prudent ones," a formidable list of qualities and practices objectionable to them might be compiled, in which together they shared their disapproval with other puritans. In such a list would be included health-drinking, drunkeness, quarrelling, bear-baiting, fencing, bad manners, dancing, evil company, misspending time, poetry, plays, idle compliment, untruths, idleness, jesting, pranks, boldness, oaths, lack of regard for proper place and proper time, singing, disorderly conduct, staying out late at night, feasting, music, discourtesy, disrespect of persons, folly, fashionable dress, shallowness. The sure hand of the master dramatist has touched Malvolio's and Olivia's dislike of these habits lightly, but sufficiently to score his points with an audience alive to the significance of each touch. In forming our opinion of Olivia and of Malvolio with regard to this list, it is well to keep in mind that in an age of greater license than our own, some of the habits objected to by Malvolio, such as excessive drinking, bear-baiting and oaths, which are offensive to us, were not objectionable to most people.

At the end of *Twelfth Night* is a song sung by Feste that is thought by some to be full of wisdom and by others to be hardly intelligible. The refrain to each couplet omitted, the words of the song are as follows:

When that I was and a little tiny boy,
A foolish thing was but a toy.

But when I came to man's estate,
Gainst Knaves and Thieves men shut their gate.

But when I came alas to wive,
By swaggering could I never thrive.

But when I came unto my beds,
With tosspots still had drunken heads.

A great while ago the world begun,
But that's all one, our play is done,
And we'll strive to please you every day.

In these words we have Feste touching lightly upon the fundamental idea of the play. Experience, coming to him with man's estate, has taught him the difference between men who are knaves and men who are not. The third and fourth stanzas of his song give his division of knaves into two classes, representatives of each of which he finds in his fellows of the sub-plot. Malvolio, who by swaggering tries to thrive in his suit for Olivia's hand, is his reference to the one class; and Sir Toby, Olivia's drunken cousin, and his foolish dupe Sir Andrew Aguecheek, whom canary has put down, are the point of his allusion to the tosspots, who go to bed with drunken heads. This division of knaves by Feste is his reference to the followers of the two extremes in the play. Experience has taught him that against both "men shut their gates."

"A great while ago the world begun," he adds. This matter of good and evil is as old as the world, is his thought. You have seen the folly of the fools, and the disappointments that they have reaped from their folly. "But that's all one, the play is done, we will strive to please you every day."

Thus it is that Feste, the wise discerner of motives throughout the play, gives us in this his song, and the last words of the comedy, assistance in penetrating to its fundamental idea; and in so doing adds his word to the support of the theory that Shakespeare in *Twelfth Night* scorns the folly of extremes, and holds up to high praise the mean that we term golden.

NOTES

1. *Twelfth Night*. Ed. by Morton Luce. p. xxxiv (foot-notes).
2. *Ibid*.
3. *Twelfth Night*. Ed. by Morton Luce, p. xxix.
4. Brandes, *Shakespeare*, vol. 1, p. 273.
5. *An Apologie of the Schools of Abuse*, Arber Reprint edition, p. 72.
6. *A Short Treatise against Stage Plays* (1625), p. 241. In *English Drama and Stage* (Rox. Lib. 1869).
7. *A Short Treatise against Stage Plays* (1625), pp. 240, 241.
8. *A Short Treatise against Stage Plays* (1625), pp. 240, 241.
9. Stubbes, *Anatomie of Abuses*, p. 111.
10. *Defense of Poesy*. Ed. by A. S. Cook (1890), p. 36.
11. T. Kenny (1864). Furness, *Twelfth Night*, p. 382: "There is nothing in his conduct to justify the unscrupulous persecution of his tormentors." Wm. Archer, in Furness, *Twelfth Night*, p. 399: "Punishment excessive to the point of barbarity."
12. Furness, *Twelfth Night*, pp. 399, 400.

—◦◦◦— —◦◦◦— —◦◦◦—

1915—William Winter. "Character of Viola," from *Shakespeare on the Stage*

William Winter (1836–1917) was a literary and drama critic for the *New York Tribune*, among other publications. His books include *Shakespeare's England, Henry Irving*, and many more. His *Shakespeare on the Stage* includes information on the origin and date of the plays as well as on various performances and actors.

The prominence of *Malvolio* in the comedy does not lessen that of *Viola*. If the humor and satire eddy and crystallize around him, the loveliness, poetry, ardent, unselfish emotion, exquisite glee and radiant grace crystallize around her. *Viola* is Shakespeare's ideal of the patient idolatry and silent self-sacrifice of perfect love. In the simple, earnest words, "I'll serve this Duke," the shipwrecked, bereaved, lonely, almost destitute girl, who, cast away on a strange sea-coast, must seek her fortune, practically beginning life anew, reveals more than her adventurous intention, because she also reveals the steadfast quality,—blending meek endurance with buoyant self-control,—of her strong as well as lovely character. As to the *Duke Orsino* she knows only that he is reputed noble, that he is a bachelor, and that he loves the *Lady Olivia*, who is mourning the death of her father and brother, and who will admit no one to her presence. *Viola* is not impelled by passion, or by sentiment, or by curiosity. She must find a new home, and she must obtain subsistence. Her first impulse is to serve *Olivia*, but that plan is rejected as impracticable. She will seek service in the household of the *Duke*,—for she can sing and can speak to him in many sorts of music,—and she will hide her sex, and proceed thither in disguise. A happy chance has saved her from the sea, and meanwhile the same happy chance may also have saved *Sebastian*, her brother. She will be hopeful and will go forward, and the events of her future shall be trusted to propitious time.

After her plan has succeeded and she has become a resident of *Orsino*'s palace and is established, as a *Page*, in the *Duke*'s favor, *Viola* spreads no lure, resorts to no subterfuge. In such cases the first advance is usually made by the female. It is so made by *Rosalind*, for example,—a character commonly, and erroneously, named as the perfection of poetic spirituality and refinement,—but it is not made by *Viola*. She is a sweet, constant woman, and she is specially blessed with that cheerful courage, as to worldly fortune, for which good women are usually more remarkable than men, and she is young, handsome, attractive and, unconsciously, well qualified to prove victorious. She loves and she is simply herself and will submit, without a murmur, to any sorrow that may await her. "She never told her love." *Rosalind* is a woman. *Viola* is a poem. *Rosalind* is human. *Viola* is human, too, but also she is celestial. In her disguise, as a boy, she will follow the fortunes of her lord, and she will even plead his cause, as a lover, with the beautiful *Olivia*, who has captured his physical longing and his languishing, sentimental fancy.

A woman, under such circumstances, commonly hates her rival, with bitter resentment. *Viola* never harbors hate, never speaks one word of antagonism or malice. She does not assume that *Orsino* is her property because she happens to love him, or that he is in any way responsible for the condition of her feelings, or that *Olivia* is reprehensible because she has fascinated him. There is no selfishness in her love, because there is no selfishness in her nature. Her desire to see the face of *Olivia* is the pathetic desire to know what it is that has charmed the man whom she worships, and, through her simulated glee, when she does see it, shines the touching consciousness that the beauty of *Olivia* might well inspire a man's devotion. Nothing could be more fervent and generous than the candour and enthusiasm with which she recognizes that beauty and pleads with its possessor for compassion upon a suffering worshiper. She knows *Orsino's* sorrow by her own, and she pities him and would help him if she could. That is true love, which desires not its own happiness first, but the happiness of its object, and which feels, without conscious knowledge, that itself is the perfection of human attainment and that it may be better to lose than to win. Shakespeare has incarnated that lovely spirit in a person of equal loveliness, and has inspired it with the exuberant glee that is possible only to perfect innocence. *Viola* is as gay as she is gentle, and as guileless and simple as she is generous and sincere. The poet has emphasized his meaning, furthermore, by the expedient of contrast between the two women. *Olivia*,—self-absorbed, ostentatious in her love, self-willed in her conduct, conventional to her character, physically beautiful, but spiritually insignificant,—while she is precisely the sort of woman for whom men in general go wild, serves but to throw the immeasurable superiority of *Viola* into stronger relief.

<hr />

1916—A. C. Bradley. "Feste the Jester," from *A Book of Homage to Shakespeare*

A. C. Bradley (1851–1935) was a professor at Oxford and other institutions. His book *Shakespearean Tragedy* was one of the most significant works of Shakespeare criticism of the twentieth century.

Lear's Fool stands in a place apart—a sacred place; but, of Shakespeare's other Fools,[1] Feste, the so-called Clown in *Twelfth Night*, has always lain nearest to my heart. He is not, perhaps, more amusing than Touchstone, to whom I bow profoundly in passing; but I love him more.

Whether Lear's Fool was not slightly touched in his wits is disputable. Though Touchstone is both sane and wise, we sometimes wonder what would happen if he had to shift for himself. Here and there he is ridiculous as well as humorous; we laugh at him, and not only *with* him. We never laugh at Feste. He would not dream of marrying Audrey. Nobody would hint that he was a 'natural' or propose to 'steal' him (*A.Y.L.I.* 1. ii. 52, 57; iii. 131). He is as sane as his mistress; his position considered, he cannot be called even eccentric, scarcely even flighty; and he possesses not only the ready wit required by his profession, and an intellectual agility greater than it requires, but also an insight into character and into practical situations so swift and sure that he seems to supply, in fuller measure than any of Shakespeare's other Fools, the poet's own comment on the story. He enters, and at once we know that Maria's secret is no secret to him. She warns him that he will be hanged for playing the truant. 'Many a good hanging', he replies, 'prevents a bad marriage'; and if Maria wants an instance of a bad marriage, she soon gets it: 'Well, go thy way; if Sir Toby would leave drinking, thou wert as witty a piece of Eve's flesh as any in Illyria.' (Gervinus, on the contrary, regarded this marriage as a judgement on Sir Toby; but then Gervinus, though a most respectable critic, was no Fool.) Maria departs and Olivia enters. Her brother is dead, and she wears the deepest mourning and has announced her intention of going veiled and weeping her loss every day for seven years. But, in Feste's view, her state of mind would be rational only if she believed her brother's soul to be in hell; and he does not conceal his opinion. The Duke comes next, and, as his manner ruffles Feste, the mirror of truth is held firmly before him too: 'Now, the melancholy god protect thee, and the tailor make thy doublet of changeable taffeta, for thy mind is a very opal.' In these encounters we admire the Fool's wisdom the more because it makes no impression on his antagonists, who regard it as mere foolery. And his occasional pregnant sayings and phrases meet the same fate. His assertion that he is the better for his foes and the worse for his friends the Duke takes for a mere absurdity or an inadvertence of expression, though he is tickled by Feste's proof of his affirmation through double negation.[2] The philosopher may speak to Sebastian of 'this great lubber the world'; he may tell Viola how 'foolery, sir, does walk about the orb like the sun; it shines everywhere'; he may remark to the whole company how 'the whirligig of time brings in his revenges'; but nobody heeds him. Why should any one heed a man who gets his living by talking nonsense, and who may be whipped if he displeases his employer?

All the agility of wit and fancy, all the penetration and wisdom, which Feste shows in his calling, would not by themselves explain our feeling for him. But his mind to him a kingdom is, and one full of such present joys that he finds contentment there. Outwardly he may be little better than a slave; but Epictetus was a slave outright and yet absolutely free: and so is Feste. That world of quibbles which are pointless to his audience, of incongruities which nobody else can see, of flitting fancies which he only cares to pursue, is his sunny realm. He is alone when he invents that aphorism of Quinapalus and builds his hopes on it; and it was not merely to get sixpence from Sir Andrew that he told of Pigrogromitus and the Vapians passing the equinoctial of Queubus. He had often passed it in that company himself. Maria and Sir Toby (who do enjoy his more obvious jests) are present when, clothed in the curate's gown and beard, he befools the imprisoned Malvolio so gloriously; but the prisoner is his only witness when, for his own sole delight, himself as Sir Topas converses with himself the Fool. But for this inward gaiety he could never have joined with all his heart in the roaring revelry of Sir Toby; but he does not need this revelry, and, unlike Sir Toby and Sir Toby's surgeon, he remains master of his senses. Having thus a world of his own, and being lord of himself, he cares little for Fortune. His mistress may turn him away; but, 'to be turned away, let summer bear it out.' This 'sunshine of the breast' is always with him and spreads its radiance over the whole scene in which he moves. And so we love him.

We have another reason. The Fool's voice is as melodious as the 'sweet content' of his soul. To think of him is to remember 'Come away, come away, Death', and 'O Mistress mine', and 'When that I was', and fragments of folk-song and ballad, and a catch that 'makes the welkin dance indeed'. To think of *Twelfth Night* is to think of music. It opens with instrumental music and ends with a song. All Shakespeare's best praise of music, except the famous passage in *The Merchant of Venice*, occurs in it. And almost all the music and the praise of music come from Feste or have to do with Feste. In this he stands alone among Shakespeare's Fools; and that this, with the influence it has on our feeling for him, was intended by the poet, should be plain. It is no accident that, when the Duke pays him for his 'pains' in singing, he answers, 'No pains, sir; I take pleasure in singing, sir'; that the revelry for which he risks punishment is a revelry of song; that, when he is left alone, he still sings. And, all this being so, I venture to construe in the light of it what has seemed strange to me in the passage that follows the singing of 'Come away'. Usually, when Feste receives his 'gratillity', he promptly tries to get it doubled; but here he not only abstains from any such effort but is short, if not disagreeably sharp, with the Duke. The fact is, he is offended, even disgusted; and offended, not as Fool, but as music-lover and artist. We others know what the Duke said beforehand of the song, but Feste does not know it. Now he sings, and his soul is in the song. Yet, as the last note dies away, the comment he hears from this noble aesthete is, 'There's for thy pains'!

I have a last grace to notice in our wise, happy, melodious Fool. He was little injured by his calling. He speaks as he likes; but from first to last, whether he is revelling or chopping logic or playing with words, and to whomsoever he speaks or sings, he keeps his tongue free from obscenity. The fact is in accord with the spirit of this ever-blessed play, which could not have endured the 'foul-mouthed' Fool of *All's Well*, and from which Aldis Wright in his school edition found, I think, but three lines (not the Fool's) to omit. But the trait is none the less characteristic of Feste, and we like him the better for it.

It remains to look at another side of the whole matter. One is scarcely sorry for Touchstone, but one is very sorry for Feste, and pity, though not a painful pity, heightens our admiration and deepens our sympathy. The position of the professional jester we must needs feel to be more or less hard, if not of necessity degrading. In Feste's case it is peculiarly hard. He is perfectly sane, and there is nothing to show that he is unfit for independence. In important respects he is, more than Shakespeare's other fools, superior in mind to his superiors in rank.

And he has no Celia, no Countess, no Lear, to protect or love him. He had been Fool to Olivia's father, who 'took much delight in him'; but Olivia, though not unkind, cannot be said to love him. We find him, on his first appearance, in disgrace and (if Maria is right) in danger of being punished or even turned away. His mistress, entering, tells him that he is a dry fool, that she'll no more of him, and (later) that his fooling grows old and people dislike it. Her displeasure, doubtless, has a cause, and it is transient, but her words are none the less significant. Feste is a relic of the past. The steward, a person highly valued by his lady, is Feste's enemy. Though Maria likes him and, within limits, would stand his friend, there is no tone of affection in her words to him, and certainly none in those of any other person. We cannot but feel very sorry for him.

This peculiar position explains certain traits in Feste himself which might otherwise diminish our sympathy. One is that he himself, though he shows no serious malevolence even to his enemy, shows no affection for any one. His liking for Maria does not amount to fondness. He enjoys drinking and singing with Sir Toby, but despises his drunkenness and does not care for him. His attitude to strangers is decidedly cool, and he does not appear to be attracted even by Viola. The fact is, he recognizes very clearly that, as this world goes, a man whom nobody loves must look out for himself. Hence (this is the second trait) he is a shameless beggar, much the most so of Shakespeare's Fools. He is fully justified, and he begs so amusingly that we welcome his begging; but shameless it is. But he is laying up treasures on earth against the day when some freak of his own, or some whim in his mistress, will bring his dismissal, and the short summer of his freedom will be followed by the wind and the rain. And so, finally, he is as careful as his love of fun will allow to keep clear of any really dangerous enterprise. He must join in the revel of the knights and the defiance of the steward; but from the moment when Malvolio retires with a threat to Maria, and Maria begins to expound her plot against him, Feste keeps silence; and, though she expressly assigns him a part in the conspiracy, he takes none. The plot succeeds magnificently, and Malvolio is shut up, chained as a lunatic, in a dark room; and that comic genius Maria has a new scheme, which requires the active help of the Fool. But her words, 'Nay, I prithee, put on this gown and this beard,' show that he objects; and if his hesitation is momentary, it is not merely because the temptation is strong. For, after all, he runs but little risk, since Malvolio cannot see him, and he is a master in the management of his voice. And so, agreeing with Sir Toby's view that their sport cannot with safety be pursued to the upshot, after a while, when he is left alone with the steward, he takes steps to end it and consents, in his own voice, to provide the lunatic with light, pen, ink, and paper for his letter to Olivia.

We are not offended by Feste's eagerness for sixpences and his avoidance of risks. By helping us to realize the hardness of his lot, they add to our sympathy and make us admire the more the serenity and gaiety of his spirit. And at the close of the play these feelings reach their height. He is left alone; for Lady Belch, no doubt, is by her husband's bed-side, and the thin-faced gull Sir Andrew has vanished, and the rich and noble lovers with all their attendants have streamed away to dream of the golden time to come, without a thought of the poor jester. There is no one to hear him sing; but what does that matter? He takes pleasure in singing. And a song comes into his head; an old rude song about the stages of man's life, in each of which the rain rains every day; a song at once cheerful and rueful, stoical and humorous; and this suits his mood and he sings it. But, since he is even more of a philosopher than the author of the song, and since, after all, he is not merely a Fool but the actor who is playing that part in a theatre, he adds at the end a stanza of his own:

> A great while ago the world begun,
>> With hey, ho, the wind and the rain;
> But that's all one, our play is done,
>> And we'll strive to please you every day.[3]

Shakespeare himself, I feel sure, added that stanza to the old song; and when he came to write *King Lear* he, I think, wrote yet another, which Feste might well have sung. To the immortal words,

> Poor Fool and knave, I have one part in my heart
> That's sorry yet for thee,

the Fool replies,

> He that has and a little tiny wit,
>> With hey, ho, the wind and the rain,
> Must make content with his fortunes fit,
>> Though the rain it raineth every day.

So Shakespeare brings the two Fools together; and, whether or no he did this wittingly, I am equally grateful to him. But I cannot be grateful to those critics who see in Feste's song only an illustration of the bad custom by which sometimes, when a play was finished, the clown remained, or appeared, on the stage to talk nonsense or to sing some old 'trash'; nor yet to those who tell us that it was 'the players' who tacked this particular 'trash' to the end of *Twelfth Night*. They may conceivably be right in perceiving no difference between the first four stanzas and the last, but they cannot possibly be right in failing to perceive how appropriate the song is to the singer, and how in the line

> But that's all one, our play is done,

he repeats an expression used a minute before in his last speech.[4] We owe these things, not to the players, but to that player in Shakespeare's company who was also a poet, to Shakespeare himself—the same Shakespeare who perhaps had hummed the old song, half-ruefully and half-cheerfully, to its accordant air, as he walked home alone to his lodging from the theatre or even from some noble's mansion; he who, looking down from an immeasurable height on the mind of the public and the noble, had yet to be their servant and jester, and to depend upon their favour; not wholly uncorrupted by this dependence, but yet superior to it and, also, determined, like Feste, to lay by the sixpences it brought him, until at last he could say the words, 'Our revels now are ended,' and could break—was it a magician's staff or a Fool's bauble?

NOTES

1. I mean the Fools proper, i.e. professional jesters attached to a court or house. In effect they are but four, Touchstone, Feste, Lavache in *All's Well*, and Lear's Fool; for it is not clear that Trinculo is the court-jester, and the Clown in *Othello*, like the Fool (a brothel-fool) in *Timon*, has but a trivial part. Neither humorists like Launce and Launcelot Gobbo, nor 'low' characters, unintentionally humorous, like the old peasant at the end of *Antony and Cleopatra* or the young shepherd called 'clown' in *The Winter's Tale*, are Fools proper. The distinction is quite clear, but it tends to be obscured for readers because the wider designation 'clown' is applied to persons of either class in the few lists of Dramatis Personae printed in the Folio, to the complete lists of our modern editions, and also, alike in these editions and in the Folio, in stage-directions and in the headings of speeches. Such directions and headings were meant for the actors, and the principal comic man of the company doubtless played both Launce and Feste. Feste, I may observe, is called 'Clown' in the stage-directions and speech-headings, but in the text always 'Fool'. Lear's Fool is 'Fool' even in the former.

2. Feste's statement of his proof can hardly be called lucid, and his illustration ('conclusions to be as kisses, if your four negatives make your two affirmatives') seems to have cost the commentators much fruitless labour. If anything definite was in the Fool's mind it may have been this. The gentleman asks for a kiss. The lady, denying it, exclaims 'No no no no.' But, as the first negative (an adjective) negates the second (a substantive), and the third in like manner the fourth, these four negatives yield two enthusiastic affirmatives, and the gentleman, thanks to the power of logic, gets twice what he asked for. This is not Feste's only gird at the wisdom of the schools. It has been gravely surmised that he was educated for the priesthood and, but for some escapade, would have played Sir Topas in earnest.

3. Those who witnessed, some years ago, Mr. Granville Barker's production of *Twelfth Night* and Mr. Hayden Coffin's presentment of the Fool's part must always remember them with great pleasure, and not least the singing of this song.

4. 'I was one, sir, in this interlude; one Sir Topas, sir; *but that's all one.*' No edition that I have consulted notices the repetition.

1925—J. B. Priestley. "The Illyrians," from *The English Comic Characters*

J. B. Priestley was a prolific and popular author, playwright, broadcaster, and scriptwriter. His nonfiction works include *English Humour* and *The Art of the Dramatist*.

If you take ship from the coast of Bohemia—having made your last bow to Perdita and Florizel—and sail for a day in a westerly direction, you will presently arrive at Illyria. There you will find the love-sick melancholy Duke, seated among his musicians, polishing his images and doting upon the "high-fantastical"; and go but a little way out of the city and you will come upon the stately Countess Olivia among her clipped box-trees, pacing the lawns like some great white peacock, while her steward Malvolio, lean, frowning, and cross-gartered, bends at her elbow. There too, if you are lucky, you may catch a glimpse of the rubious-lipped lovely Viola, stretching her slim legs and swinging her pert page's cloak between the Duke's palace and Olivia's house, delicately breathing blank verse. And if there should come to your ears the sound of drunken catches, and to your nose the smell of burnt sack and pickled herrings, then look for Olivia's uncle, Sir Toby Belch, and his friend, Sir Andrew Aguecheek, and with them, it may be, that dainty rogue, Maria, darting about like some little black and white bird, and Feste the Clown, with his sharp tongue, bright eyes and strange bitter-sweet songs. In and out of doors, there is good company in Illyria, good company whether it is high or low, sober or drunk.

Our present inquiry takes us into the society of the low, the drunken and disreputable company, the comic Illyrians. (It is difficult even to sound the name and remain sober.) Whether Malvolio, who was himself neither drunken nor disreputable but essentially a "grave liver," should have place in the company, is a very debatable question. Most of the comic scenes in the play revolve around him, and it is his antics, his sudden rise and his awful collapse, that form the basis of most of the broader comedy of the piece; his self-love and swelling vanity, which make him an easy butt for Maria and her grinning troupe, his gravity and pompous airs, are all served up, without mercy, for our entertainment. Yet Malvolio, strictly speaking, is not a comic character. He stands outside the real comic tradition. Although Shakespeare gives some of his speeches a most delicious flavour of absurdity, he does not treat Malvolio as he treats his purely comic figures, whom he regards not merely with a humorous tolerance but with positive delight and relish, encouraging them, as it were, to indulge their every whim. The difference between, let us say, Malvolio and Sir Andrew Aguecheek is that Shakespeare handles the one and dandles the other. Sir Andrew is really a much more contemptible figure than the serious and capable steward, but then he is so manifestly ridiculous that he evades criticism altogether, escapes into a world of his own, where every fresh piece of absurdity he commits only brings him another round of laughter and applause. Times change, and we are more likely to regard Malvolio with some measure of sympathy than was Shakespeare; indeed, in spite of his vanity, to us he is a figure not untouched by pathos, for the possibility of Olivia falling in love with him (and she admits his value as an employee) appears to us not entirely preposterous, nor do his portentous gravity and puritanical airs seem to us so offensive, now that our Sir Tobies have been steadily rebuked in the manner of Malvolio for at least two generations. Sir Toby's famous reply—"Dost thou think, because thou art virtuous, there shall be no more cakes and ale"—cuts the ground from under the feet of a very large number of our energetic fellow-citizens, whose apparent business it is, Malvolio-like, to attend to our private affairs and superintend our morals; and Sir Toby was fortunate in being able to make such a rejoinder without being suppressed. Malvolio, we may say, has been steadily coming into his own for a long time, so that it is difficult for us to regard him as an unpleasant oddity as Shakespeare did. And perhaps it says something for our charity that, sitting as we are among ever-diminishing supplies of cakes and ale, we can still see something pathetic in this figure.

Shakespeare's sympathies were so wide and his dramatic genius so universal that it is always dangerous to give him a point of view and dower him with various likes and dislikes. Nevertheless it is true to say that certain types of character very clearly aroused his dislike; and it is also true to say that these are the very types of character that appear to have some fascination for our world. In short, his villains are rapidly becoming our heroes. Thus, Shakespeare clearly detested all hard, unsympathetic, intolerant persons, the over-ambitious and overweening, the climbers and careerists, the "get on or get outs" of this world. When the will and the intellect in all their pride were divorced from tolerance, charity, a love of the good things of this world, they formed the stuff out of which the Shakespearean villains were made. But the Bastard and Iago and Richard the Third are the very characters that some of our modern dramatists would select to adorn three acts of hero-worship. So too, to come down the scale, our friend Malvolio, the pushing puritan, is, under various disguises, the hero of almost one-half of all the American novels that were ever written. Shakespeare, looking steadily at Malvolio with his self-love ("O, you are sick of self-love," cries Olivia to him) and his intolerance, contrives that he shall be covered with ridicule, but never regards him as a comic figure. In spite of his absurdities there are fermenting in him too many of those qualities that Shakespeare detested for him to be a figure of fun. While this conceited and over-ambitious steward struts cross-gartered on the lawn for our entertainment, there flutters across his path, for one fleeting moment, the terrible shadow of that other ambitious underling,

Iago. So Malvolio is deceived, abused, locked up and treated as a madman for a short space, and this is his purgation, for Shakespeare saw that his soul was in danger and so appointed for him two angels of deliverance, namely, Maria and Sir Toby Belch.

In the very first speech that Sir Toby makes, when we discover him talking with Maria, he remarks that "care's an enemy to life," and this we may take to be his philosophy. His time is spent in putting a multitude of things, oceans of burnt sack, mountains of pickled herrings, between himself and the enemy, Care; and he may be shortly described as a Falstaff without genius, who would have made the fat knight a very able lieutenant. Undoubtedly, he is a very idle and drunken old rip, who forgets his position, which, as the uncle of the Countess, is considerable, his years and his manners, and passes all his time in low company, in the society of his inferiors, either because, like Maria, his niece's chambermaid, they devise entertainment for him, or because, like Sir Andrew, they serve as butts and cat's-paws. But notwithstanding his devotion to sherris sack—and it is doubtful if we ever see him sober—unlike Falstaff Sir Toby does not live altogether in an ideal comic world of ease and merriment; by much drinking of healths and singing of catches and fool-baiting, and with the assistance of a kind of rough philosophy, a tap-room epicureanism, he certainly tries to live in such a world; but common-sense and a knowledge of this world's uses keep breaking in from time to time. In spite of his idleness and love of mischief, he is shrewd enough on occasion. Thus, he does not propose to deliver Sir Andrew's ridiculous challenge to the supposed Cesario, because, he declares, "the behaviour of the young gentleman gives him out to be of good capacity and breeding; his employment between his lord and my niece confirms no less: therefore this letter, being so excellently ignorant, will breed no terror in the youth,—he will find it comes from a clod-pole." He is in no doubt as to the capacity of his admiring dupe, Sir Andrew, who is only encouraged to remain as the suitor of Olivia in order that Toby may amuse himself and mulct the foolish knight of his ducats. His apparently innocent defence of Sir Andrew in the opening dialogue with Maria ("He's as tall a man as any's in Illyria"—and the rest) is, of course, mere impudence, one wag winking at another. Then later, when the confusion between Viola and her brother complicates the action, Sir Toby changes his mind about Cesario, as he has a right to do on the evidence before him, and remarks: "A very dishonest, paltry boy, and more a coward than a hare: his dishonesty appears in leaving his friend here in necessity, and denying him. . . ." And he it is who has the wit to see that the joke against Malvolio has gone far enough—"I would we were well rid of this knavery." Although he vastly enjoys stirring up unnecessary strife and egging on two apparent cowards to fight one another, he shows no reluctance to taking part in any quarrel himself and is certainly no coward. When he himself is hurt, it will be remembered, he makes no complaint ("That's all one: 'has hurt me, and there's the end on 't.—Sot, didst see Dick surgeon, sot?"), and though this stoicism simply covers a fear of being ridiculed, it does argue a stout nature.

Sir Toby, then, is by no means a simpleton. Nor is he, on the other hand, a comic genius like Falstaff, whose world has been transformed into an ideally comic world, whose whole life, whose every speech and action, are devised to further ease, enjoyment, and laughter. Sir Toby, in his own coarse, swashbuckling manner, is witty, but he is not the cause of wit in other men. He does not transform himself into an object of mirth, content so long as men are laughing and the comic spirit is abroad, but, like any bullying wag of the tap-room, looks for a butt in the company. He is really nothing more than an elderly schoolboy with a prodigious thirst and far too much spare time on his hands: the type is not uncommon. Having a more than usual amount of energy, both of brain and body, and no serious powers of application and no sensible objects upon which to expend such energy, his one problem is how to pass the time pleasantly. As he happens to have his existence in a romantic and idyllic world of love and dalliance and fine phrases that offers no employment to a robust and prosaic middle-aged gentleman, and as he, unlike our country squires and retired majors, cannot turn to golf and bridge, there is nothing for it but cakes and ale, the roaring of catches, verbal bouts with the chambermaid and the clown, and mischievous antics played at the expense of such creatures as Malvolio and Sir Andrew. Men so situated always seek out low company and are never at ease among their equals. But once among his cronies, Toby enjoys himself with such rollicking abandon that he communicates his enjoyment to us, so that we would not for the world have him different. There is about this drunken, staggering, swaggering, roaring knight, such a ripeness and gusto that his humours are infectious, and once we are in his riotous company decency and order seem intrusive and positively ill-natured. He has leave to keep us out of bed all night, and we would not stint him of a drop of sack or a single pickled herring. Falstaff apart, there never was a better bear-leader of a fool. With what a luxury of enjoyment he draws out and displays to us the idiocies of the guileless Sir Andrew:

> *Sir Andrew.* I'll stay a month longer. I am a fellow o' the strangest mind
> i' the world; I delight in masques and revels sometimes altogether.
> *Sir Toby.* Art thou good at these kickshawses, knight?
> *Sir Andrew.* As any man in Illyria, whatsoever he be, under the degree
> of my betters; and yet I will not compare with a nobleman.
> *Sir Toby.* What is thy excellence in a galliard, knight?
> *Sir Andrew.* Faith, I can cut a caper.
> *Sir Toby.* And I can cut the mutton to 't.
> *Sir Andrew.* And I think I have the back-trick simply as strong as any
> man in Illyria.

Sir Toby. Wherefore are these things hid? wherefore have these gifts a curtain before 'em? are they like to take dust, like Mistress Mall's picture? why dost thou not go to church in a galliard, and come home in a coranto? My very walk should be a jig; I would not so much as make water but in a sink-a-pace. What dost thou mean? is it a world to hide virtues in? I did think, by the excellent constitution of thy leg, it was form'd under the star of a galliard.
Sir Andrew. Ay, 'tis strong, and it does indifferent well in a flame-coloured stock. Shall we set about some revels?
Sir Toby. What shall we do else? were we not born under Taurus?
Sir Andrew. Taurus! that's sides and heart.
Sir Toby. No, sir; it is legs and thighs. Let me see thee caper . . . .

Once in his cups, how magnificently he overrides mere precision in speech and commonsense and rises into a poetical kind of nonsense of his own: "To hear by the nose, it is dulcet in contagion. But shall we make the welkin dance indeed? shall we rouse the night-owl in a catch that will draw three souls out of one weaver? shall we do that?" With what gusto does he enter into the matter of the duel between Sir Andrew and the disguised Viola, alternately breathing fire into them and then damping it with a report to each one of the other's fury and prowess. He bustles from one to the other in a very ecstasy of pleasure. Sir Andrew, he tells Fabian, "if he were open'd, an you find so much blood in his liver as will clog the foot of a flea, I'll eat the rest of the anatomy"—a remark worthy of Falstaff himself—Sir Andrew is not anxious to fight, but Toby fans his few smouldering embers of courage into a blaze and compels him to send a challenge:

Go, write it in a martial hand; be curst and brief it is no matter how witty, so it be eloquent and full of invention: taunt him with the license of ink: if thou *thou'st* him some thrice, it shall not be amiss; and as many lies as will lie in thy sheet of paper, although the sheet were big enough for the bed of Ware in England, set 'em down: go, about it. Let there be gall enough in thy ink; though thou write with a goose-pen, no matter: about it.

Then gives him some further encouragement when the challenge is written:

Go, Sir Andrew; scout me for him at the corner of the orchard, like a bumbaily: so soon as ever thou see'st him, draw; and, as thou drawest, swear horrible; for it comes to pass oft, that a terrible oath, with a swaggering accent sharply twang'd off, gives manhood more approbation than ever proof itself would have earned him. Away!

We can almost hear Toby smacking his lips over the vision of Sir Andrew letting fly a terrible oath, with a swaggering accent sharply twang'd off. Then, with an ever-increasing relish for the situation and with his images swelling at every fresh turn of the farce, Sir Toby confronts Viola with a tale of her incensed opponent awaiting her, "bloody as a hunter," "a devil in private brawl: souls and bodies hath he divorced three; and his incensement at this moment is so implacable, that satisfaction can be none but by pangs of death and sepulchre: hobnob is his word; give 't or take 't . . . "—a terrifying picture. Back again he goes to Sir Andrew, now to damp the knight's faint ardour with an equally terrifying account of his adversary: "Why, man," roars the mischievous old toper, "he's a very devil; I have not seen such a firago. I had a pass with him, rapier, scabbard, and all, and he gives me the stuck-in with such a mortal motion, that it is inevitable; and, on the answer, he pays you as surely as your feet hit the ground they step on. They say he has been fencer to the Sophy." "Pox on 't," cries the startled Sir Andrew, out of his simplicity, "I'll not meddle with him." But there is no escape for him, even though he should part with his horse as the price of that escape. It is only the unexpected entry of Antonio that robs us of the climax and, possibly, Sir Toby of the horse, but the artful and mischievous knight, who has known something of the satisfaction of those lesser gods who prompt our tyrants and prophets and further our wars and revolutions to pass pleasantly their idle aeons, has had his fun. He has contrived a tale that, with humorous embellishment, will keep any company uproarious between one round of sack and the next, between chorus and chorus.

But if we have enjoyed Sir Toby's antics so much that we have no desire for his immediate amendment, we must leave him with some misgiving, for at the conclusion of the piece we plainly see that those very gods of mischief whom he has emulated in this affair of the duel have now selected him as the victim of their sport. They who have allowed him to season his sack with so many herrings in pickle, have now devised for him a rod in pickle. This is nothing less than his marriage with Maria, of which we learn from Fabian's explanation of the joke against Malvolio at the end of the play. We are told: "Maria writ the letter at Sir Toby's great importance (*i.e.* importunity—though this is not strictly true); in recompense whereof he hath married her." Alas!—poor Toby. We had seen the possibility of such an alliance throughout the play; indeed, scene after scene had shown us Toby edging nearer and nearer to his doom. We had heard him declare, "She's a beagle, true-bred, and one that adores me," in all his fateful masculine complacency. When the Malvolio jest was at its intoxicating height, we had heard him shower compliments on the artful little soubrette, "Excellent wench" and the rest, had caught him declaring to Sir Andrew and Fabian, in the ecstasy of his enjoyment, "I could marry this wench for this device, and ask no other dowry with her but such another jest." We have heard him cry to her, "Wilt thou set thy foot o' my neck?" and "Shall I play my freedom at tray-trip, and become thy bond-slave?" Yet, with the sound of such dangerous speeches, verbal gun-cotton, still ringing in our ears, we had thought that the old fox might yet sniff the air, scent danger and then bolt for freedom. But no, he has walked into the trap. He has been snared, like many another man, not only by a woman but by his own philosophy. "Care's an enemy to life" he has told himself, and with so much idleness on his hands, with so rich an appreciation of japes and jests, with so great a capacity for mischief and the staging of whims, what could be better than an alliance with Maria, who has proved herself the very queen of humorous strategy, a "most excellent devil of wit," and a most generous purveyor of cakes and ale? Alas!—had this been any other man's reasoning, he would have seen the folly of it. As it is, he marries, so that the perfect life of comic ease and merriment that he is always attempting to build up may have another prop, and does not realise that he is simply bringing it all down in one awful crash. Who doubts for a moment that what Olivia, with her stately displeasure, could not do, Maria, the erstwhile accomplice and fellow mischief-maker, but now the wife, will accomplish within a very short space; that Maria the chambermaid, with a comically sympathetic view of sack, catches, and late hours, is one thing, and Maria the wife, with a husband to reform, is another; that the very wit that could devise such unseemly jests will henceforward be occupied, not in devising others, but in schemes, equally efficacious, for preventing husband Toby from reaching that large freedom he hitherto enjoyed? As a last bulwark against care, he has taken Maria to wife, and now, without a doubt, the old freedom has vanished and care is about to return in an undreamed-of measure. Toby's philosophy has undone him, and he falls; but he falls like a great man. We have caught his days at their highest point; nevermore shall we see him, free, spacious, as rich and ripe as a late plum, all Illyria his tavern, a prince of gusto, good living, and most admirable fooling; from now on he will dwindle, take on a cramped and secretive air, and lose his confidence and zest, for now he will always be discovered, his Maria's reproaches still shrilling in his ear, a cup too low.

Of one of Sir Toby's boon companions, Feste the Clown, there is little to be said. Viola, after a bout of wit with him, sums up the matter admirably:

This fellow's wise enough to play the Fool;
And to do that well craves a kind of wit:
He must observe their mood on whom he jests,
The quality of persons, and the time;
Not, like the haggard, check at every feather
That comes before his eyes. This is a practice
As full of labour as a wise man's art:
For folly, that he wisely shows, is fit;
But wise men's folly, shown, quite taints their wit.

This is an accurate description of Feste's own practice, for as he lounges in and out of the scene, it will be noticed that always he plays up to his company. He is a professional entertainer and gives his audiences what he knows will please them. The love-sick Duke feeds upon melancholy, and so to him Feste sings "old and antique" songs and takes delight in his art, but as soon as he has finished the last note of *Come Away, Death*, like the brisk professional he is, he himself shows no trace of melancholy or of any emotion, but is his usual self in a moment, detached, observant, critical, taking his leave with a sly dig at the Duke's melancholy and inconstancy. With the other serious characters, he acts the professional fool but always with a certain reserve and dignity and always with one eye upon the main chance, conjuring another coin into his hand with an ingratiating witticism. Malvolio he really dislikes because the proud and puritanical steward has a contempt for both him and his office (a contempt that Shakespeare himself had probably met with in some Malvolios of his acquaintance), and so he does not scruple to play Malvolio the cruellest trick of all by pretending to be Sir Tobas the parson. With Sir Toby and Maria, Feste appears at his ease and, as it were, with his wit unbuttoned, bandying broad jests with them; while for the delectation of Sir Andrew, a great admirer of his, he utters the first nonsense that comes into his head. Indeed, in this company of boon companions and midnight caterwaulers, his humour is all for wild nonsense of a Rabelaisian cast. Such ridiculous speeches as "I did impeticos thy gratillity; for Malvolio's nose is no whipstock; my lady has a white hand, and the Myrmidons are no bottle-ale houses" cast a spell over the rural wits of Sir Andrew, who pronounces it to be "the best fooling, when all is done." (There is apparently a lower level of intelligence and humour than Sir Andrew's; it is to be found in those commentators who have pored for hours over these nonsensical speeches of the Clown's and have then complained that they could make little of them.) And though we may not agree that this "is the best fooling, when all is done," most of us have regretted that we were not present at the previous meeting of Sir Toby, Sir Andrew, and the Clown, when, according to Sir Andrew, the Clown was in very gracious fooling and spoke of Pigrogromitus and of the Vapians passing the equinoctial of Queubus. Perhaps this is one of the delights that Heaven has in store for us, or for those of us who are only fit for a Heaven slightly damaged and humanised. Wind and rain outside; indoors a clear fire and a few tall candles, with sack in plenty; Sir Toby, straddling and with nose aglow, on one side; Sir Andrew gaping on the other; and the Clown before us, nodding and winking through his account of Pigrogromitus and the Vapians passing the equinoctial of Queubus; the whole to be concluded by the catch of *Hold thy peace, thou knave*, with the possibility of being interrupted at any moment by a Malvolio in his nightshirt—here is a hint for the commander of the starry revels.

Sir Andrew Aguecheek is one of Shakespeare's family of simpletons: he is first cousin to Slender and Silence. Life pulses so faintly in this lank-haired, timid, rustic squire that he is within a stride of utter imbecility. He is really the very opposite of Sir Toby, who is for ever in mischief simply because he has more energy and brains than he knows what to do with, being without any serious purpose, whereas Sir Andrew follows Toby into mischief simply because he is deficient in both energy and brains, and for ever takes the line of least resistance. Without a shred of either self-respect or self-confidence, without volition, courage or sense, he is any man's prey, a toy-balloon blown hither and thither by the slightest breeze. His social standing and wealth are just sufficient to leave him independent of any occupation or control, a free agent, but being what he is, it means that they are just sufficient to leave him at the mercy of the first rascal he meets. At first sight, it seems astonishing that a comic character of any dimensions could possibly be created out of such material, and, indeed, only a great genius could have taken these few straws and made of them a creature whose every odd remark and quaint caper is a delight. But it is Sir Andrew's amazing simplicity, his almost pathetic naïvety, his absolute lack of guile, that make him so richly absurd. And with these there goes a certain very characteristic quality, the unanalysable factor, that is present in every remark he makes; every speech has a certain Aguecheek flavour or smack that is unmistakable; even as we read we can hear the bleating of his plaintive little voice. His best trait is one that he shares with every simpleton, and that is a childlike capacity for enjoyment, which is really born of a sense of wonder, the ability to marvel at and relish the commonest things, to see the world innocently and freshly, a sense that withers among brighter wits and natures richer in experience but blooms for ever with the extremes of humankind, the utter simpletons and the great geniuses. Sir Andrew has this capacity, and it entitles him to a place at the revels. In spite of his starts and frights, his loss of two thousand ducats and his broken head, it is clear that he has enjoyed himself hugely in the company of his admired Sir Toby, and that he will return to his distant estate bubbling with a confused tale of strange happenings and great personages that will be meat and drink to him for years. It is true that he has been everybody's butt, but then he does not know it; he is happily protected from all such discoveries and will be all his life; so that he might almost be said to have the best of the laugh, for whereas the others are living in this world, he is still dwelling in Eden.

There are a thousand things that could be said of this simple creature, for there is probably no better text than a fool, but one particular aspect of him invites our attention. What really tickles us about Sir Andrew, over and above the unanalysable drollery of his speeches, is not what he thinks and feels but the fact that he should not be able to conceal what he thinks and feels. There is somewhere at the back of all our minds a little Sir Andrew Aguecheek, giggling and gaping, now strutting and now cowering, pluming himself monstrously at one word and being hurled into a fit of depression by the next; but most of us contrive to keep this little fellow and his antics carefully hidden from sight for the sake of decency and our own self-respect. Some of Sir Andrew's ingenuous remarks have the same effect, or should have the same effect, upon us as the sight of a monkey, which presents us with a parody of human life that is highly diverting but that leaves us somewhat shamefaced: after seeing so many things done openly that we ourselves do in secret, we blush, partly for the monkey that it should make a public show of itself, and partly for ourselves who have so much that is better concealed. The mind of Sir Andrew, such as it is, is as plain to sight as the dial of the parish clock. Almost every remark he makes, innocently revealing, as it does, the ebb and flow of his poor self-esteem, is not only a piece of self-revelation but also a revelation of all our species: this zany, naked to our sight, is uncovering the nakedness of statesmen and philosophers, popes and emperors. How delicious in its candour is his reply to Sir Toby's bantering charge of being "put down": "Methinks sometimes I have no more wit than a Christian or an ordinary man has: but I am a great eater of beef, and I believe that does harm to my wit." How swiftly following the thought that he may be no better than the ordinary in some particular comes the possible explanation, the eating of beef, to raise the phoenix of his vanity again from its ashes. He remains, at some charge to his purse, with Sir Toby as a suitor to Olivia; and yet it is clear that the whole idea is Sir Toby's, for Olivia plainly does not favour Sir Andrew, and he knows it, nor does he himself feel any passion for the lady: he has simply allowed himself to be persuaded, caught in the web of Sir Toby's imagination and rhetoric. How swiftly too his vanity plumes itself again at Sir Toby's artful prompting in the matter of his accomplishments; he can cut a caper, he tells us with a delicious affectation of detachment, and thinks he has the back-trick simply as strong as any man in Illyria.

In the matter of scholarship, which most gentlemen of his time affected, his simplicity and candour are nothing less than wholesome and refreshing. When Sir Toby declares that "not to be a-bed after midnight is to be up betimes"—and then, plunging into the depths of his learning, brings forth an adage from Lily's grammar—"And *diliculo surgere*, thou know'st—" Sir Andrew provides us with the rare spectacle of a man acting honestly in the face of a classical quotation, by replying: "Nay, by my troth, I know not: but I know, to be up late is to be up late." So too when Sir Toby asks if our life does not consist of the four elements, he replies, indifferently, "Faith, so they say; but I think it rather consists of eating and drinking"—a notable answer. Again, when the Clown asks whether they will have a love-song or a song of good life, and Sir Toby decides for the former, Sir Andrew speaks for all the novel-readers of our circulating libraries but with more sincerity than they can ever muster when he adds: "Ay, ay: I care not for good life." Most excellent too is his critical observation in reply to the Clown's remark that the knight, Sir Toby, is "in admirable fooling": "Ay, he does well enough if he be disposed, and so do I too: he does it with a better grace, but I do it more natural." And what could be more revealing than his cry at the indignation meeting after the visit of Malvolio. Maria has said that the steward is sometimes a kind of Puritan. "O!" cries Sir Andrew, "if I thought that, I'd beat him like a dog." When pressed for his exquisite reason, he confesses to having none: indeed, he has no reason at all, but the excitement of the occasion has heated his poor wits and he wishes to make some full-blooded declaration and stand well with the company, like our Sir Andrews who sit in their clubs and tell one another they would "shoot 'em down." How pathetically he echoes Sir Toby. Even when the latter remarks that Maria adores him, Sir Andrew, not to be left out, instantly lights a pitiful rushlight of amatory remembrance: "I was adored once." Yes, he, Sir Andrew, was adored once: it is not true, but for the moment he thinks it is and so contrives to take his place among the swaggering fellows, alongside Sir Toby. And perhaps best of all, the very sweet distillation of ingenuousness, is his whisper in the shrubbery when Malvolio, having read the letter, is rehearsing his part as the Countess's husband. As soon as mention is made of "a foolish knight," Sir Andrew is in no doubt as to the person—"That's me, I warrant you." And when his guess is confirmed by the actual sound of his name, he is almost triumphant—"I knew 'twas I, for many do call me fool," a remark that smacks more of complacency than resignation, as if to be known as a fool did at least single him out for some notice. And how revealing, too, is his conduct during the duel episode. He has been told that Olivia has only shown favour to Cesario in order that her more backward suitor, the knight, should be encouraged to accost: he must redeem his credit either by valour or by policy; and so he declares for valour, for policy he hates. And so he sends a challenge that, notwithstanding his complacent view of its "vinegar and pepper," deserves a prominent place in any collection of diplomatic documents:

> *Youth, whatsoever thou art, thou art but a scurvy fellow. Wonder not, nor admire not in thy mind, why I do call thee so, for I will show thee no reason for 't. Thou comest to the Lady Olivia, and in my sight she uses thee kindly: but thou liest in thy throat; that is not the matter I challenge thee for. I will waylay thee going home; where if it be thy chance to kill me, thou kill'st me like a rogue and a villain. Fare thee well; and God have mercy upon one of our souls! He may have mercy upon mine; but my hope is better, and so look to thyself. Thy friend, as thou usest him, and thy sworn enemy, ANDREW AGUECHEEK.*

Never, in the whole history of the duello, was such good citizenship exhibited in a challenge. And when Sir Andrew learns that his adversary has been fencer to the Sophy and is a fire-eater, he is swift to declare that he will not meddle with him, and that had he known that the fellow had been so valiant and so cunning in fence, he would have seen him damned before he would have challenged him. And, of course, Sir Andrew is only talking sense: it would have served the fellow right not to have been challenged. Later, when he has struck Sebastian and has received a pummelling in exchange, he tells Sir Toby to let Sebastian alone: "I'll go another way to work with him; I'll have an action of battery against him, if there be any law in Illyria: though I struck him first, yet it's no matter for that." No matter at all: he feels, as we all do, that the law is on his side. Our last glimpse of him is somewhat moving, for he has a broken head, received in the company of Sir Toby, who has himself been given "a bloody coxcomb," but nevertheless his admiration and faith are undiminished; had Sir Toby not been in drink, he tells the company, things would have fallen out very differently; and at the last, he cries: "I'll help you, Sir Toby, because we'll be dressed together." But his idol turns and rends him, calling him an ass-head and a coxcomb and a knave, a thin-faced knave, a gull. These are hard sayings but not too hard for Sir Andrew to swallow, and perhaps they made their peace together afterwards. If not, we can only hope that our simpleton went on his travels and somehow in the end contrived to find his way into Gloucester and into the orchard of Justice Shallow, for there he would find company after his own heart, the great Shallow himself and Silence and Slender, and take his place among such boon companions, seat himself at the pippins and cheese and try to disengage from his tangled mind such confused memories as remained there of Illyria and the roystering Illyrians, his foolish face aglow beneath the unfading apple blossom.

—◇◇◇— —◇◇◇— —◇◇◇—

1932—G. Wilson Knight. From "The Romantic Comedies," from *The Shakespearian Tempest*

G. Wilson Knight (1875–1965) was a professor of English at Leeds University and also taught at the University of Toronto. At both universities he produced and acted in Shakespeare plays. In addition, Knight wrote plays for the British stage and television. His critical books include *The Wheel of Fire, Shakespearean Production,* and *Lord Byron: Christian Virtues.*

Twelfth Night is an exquisite blending of *The Comedy of Errors* and *The Merchant of Venice:* the plot of the one charged with the imaginative richness and deep emotions of the other. Again the tempest-music opposition is exquisitely developed. Wrecked and divided, the twins, Viola and Sebastian, find themselves in Illyria, land of music and romance. Music is here stronger than in any other of these romantic comedies, and the pattern of romantic love more exquisitely therewith entwined. The tempest which prologues the action is described for us:

> *Viola.* And what should I do in Illyria?
> My brother he is in Elysium.
> Perchance he is not drown'd: what think you, sailors?
> *Captain.* It is perchance that you yourself were saved.
> *Viola.* O my poor brother! and so perchance may he be.
> *Captain.* True, madam: and, to comfort you with chance,
> Assure yourself, after our ship did split,
> When you and those poor number saved with you
> Hung on our driving boat, I saw your brother,
> Most provident in peril, bind himself,
> Courage and hope both teaching him the practice,
> To a strong mast that lived upon the sea;
> Where, like Arion on the dolphin's back,
> I saw him hold acquaintance with the waves
> So long as I could see.   (I. ii. 3)

The association of the sea and 'chance' is important. The thought is often embedded in this tempest-imagery: waves are fickle as fortune, the sea suggests all the chances of mortality. This description of Sebastian in the waters is close to a similar passage on Ferdinand in *The Tempest*. Now Sebastian, too, recalls the wreck. He is with Antonio, bereft of his loved sister, derelict and purposeless: 'my determinate voyage is mere extravagancy' (II. i. II): here all human adventure is a 'voyage' and nearly every one employs the metaphor. Sebastian tells Antonio of his father, and twin sister; then,

> . . . some hour before you took me from the breach of the sea was my
> sister drowned.   (II. i. 23)

There follows a characteristic image:

> . . . She is drowned already, sir, with salt water, though I seem to drown
> her remembrance again with more.   (II. i. 32)

It is the same as Laertes' thought about the drowned Ophelia:

> Too much of water hast thou, poor Ophelia,
> And therefore I forbid my tears.
>   (Hamlet, IV. vii. 186)

Antonio later recalls how he rescued Sebastian

> From the rude sea's enraged and foamy mouth.   (V. i. 81)

'Enraged' again. 'A wreck past hope he was', says Antonio. So a tempest here disperses and divides, setting the stage for reunion and joy.

Twelfth Night takes us to a world of music:

> If music be the food of love, play on;
> Give me excess of it, that, surfeiting,
> The appetite may sicken and so die.
> That strain again! it had a dying fall:
> O, it came o'er my ear like the sweet sound,
> That breathes upon a bank of violets,
> Stealing and giving odour.   (I. i. I)

'Violets'. The name Viola suggests both flowers and music, music of the 'viol', mentioned in *Pericles*. Music and soft zephyrs: we shall find them again in the person of Imogen. Viola can speak 'in many sorts of music' (I. ii. 58). This is a natural phrase. Personal qualities tend to reflect poetic associations. Thus love-heroines are continually gifted with love-associations: Portia has riches, Viola, Desdemona, Marina and many others are musical, Perdita and Ophelia carry flowers, Imogen is 'a piece of tender air'. But in this play music is more important than any other love-suggestion:

> *Duke.* Give me some music. Now, good morrow, friends.
> Now, good Cesario, but that piece of song,
> That old and antique song we heard last night:
> Methought it did relieve my passion much,
> More than light airs and recollected terms
> Of these most brisk and giddy-paced times:
> Come, but one verse.   (II. iv. I)

Orsino reminds us of Cleopatra: 'music, moody food of us that trade in love' (where, by the way, we may observe the typical merchandise metaphor 'trade'). Music plays.

> *Orsino.*   . . . How dost thou like this tune?
> *Viola.* It gives a very echo to the seat
> Where Love is throned.   (II. iv. 20)

Here is another fine love-music comparison:

> *Olivia.* But, would you undertake another suit,
> I had rather hear you to solicit that
> Than music from the spheres.   (III. i. 119)

Feste sings a song which 'dallies with the innocence of love' (II. iv. 48). Feste embodies the play's essence. Humour and music are blent in his person. And in his earlier song, too, singing and love are close-twined:

> O mistress mine, where are you roaming?
> O stay and hear; your true love's coming,
>   That can sing both high and low.   (II. iii. 40)

And there are some fine phrases spoken in Viola's embassy of love to Olivia. First she tells how her master loves

> With adorations, fertile tears,
> With groans that thunder love, with sighs of fire.
>   (I. v. 274)

A curious passage where love, to suit Viola's purpose, itself becomes imaginatively a thing of terrible, god-like power to which mortality must submit. Next, she tells how she, in her master's place, would sing her love:

> *Olivia.*   Why, what would you?
> *Viola.* Make me a willow cabin at your gate,
> And call upon my soul within the house;
> Write loyal cantons of contemned love
> And sing them loud, even in the dead of night;
> Holla your name to the reverberate hills,
> And make the babbling gossip of the air
> Cry out 'Olivia!' O you should not rest
> Between the elements of air and earth
> But you should pity me!   (I. v. 286)

Throughout, however, sea-thought and voyages are inwoven in our world of music. Sebastian's sudden love-joy at the end is a 'flood of fortune' (IV. iii. II). Orsino's love, 'receiveth as the sea' and is 'all as hungry as the sea', infinite as the ocean itself (I. i. II; II. iv. 103). And, like the ocean, he is changeable, uncertain. Says Feste:

... I would have men of such constancy put to sea, that their business
might be every thing and their intent every where; for that's it that
always makes a good voyage of nothing.   (II. iv. 77)

'I am for all waters', he says later (IV. ii. 68). Sir Toby is 'drowned' in drink (I.
v. 140), just as the mind is often imaged as 'drowned' by any mastering emotion.
Malvolio says of Cesario: ''tis with him in standing water, between boy and man'
(I. v. 168), a queer image such as we find in *Antony and Cleopatra*. Viola is love's
ambassador and therefore, as happens elsewhere in *The Merry Wives of Windsor*,
and *Troilus*, imaged as a ship:

> *Maria.* Will you hoist sail, sir? here lies your way.
> *Viola.* No, good swabber; I am to hull here a little longer.
>   (I. v. 215)

Again:

> *Sir Toby.* Will you encounter the house? my niece is desirous you should
> enter, if your trade be to her.
> *Viola.* I am bound to your niece, sir; I mean, she is the list of my voyage.
>   (III. i. 82)

'Board' is used in relation to love in Sir Toby's 'Board her, woo her, assail her'
(I. iii. 60). There is rich jewel imagery, too. Rings and pearls are associated with
love, and Orsino makes a fine 'jewel' comparison:

> But 'tis that miracle and queen of gems
> That nature pranks her in, attracts my soul.   (II. iv. 88)

Maria, whom Sir Toby eventually marries, is his 'metal of India' (II. v. 17). Such
Eastern imagery variously accompanies Shakespearian love. So Orsino compares
himself to an angry lover of legend: 'the Egyptian thief' (V. i. 121), and a lover's
smile is compared to a map of the 'Indies' (III. ii. 86). But tragic sea-adventures
are in our background. Antonio is throughout a tragic figure, associated with
sea-fights and stern events:

> Once, in a sea-fight, 'gainst the count his galleys
> I did some service.   (III. iii. 26)

Orsino describes the action:

> That face of his I do remember well;
> Yet, when I saw it last, it was besmear'd

As black as Vulcan in the smoke of war:
A bawbling vessel was he captain of,
For shallow draught and bulk unprizable,
With which such scathful grapple did he make
With the most noble bottom of our fleet,
That very envy and the tongue of loss
Cried fame and honour on him.   (V. i. 54)

He is a 'notable pirate' and 'salt-water thief' (V. i. 72), according to Orsino. His passionate love of Sebastian causes him to make a metaphorical 'voyage' in following him. (III. iii. 7). His love is tragically passionate, a more dangerous reality than our other love-themes: he is a forecast of Othello. But tragedy is not given much freedom here. Terror is often humorous, as in the duel scene. There a 'bear' is mentioned as an image of terror (III. iv. 323). Malvolio was originally annoyed about a bear, too (II. v. 10). All, however, if we except Malvolio, is blended in a final joy. At the moment of reunion the amazed Sebastian cries:

I had a sister,
Whom the blind waves and surges have devour'd . . . .
                                                (V. i. 235)

Sebastian, too, has risen from 'his watery tomb' (V. i. 241). Both find that 'tempests are kind and salt waves fresh in love' (III. iv. 419).

Here, then, we find a pattern of music, love, and precious stones, threaded by the sombre strands of a sea tempest and a sea-fight. Finally there is love, reunion, and joy. Even Orsino has a share 'in this most happy wreck' (V. i. 273). 'Journeys end in lovers meeting', sings Feste (II. iii. 44): they are sea-journeys, the storm-tossed life of man voyaging to love's Illyrian coasts. Like Christopher Sly's strange experience, this golden romance is all like a sweet dream come true, or a bad dream gone:

What relish is in this? How runs the stream?
Or I am mad, or else this is a dream:
Let fancy still my sense in Lethe steep;
If it be thus to dream, still let me sleep!   (IV. i. 64)

Continually the Shakespearian imagination plays on this thought of dream; and his romances are dreamland actualized. But never was the whole world of sweet dream so perfectly and harmoniously bodied into a purely human plot as here. And even Malvolio only falls by aspiring to the fine and rich delight of an impossible love. All tragic and tempestuous things are finally blended in the music of Feste's final song, with its refrain,

With hey, ho, the wind and the rain . . . .

and

The rain it raineth every day.

Which song presents a microcosm of the play: tempests dissolved in music. Perhaps this is the most harmonious of Shakespeare's human romances.

━⁓⁓━ ━⁓⁓━ ━⁓⁓━

1951—Harold C. Goddard. *"Twelfth Night,"* from *The Meaning of Shakespeare*

Harold C. Goddard (1878-1950) was head of the English department at Swarthmore College. One of the most important twentieth-century books on Shakespeare is his *The Meaning of Shakespeare*, published after his death.

I

Twelfth Night, as its stage history proves, is one of the most effective theater pieces Shakespeare ever wrote. It is an almost unbroken succession of telling scenes. As has often been pointed out, the play is a sort of recapitulation. It is as if Shakespeare, for his last unadulterated comedy, summoned the ghosts of a dozen characters and situations with which he had triumphed in the past and bade them weave themselves into a fresh pattern. *The Comedy of Errors*, *The Two Gentlemen of Verona*, *The Merchant of Venice*, *Henry IV*, and even such recent successes as *Much Ado about Nothing* and *As You Like It* were laid under contribution. He pilfered from himself in this play as shamelessly as he ever had from others but, as usual, turned all his thefts to original account. And he named what came out of it all *Twelfth Night; or, What You Will*—as if he had selected the first title that came into his head and were quite willing that any auditor should rechristen the play to his own liking. All this seems to stamp *Twelfth Night* as a potboiler. But we had better beware, for whenever Shakespeare tried a potboiler some of his genius had a habit of boiling over into the pot.

In general, we go to the theater to be entertained. As we enter we are either in a gay mood already or in search of gaiety—of something at any rate that will carry us out of ourselves. And everything before the play begins collaborates. The bright costumes, the chatter, the laughter—in the modern theater the lights and the music—to say nothing of the mere fact of becoming part of a crowd, all tend to one end. They prepare us for emotion, make us ready to laugh and weep, to be amused or absorbed. Of anything that will achieve these results we are not too critical. So with *Twelfth Night*. In spite of Fabian's remark at one point, "If this were played upon a stage now, I could condemn it as an improbable fiction," we do not submit it in the theater to the tests or judge it by the standards we would use in real life, nor even to those we may apply to it afterward when we recollect it in solitude and tranquility. With the crowd around us to suggest what our own reaction should be, Sir Toby's drunkenness, even to his belchings, is without reservation funny; Maria's practical joking, even to Malvolio's confinement as a madman, without qualification clever and side-splitting; the steward's combined vanity and virtue fair game to any limit, and his discomfiture, even in the dark house, nothing but deserved. And when at the end we reach for coat and hat we are too theatrically intoxicated to pay much attention to the Clown's closing song, which, if we listened to it, might have a sobering effect.

It is only afterward, if at all, that we realize we might have probed a little deeper, might even have seen a little deeper in the theater with the aid of actors of genius, especially such a one in the part of Malvolio, as Charles Lamb's superlative criticism of this play in "On Some of the Old Actors" makes clear. *Twelfth Night!* So far from being a casual title, it is one of the most revealing ones Shakespeare ever used, however aware or unaware he may have been of all it implied. For Twelfth Night, January 6—though it is something else too—marks the end of the Christmas festivities. In half-a-dozen senses Shakespeare's *Twelfth Night* brings festivity to an end. To begin with, it is the third and last of the poet's own farewells to "wit" (*Much Ado* and *As You Like It* of course being the other two). In a wider sense it is his farewell to comedy. It is his transition from prince to king, his rejection of "Falstaff," not for the purpose of ascending the throne and conquering France, but of becoming "king" in the sense of mastering the domain of tragedy and tragicomedy. It marks an end too in more than a personal and professional way. It marks the end of Merry England, of the great day of the great Tudor houses where hospitality and entertainment were so long dispensed, one of the ends even (if I may use that expression) of feudalism itself whose long-drawn-out death never permits the historian to put a finger on any particular hour or event and say, Here it finally died. With its own reference to the pendulum swing of things, the whirligig of time that brings in his revenges, it seems like an intimation of the Puritan revolution with its rebuke to revelry—down even to the closing of the theaters. Merry England after the Armada certainly has its points of difference from the America of the twenties after World War I. (In the amount of genius produced that difference is abysmal.) But it has its points of likeness too. There was a descent and, if in a different sense, a Great Depression in store in both cases.

Did Shakespeare know what he was doing when he wrote and named this play? Did he appreciate its irony? Not entirely, of course. We have to wait for history to read its ironies into literature as it does into its own facts. But if Shakespeare's own development means anything, *Twelfth Night* is merely the culmination and consummation of something he had been saying almost from the beginning. If in *The Two Gentlemen of Verona* he gives us two revealing specimens of the species gentleman; if in *Romeo and Juliet* he shows us to what tragedy the code of the gentleman may lead; if in *The Merchant of Venice* he exposes the hollowness, and even cruelty, lurking under the silken surface of a leisured society; if in all these plays and in *Much Ado about Nothing* and *As You Like It* he tears the mask off wit and word-play, he does all these things at once in *Twelfth Night* (except that the tragedy that emerges fully in *Romeo and Juliet* is here only hinted at), but does them so genially that his very victims were probably loudest in their applause. We can imagine the Elizabethan gentlemen swarming to see *Twelfth Night* and paying for the privilege! It is almost as if the dead man were expected to pay an entrance fee to his own funeral and enjoy the proceedings. The poet just holds the mirror up to nature and gets a more devastating effect than the fiercest satire could achieve. It is the Chaucerian method. Indeed *Twelfth Night* makes one wonder whether justice has been done to the indebtedness of Shakespeare to the spirit of his great predecessor as distinguished from his indebtedness to him as source in the narrower sense (as in *Troilus and Cressida*). In *Twelfth Night* at any rate Shakespeare does something similar to what Chaucer does in *The Legend of Good Women*: so sweetens the medicine he is administering to his victims (in Chaucer's case the women) that they swallow it as if it were the most refreshing draught.

And yet there have been critics so incapable of shaking off their theater mood as to suggest that in this play Shakespeare is unreservedly on the side of revelry, of cakes and ale as against "virtue," of drunkenness and riot and quarreling as against sobriety and decency and some semblance of order. (Not that he is on the side of those things either!) In their dislike of Malvolio they forget that he is merely carrying out Olivia's orders, in however annoying a manner. She objects quite as much as he to having her house turned into a bedlam at any and all hours; she calls her drunken parasite of an uncle a wretch and a ruffian and declares that he is

> Fit for the mountains and the barbarous caves,
> Where manners ne'er were preach'd,

which, according to any considered judgment, he is. The unconscious logic of these critics seems to run something like this: (1) Shakespeare believed in laughter; (2) Sir Toby and his cronies make us laugh; therefore (3) Shakespeare approved of Sir Toby and his cronies. Imagine thinking that of the man who at this very time may have been creating the drunken court at Elsinore and its princely critic! Imagine thinking it of the author of the 146th sonnet:

> Why so large cost, having so short a lease,
> Dost thou upon thy fading mansion spend?

Shall worms, inheritors of this excess,
Eat up thy charge? Is this thy body's end?
Then, soul, live thou . . . .

II

If ever there were mansions fading from excess, they were those of Olivia
and the Duke in this play, and that that is what Shakespeare set out to show is
strongly indicated by the opening and the close of the piece (of its end we will
speak at the end). Taken together they practically prove as much. The familiar
speech of the Duke with which *Twelfth Night* opens is like a musical overture in
which Shakespeare, as so often, announces his main theme:

If music be the food of love, play on;
Give me excess of it, that, surfeiting,
The appetite may sicken, and so die.
That strain again! It had a dying fall.
. . . Enough, no more!
'Tis not so sweet now as it was before.

Excess! Surfeit! Sicken! Dying fall! Enough, no more! 'Tis not so sweet now as it
was before! Even at a second reading this play is not so sweet as it was before—
but it is more tartly significant. Pretty nearly everybody in it but Viola and
Sebastian—and those two outskirt characters the sea captains—is at the extreme
point where from excess of something or other he is about to be converted into
something else. Sir Toby, who is the feudal retainer at his vanishing point, is
in the "third degree of drink," drowned in it, namely. (Those who liken him to
Falstaff are in some still higher degree of obfuscation.) Feste the jester is in the
third degree of "wit." (There is another wiser Feste, emerging from the "dry" one
like a butterfly from a chrysalis, of whom we will speak later.) Sir Andrew is in
the third, nay, the *n*th, degree of fatuity—the complete gentleman so attenuated
that he is indistinguishable from the complete fool. He is class transmigrated
into ass, with not "so much blood in his liver as will clog the foot of a flea." He
is a great consumer of beef and thinks that life consists of eating and drinking—
and pretending to fight. He is Sir Toby's gull, as Roderigo is Iago's.

Maria's third degree is of another sort. She is a lively, alert, resourceful,
mocking person. Her vitality and intelligence (to call it that) have, in her servile
position, made her ambitious and envious, especially so of the steward whose
merits her mistress prizes so highly. It is important to realize that it is not just
because he is Malvolio that she hates him. She would have resented anyone in
his place. "I can hardly forbear hurling things at him." The remark is a giveaway.
There is a vague premonition of the Iago-Cassio theme here on the comic level
as her simile, "I have dogged him like his murderer," is enough to show. Her
"humor" is of that low order that must always have a physical outlet. She has

her jests, she says, at her fingers' ends (not at her tongue's). She will make her fellow-conspirators laugh themselves into stitches. Her sport must always bear immediate fruit that others can see and feel. In this case to show off her talents before Sir Toby is as strong a motive as to humiliate Malvolio. She tickles and catches her trout. And Toby rewards her by asking, "Wilt thou set thy foot o' my neck?" (which she doubtless did with a vengeance after they were married) and calling her "thou most excellent devil of wit!" What wonder that in her the spirit of fun passes from the cathartic prank of the cross garters and yellow stockings to the cruel and perilous practical joke of the dark room. Fabian and finally Sir Toby himself see that they have gone too far. But Maria plainly means it when she says that if Malvolio really does go mad, it will be well worth it: the house will be the quieter! There is a cruel streak in her as there generally is in practical jokers. She is in that third degree of fun where what might originally have been a sense of humor becomes perverted and commits suicide. But her excesses will trouble few people in the theater. They have made them laugh too heartily.

Malvolio and his function in the play seem plain enough during its performance or at a first reading. He is simply the antitype of the revelers, their excess drawn out equally in the opposite direction. If they are levity, he is gravity—dignity, decency, decorum, servility and severity in the cause of "good order," carried to the third degree and beyond—and as such fair game for his tormentors. No more than this is necessary to make Malvolio a success on the stage. But that more is possible even there, and much more in the imagination of a reader who reads deeper, is shown in Charles Lamb's famous reminiscences of Bensley and his own comments on the part. Lamb's main point, it will be remembered, is that Malvolio is not essentially ludicrous, that his pride is neither mock nor affected—and so not a fit object, as such, to excite laughter. He thinks the man had it in him to be brave, honorable, accomplished. Maria calls him a kind of puritan, but quickly takes it back and calls him a time-pleaser instead. She could not have been more mistaken. Malvolio is a man of principle rather, and being, like all "men of principle," lacking in imagination in its creative sense, is all the more prone to become a victim of it in its primitive form. In Malvolio's love of Olivia, Shakespeare has stolen from his own account of Bottom's love of Titania. Like that, this love is calculated in the theater to excite nothing but laughter. Bottom's love, however, eventuating as it did in Bottom's dream, was, we saw, "at bottom" beautiful, a sort of allegory of the birth of imagination in matter. But if inexpressible things can be born in the head of a weaver, why not in the head of a steward? If that seem fanciful, again we have Charles Lamb for authority, Lamb and the man who inspired him here, the actor Bensley, who showed that a different and subtler reading of Malvolio is possible even on the stage: "You would have thought that the hero of La Mancha in person stood before you. . . . You rather admired than pitied the lunacy while it lasted; you felt that an hour of such mistake was worth an age with the eyes open. . . . The man seemed to tread upon air, to taste manna, to walk with his head in the clouds, to mate Hyperion." If anything can prove that a part can be one thing to the average man and something quite different to the actor or reader of genius, Lamb's interpretation of Malvolio does. It is an infallible rule after reading a play of Shakespeare's: read it once more and read deeper.

That Malvolio keeps his head during his confinement in darkness and does not lose his dignity when he charges his mistress with having done him notorious wrong is further proof of a kind of moral solidity in the man. "I confess I never saw the catastrophe of this character, while Bensley played it," Lamb concludes, "without a kind of tragic interest." Surely Lamb is right: the shadow of Shakespeare's coming tragic period casts its shadow back over Malvolio as it does over Shylock.

The Dark House in which Malvolio is incarcerated is in some respects the central symbol of the play, for the houses of Olivia and the Duke, for all their apparent brightness, are dark houses in a deeper sense.

I am as mad as he,

says Olivia (meaning as mad as Malvolio),

If sad and merry madness equal be.

It is one of the key lines of the play and opens our eyes to the fact that with an exception or two it is little more than an anthology of madnesses, sad and merry ("Are all the people mad?" asks Sebastian); for what after all is madness but a slightly stronger term for that excess of which we have been speaking?

III

Orsino and Olivia are both victims of their emotions. The Duke is the *ne plus ultra* of the melancholy characters we have met in Shakespeare. His love is the sentimentalism that idleness is sure to breed in potentially fine natures if it does not turn to something worse. He is in the third degree of "love," as much drowned in it as Toby is in drink, a fact that makes his fondness for the sea as metaphor significant. But he does not keep it consistent. (He keeps nothing consistent; his mind, as the Clown perceives, is "a very opal.") He says in one place that his love is "as hungry as the sea, and can digest as much." But unfortunately he has admitted in his opening speech that whatever enters this sea-like love begins within a minute to lose its value. Olivia, with her inordinate grief for her brother, looks at first like Orsino's twin. But when we get a glimpse behind her veil we see that her emotionalism is of another brand. Her carefully announced, absurdly long period of mourning, with its withdrawal from society, is evidently a pretext, however unconscious, for singling herself out, making herself interesting, as black does its wearer in a crowd of bright costumes. There is much of the grand lady about Olivia. She is the efficient head of a great house, managing its affairs and commanding her followers with smoothness and discretion. But like Portia, whom she resembles at more than one point, she cannot take her own advice: "O, you are sick of self-love, Malvolio, and taste with a distempered appetite. To be generous, guiltless, and of free disposition, is to take those things for birdbolts that you deem cannon bullets." If in proper degree she could have applied this principle to her grief for her brother, she might have assuaged its supposed violence and abbreviated its seven-year term by at least a little. But it is precisely her strict adherence to outer form that accounts for her highly unconventional falling in love with the Duke's "man," Cesario. We like her for that capacity, but we cannot help noticing that she inquires about his parentage and makes certain he is a gentleman before letting her emotions have their way. Also, we wish she had not taken occasion to compliment her own countenance so early in their acquaintance. If she could not hide her feelings from him, she might at least not have blurted them out so precipitately. (And she might have concealed them from her household.) There is a finer Olivia within her that senses all this and rebukes her for her headstrong love-making:

There's something in me that reproves my fault.

But that doesn't prevent her from fairly dragging the supposed Cesario to the altar, when, in the person of the wonder-struck Sebastian, the resistance of the man at whom she has fairly flung herself apparently breaks down. On the whole, criticism has been overkind to Olivia as it has to Portia.

IV

And so the "upstairs" and the "downstairs" parts of Shakespeare's plot are not so much interwoven as identified. Excessive revelry and excessive sentimental love, the poet seems to be saying, are just opposite forms of the same infection. Barbarism and "civilization" are extremes that meet.

But in the midst of all the madness of these two dark houses two figures, Viola and Feste, stand out for their essential sanity—not Feste the jester but that wiser being into whom we can see him being transformed under our eyes.

In Feste the Shakespearean clown (with intimations of it in Launce) comes, as it were, to self-consciousness. Touchstone seems perpetually delighted with himself and his vocation. But the first thing we hear about Feste is that he has been playing truant. Why he has absented himself from his duties as jester in Olivia's household we are never told. But the rest of the play makes it a fair inference that, whatever the immediate occasion, he was sick of his fool's costume, as his protestation that he does not wear motley in his brain is almost enough in itself to show. (No wonder: Olivia's is the second generation during which he has been jesting!) The main function of a clown is to juggle with words until everything, often including the truth, is upside down and inside out. All Shakespeare's clowns do it, but Feste not only does it but perceives and proclaims that he does it. "A sentence is but a cheveril glove to a good wit. How quickly the wrong side may be turned outward! . . . Words are grown so false I am loath to prove reason with them." He is not Olivia's fool, he says, but her corrupter of words. Even Viola at first mistakes him for the conventional merry fellow who cares for nothing. "I do care for something," Feste protests, and the fact that he is frequently apologetic, even a bit sad, about his joking goes far to prove it. His disillusionment about himself and his profession betokens a sense of humor that is lacking almost by definition in the mere wit. His is a gentle and attractive melancholy that avoids sentimentalism. He loves to sing, and his songs are all plaintive and in a minor key. Wise observations about life spring up like flowers amid the weeds of his professional jesting, as, for instance, his contention that his foes are his best friends because they tell him the truth about himself. They tell him plainly that he is an ass. He seems truly concerned, too, with the moral welfare of those around him. He sees through the artifice of Olivia's grief for her brother and would gladly cure her of it. He tells the Duke to his face what a hopelessly self-contradictory mind he has, and understands the nature of his "passion" for Olivia. He enters with no particular zest into the plot against Malvolio and, when he assumes his disguise as Sir Topas, remarks that "to be said an honest man and a good housekeeper goes as fairly as to say a careful man and a great scholar," an opinion which it is safe to guess his creator shared and which betokens a simplicity of mind at the opposite pole from the snobbery of Touchstone. Rosalind even called the latter a dull fool, while Viola comes to find a philosopher in Feste. And he can be friend as well as philosopher. Near the end he promises to fetch Malvolio not only ink and paper but light also and to transmit his appeal to Olivia. All of which he obviously does. With folly bringing light to darkness and "madness" we can almost feel the fool in *King Lear* being conceived.

But it is Viola far more than Feste who offers the telling contrast with the revelers and sentimentalists. She appears out of her element among them, and Shakespeare seems to be saying as much in the second line she speaks in the play:

Vio.: What country, friends, is this?
Capt.: This is Illyria, lady.
Vio.: And what should I do in Illyria?

And, sure enough, what should she?

My brother he is in Elysium,

Viola goes on,

Perchance he is not drown'd.

Illyria—Elysium. What light that echo throws! (Yes, in poetry echoes can throw
light.) Having read the play, we are in a position to see, on rereading, that Illyria
is a counterfeit Elysium, a fool's paradise, where nearly everybody *is* drowned,
drowned in pleasure. Illyria is a sort of counter-symbol of the Forest of Arden.
There there was freedom and happiness (at least a good bit of it). Here there is
pleasure and slavery to self. And this bondage is the more sad and tragic just
because the inhabitants are socially and economically free. It is the seventeenth-
century version of *Heartbreak House* with the difference that whereas Bernard
Shaw depicts his heartbreaking society with blasts of satire and on top of that
writes a blistering preface that nobody may miss his point, Shakespeare just
holds up what is essentially the same world and allows it to amuse or break our
hearts as we choose. *What You Will.*

But that does not mean that Shakespeare does not slip in at odd moments,
when we are not looking, perfectly plain statements of his main conception.

. . . nature with a beauteous wall
    Doth oft close in pollution,

says Viola on the threshold of entering a world of just that character. "Virtue
is beauty," says Antonio, as if echoing her (Antonio, that grand old sea captain
from whom Shaw might have taken a hint for his Captain Shotover):

Virtue is beauty; but the beauteous evil
Are empty trunks, o'erflourish'd by the devil.

Ironically it is Viola herself, mistaken for Sebastian, whom Antonio is charging
with ingratitude in the matter of the money he has lent her brother.

I hate ingratitude more in a man,

she retorts,

Than lying, vainness, babbling, drunkenness,
Or any taint of vice whose strong corruption
Inhabits our frail blood.

Viola is speaking to the particular situation. But when we attend to the list of sins
she has picked out, we feel that through her her creator (who agreed with her as

to which the worst of them was) was indicting one by one and all together the inhabitants of this parasitical world of which they are typical. Lying, vainness, babbling, drunkenness are pretty sure to be characteristics of any leisured society, as they were of this one. But ingratitude is certain to be, if for no other reason than that such a society rests on the unrecognized labor of others. If anyone thinks such an idea out of Shakespeare's ken, he should remember *King Lear*.

In one sense Viola herself descends to the deceptions of this world when she enters it in disguise.

Disguise, I see, thou art a wickedness,

she cries later, when she realizes in what entanglements it has involved herself and others. (And for my part, as I have said elsewhere, I hear Shakespeare the playwright, who had condescended to the conventions of Elizabethan comedy, echoing his heroine and resolving perhaps to renounce the cheap and easy ways of holding an audience that the cruder forms of disguise and mistaken identity afford.) Yet, after all, as mythology shows, how can a being of a higher order enter a lower world except in disguise?

And Viola is such a being. She is a Lady from the Sea. Sincere, modest, sweet, gentle, generous, tender, true, she is absolutely loyal and devoted to Orsino. And she is quick-witted, practical, and resourceful as well, utterly free of the sins and sentimentalisms of the world she has been washed up on from shipwreck. What an opportunity she had, if she had been willing to adopt its code, of complicating for emotional purposes the misunderstanding Olivia is under with regard to her sex! She never toys with that possibility for a moment. Though she wears masculine attire, Viola is no boy-girl as Rosalind was. She is purely feminine. Psychically it is as if Viola-Sebastian were Rosalind split in two. It takes two of them to be what she was alone, and the play here becomes one more variation on the theme of hermaphroditic man.

Prove true, imagination, O, prove true,

Viola cries when she first realizes that she may be about to be reunited with her "drowned" brother. It is one of the supremely integrating lines in all Shakespeare, and it shows in a flash that the play deals not only with madness in its lower sense but with that divine madness of the imagination that comes into being when things long or far separated are united, or when dreams too wonderful to be true nevertheless submit themselves successfully to the tests of sight and touch:

Seb.: This is the air; that is the glorious sun;
This pearl she gave me, I do feel't and see't;

And though 'tis wonder that enwraps me thus,
Yet 'tis not madness.

Probably the most disappointing thing about *Twelfth Night* to most readers
is the fact that such a rare girl as Viola should have fallen in love with such a
spineless creature as the Duke. And Sebastian seems too good for Olivia. There
is the whole point! The play leaves us with the question whether these two beings
from outside Illyria, these two who were thought drowned, this spirit, Sebastian-
Viola, from beyond ("A spirit I am indeed," says Sebastian, and we know that
Viola is) will be sucked down into the pleasure-seeking parasitical world of
Orsino-Olivia or will redeem that world by lifting it at least a little toward a
more spiritual level. These marriages are parabolic as well as realistic unions. Are
all aristocracies destined by their very nature to decay, life doomed to die off at
the top? It is the question of the ages.

V

The theme of the main plot as well as that of the enveloping action, we
suddenly see, is rescue from drowning: drowning in the sea, drowning in the sea
of drunkenness and sentimentalism. (There is a reason why with the exception
of *The Tempest* the word "drowned" occurs oftener in this play than in any other
of Shakespeare's.) Is it possible that Orsino's renunciation, repudiation rather,
of the "marble-breasted tyrant" Olivia is not just his opaline fickleness but the
indication of a genuine change under Viola's influence? His

Come, boy, with me. My thoughts are ripe in mischief,

might make us think so. They sound a new note in his role. However that
may be, Olivia's ringing rebuke of Cesario when she thinks he is denying their
marriage (which was really hers with Sebastian) gives us ground for hope in
her case. We never heard anything so fine from her lips before, though she
is doubtless unaware at the moment of the universality of the truth she is
uttering:

Alas, it is the baseness of thy fear
That makes thee strangle thy propriety.
Fear not, Cesario; take thy fortunes up;
Be that thou know'st thou art, and then thou art
As great as that thou fear'st.

All we can say with certainty is that Viola will make a man of Orsino if any
woman can and that Sebastian seems fitted to make a woman, as distinct from

a lady, of Olivia. Her defense of Malvolio at the end and the Duke's line when the steward goes out swearing revenge,

Pursue him and entreat him to a peace,

array the two squarely against those whom Charles Lamb calls the "sottish revellers."

Feste's song at the end, as we hinted, puts the keystone in place and sums it all up. The thing that this society of pleasure-seekers has forgotten is the wind and the rain. It's all right to play with toys while we are children, and later we may thrive for a little time by swaggering or crime. But knaves and thieves are soon barred out. There is such a thing as coming to man's estate, such a hard reality, for instance, as marriage, which all the cakes and ale will not turn into what it is not. The world, with its weather, is an ancient fact. There is even a kind of rain that raineth not just occasionally but every day. "Our play is done."

When that I was and a little tiny boy,
    With hey, ho, the wind and the rain,
A foolish thing was but a toy,
    For the rain it raineth every day.

But when I came to man's estate,
    With hey, ho, the wind and the rain,
'Gainst knaves and thieves men shut their gate,
    For the rain it raineth every day.

But when I came, alas! to wive,
    With hey, ho, the wind and the rain,
By swaggering could I never thrive,
    For the rain it raineth every day.

But when I came unto my beds,
    With hey, ho, the wind and the rain,
With toss-pots still had drunken heads,
    For the rain it raineth every day.

A great while ago the world begun,
    With hey, ho, the wind and the rain,
But that's all one, our play is done,
    And we'll strive to please you every day.

Was there ever a song at the end that made plainer the meaning of what has gone before? It seems almost inconceivable that the poet did not expressly intend it as his own comment on the play it brings to an end, a piece that for all its gaiety is somehow touched with an ominous shadow. But even if the author did not mean it so, time did. So it makes little difference.

When Shakespeare wrote *Twelfth Night* he could only surmise what the future had in store for him. But we know. To us this play, with the song that brings it to a conclusion, looks both ways. It is a bridge between the poet's Comedies and his Tragedies as *Julius Caesar* more obviously is between his Histories and his Tragedies. Compared with most other men, Shakespeare was a man from the beginning. Compared with himself, he is now for the first time about to confront the full force of the wind and the rain, to come to man's estate. *King Lear* is not far under the horizon. His "play" is done.

Twelfth Night. The work, like the festival, is a recapitulation and looks back over what it brings to an end. But Twelfth Night is also Epiphany, a commemoration of the coming of the Magi to Bethlehem, the first manifestation of Christ to the Gentiles! Did Shakespeare somehow sense that he was on the verge of a visitation of new wisdom from the East? It is not necessary to think so. But he was.

1958—Leo Salingar. "The Design of *Twelfth Night*," from *Shakespeare Quarterly*

Leo Salingar has been a fellow at Trinity College, Cambridge. He wrote *Shakespeare and the Traditions of Comedy* and *Dramatic Form in Shakespeare and the Jacobeans.*

Most readers of *Twelfth Night* would probably agree that this is the most delightful, harmonious and accomplished of Shakespeare's romantic comedies, in many ways his crowning achievement in one branch of his art. They would probably agree, too, that it has a prevailing atmosphere of happiness, or at least of "tempests dissolved in music". Yet there are striking differences of opinion over the design of *Twelfth Night*. Is it, for example, a vindication of romance, or a depreciation of romance[1]? Is it mainly a love-story or a comedy of humours; a "poem of escape" or a realistic comment on economic security and prudential marriage[2]? And there are further variations. The principal character, according to choice, is Viola, Olivia, Malvolio, or Feste.

To some extent, the play itself seems to invite such varying reactions: *Twelfth Night; or, What You Will*. Shakespeare here is both polishing his craftsmanship and exploring new facets of his experience[3], so that the play has the buoyancy of a mind exhilarated by discovery, testing one human impulse against another, and satisfied with a momentary state of balance which seems all the more trustworthy because its limits have been felt and recognized. But in consequence, Shakespeare's attitude towards his people comes near to humorous detachment, to a kind of Socratic irony. He refrains from emphasising any one of his themes at the expense of the rest. He carefully plays down and transforms the crisis of sentiment in his main plot, while giving unusual prominence to his comic sub-plot. He distributes the interest more evenly among his characters than in *As You Like It* or the other comedies, providing more numerous (and more unexpected) points of contact between them, not only in the action but on the plane of psychology. And the whole manner of *Twelfth Night* is light and mercurial. The prose is full of ideas, but playful, not discursive. The poetry, for all its lyrical glow, gives a sense of restraint and ease, of keenly perceptive and yet relaxed enjoyment, rather than of any compelling pressure of emotion.

Perhaps this attitude on Shakespeare's part is responsible for the inconsistency of his interpreters. Those who dwell on the romantic side of the play seem uncertain about its connection with the comic realism; while those who concentrate on the elements of realism have to meet the kind of objection gravely stated by Dr. Johnson—that "the marriage of Olivia, and the succeeding perplexity, though well enough contrived to divert on the stage, wants credibility, and fails to produce the proper instruction required in the drama, as it exhibits no just picture of life". The question to be interpreted, then, is how Shakespeare is using the instrument of theatrical contrivance, which is present, of course, in all his comedies, but which he uses here with exceptional delicacy and freedom.

Briefly, Shakespeare has taken a familiar kind of love-story and transformed it so as to extend the interest from the heroine to a group of characters who reveal varying responses to the power of love. He has modified the main situation further, and brought home his comments on it, by using methods of construction he had mastered previously in his *Comedy of Errors*. And he has added a sub-plot based on the customary jokes and revels of a feast of misrule, when normal restraints and relationships were overthrown. As the main title implies, the idea of a time of misrule gives the underlying constructive principle of the whole play.

In *Twelfth Night*, as Miss Welsford puts it, Shakespeare "transmutes into poetry the quintessence of the Saturnalia"[4]. The sub-plot shows a prolonged season of misrule, or "uncivil rule", in Olivia's household, with Sir Toby turning night into day; there are drinking, dancing, and singing, scenes of mock wooing, a mock sword fight, and the gulling of an unpopular member of the household, with Feste mumming it as a priest and attempting a mock exorcism in the manner of the Feast of Fools. Sir Andrew and Malvolio resemble Ben Jonson's social pretenders[5]; but Shakespeare goes beyond Jonson in ringing the changes on the theme of Folly and in making his speakers turn logic and courtesy on their heads. A girl and a coward are given out to be ferocious duellists; a steward imagines that he can marry his lady; and finally a fool pretends to assure a wise man that darkness is light. In Feste, Shakespeare creates his most finished portrait of a professional fool; he is superfluous to the plot, but affects the mood of the play more than any other of Shakespeare's clowns.

Moreover, this saturnalian spirit invades the whole play. In the main plot, sister is mistaken for brother, and brother for sister. Viola tells Olivia "That you do think you are not what you are"—and admits that the same holds true of herself. The women take the initiative in wooing, both in appearance and in fact; the heroine performs love-service for the lover. The Duke makes his servant "your master's mistress" and the lady who has withdrawn from the sight of men embraces a stranger. The four main actors all reverse their desires or break their vows before the comedy is over; while Antonio, the one single-minded representative of romantic devotion, is also the only character in the main plot who tries to establish a false identity and fails (III.iv.341–343); and he is left unrewarded and almost disregarded. Such reversals are, as Johnson says, devices peculiar to the stage, but Shakespeare makes them spring, or seem to spring, from the very nature of love. In the *Comedy of Errors* the confusions of identity are due to external circumstances; in *A Midsummer Night's Dream* Shakespeare begins to connect them with the capricious, illusory factor in subjective "fancy" that is common to the madman, the lover, and the creative poet. In *Twelfth Night*, he takes this similitude further. Love here will "be clamorous, and leap all civil bounds", like a lord of misrule; "love's night is noon", like Sir Toby's carousals. Love seems as powerful as the sea, tempestuous, indifferent, and changeable as the sea. And fortune, or fate, reveals the same paradoxical benevolence in this imbroglio of mistakes and disguises: "Tempests are kind, and salt waves fresh in love".

The analysis of love as a kind of folly was a common theme of Renaissance moralists, who delighted in contrasting it with the wisdom of the stoic or the man of affairs. Shakespeare's treatment of the theme in *Twelfth Night* is a natural development from his own previous work, but he could have found strong hints of it in the possible sources of his Viola–Orsino story. Bandello remarks, for instance, that it arouses wonder to hear of a gentleman disguising himself as a servant, and still more in the case of a girl: but when you realize that love is the cause, "the wonder ceases at once, because this passion of love is much too potent and causes actions much more amazing and excessive than that"; a person in love has "lost his liberty, and . . . no miracle if he commits a thousand errors"[6]. And Barnabe Riche tells his readers that in his story of *Apolonius and Silla*, "you shall see Dame Error so play her part with a leash of lovers, a male and two females, as shall work a wonder to your wise judgement"[7]. In effect, then, what Shakespeare could take for granted in his audience was not simply a readiness to be interested in romance, but a sense of the opposition between romance and reason.

On this basis, Shakespeare can unite his main action with his sub-plot, bending a romantic story in the direction of farce. By the same contrivances, he can disclose the follies surrounding love and celebrate its life-giving power. And he can do this, without sacrificing emotional reality—which is not exactly the same as Dr. Johnson's "just picture of life"—because he takes his stage machinery from the traditions of a feast of misrule, where social custom has already begun to transform normal behavior into the material of comic art[8]. The whole play is a festivity, where reality and play-acting meet. By presenting his main story on these lines, Shakespeare can develop his insight into the protean, contradictory nature of love with more economy and force than by keeping to the lines of an ordinary stage narrative. At the same time he can extend this theme through his realistic images of "uncivil rule" in the sub-plot, disclosing the conflicting impulses of an aristocratic community in a period of social change, and touching on the potentially tragic problems of the place of time and order in human affairs.

Shakespeare's intentions may stand out more clearly when one compares his treatment of the Viola story with its possible or probable sources[9]. The ultimate source is held to be the anonymous Sienese comedy, *Gl'Ingannati* (*The Deceived*), first performed at a carnival of 1531 and frequently reprinted, translated, or imitated in the course of the sixteenth century. Shakespeare may also have known Bandello's story, which follows the plot of *Gl'Ingannati* closely, omitting the subordinate comic parts; and he probably knew Riche's *Apolonius and Silla* (1581), derived indirectly and with variations from Bandello. Another source of the main plot must have been the *Menaechmi* of Plautus, which presumably had already contributed something to *Gl'Ingannati*, but affects the composition of *Twelfth Night* more directly by way of *The Comedy of Errors*. In any case, Shakespeare's situations were part of the common stock of classical and medieval romance, as Manningham saw at one of the first performances of *Twelfth Night*, when he noted in his diary that it was "much like the Commedy of Errores, or Menechmi in Plautus, but most like and neere to that in Italian called *Inganni*" (one of the offshoots of *Gl'Ingannati*).

There are four essential characters common to *Gl'Ingannati*, Bandello, Riche, and Shakespeare; namely, a lover, a heroine in his service disguised as a page, her twin brother (who at first has disappeared), and a second heroine. The basic elements common to all four plots are: the heroine's secret love for her master; her employment as go-between, leading to the complication of a cross-wooing; and a final solution by means of the unforeseen arrival of the missing twin.

If Shakespeare knew Bandello or *Gl'Ingannati*, he altered their material radically. The Italians both take the romance motif of a heroine's constancy and love-service, set it in a realistic bourgeois environment, and rationalize it with respectful irony. In Bandello, the irony is severely rational—because it is a tale of love, "the wonder ceases at once". In *Gl'Ingannati*, the tone is whimsical. "Two lessons above all you will extract from this play", says the Prologue: "how much chance and good fortune can do in matters of love; and how much long patience is worth in such cases, accompanied by good advice"[10]. Both Italian authors give the heroine a strong motive for assuming her disguise, in that the lover has previously returned her affection, but has now forgotten her and turned elsewhere. Both provide her with a formidable father in the background and a foster-mother like Juliet's Nurse, who admonishes and helps her; and both credit her with the intention of bilking her rival if she can. On the other side, they both respect the code of courtly love to the extent of stressing the lover's penitence at the end, and his recognition that he must repay the heroine for her devotion. "I believe", he says in the play, "that this is certainly the will of God, who must have taken pity on this virtuous maiden and on my soul, that it should not go to perdition. . . . "[11]

Riche keeps this framework of sentiment, vulgarizes the narrative, and changes some of the material circumstances, generally in the direction of an Arcadian romance.

Shakespeare, for his part, changes the story fundamentally, broadening the interest and at the same time making the whole situation more romantically improbable, more melancholy at some points, more fantastic at others. He stiffens the heroine's loyalty, but deprives her of her original motive, her initiative, and her family. In place of these, he gives her the background of a vague "Messaline" and a romantic shipwreck, for which he may have taken a hint, but no more, from the episode of the shipwreck in Riche. Shakespeare's Viola, then, is a more romantic heroine than the rest, and the only one to fall in love *after* assuming her disguise. At the same time, however, Shakespeare enlarges the role of her twin brother and gives unprecedented weight to coincidence in the dénouement, which in both Italian stories is brought about more rationally, by the deliberate action of the heroine and her nurse; so that Shakespeare's Viola is also unique in that her happiness is due to "good fortune" more than "long patience", and to "good advice" not at all.

In his exposition, therefore, Shakespeare sketches a situation from romance in place of a logical intrigue. But the purpose, or at any rate, the effect, of his plan is to shift attention at the outset from the circumstances of the love story to the sentiments as such, especially in their more mysterious and irrational aspects. Shakespeare may have taken hints, for Orsino and Olivia, from his predecessors' comments on the "error" of "following them that fly from us". But however that may be, his comedy now consists in the triumph of natural love over affectation and melancholy. And, taken together, the leading characters in *Twelfth Night* form the most subtle portrayal of the psychology of love that Shakespeare had yet drawn.

Viola's love is fresh and direct, and gathers strength as the play advances. When she first appears, Viola mourns her brother, like Olivia, and by choice would join Olivia in her seclusion:

> O, that I serv'd that lady,
> And might not be deliver'd to the world,
> Till I had made mine own occasion mellow,
> What my estate is.   (I.ii.40)

Shakespeare makes the most here of the vagueness surrounding Viola; she seems the child of the sea, and of time. But even when her feelings and her problem have become distinct she still commits herself to "time" with a gentle air of detachment:

> What will become of this? As I am a man,
> My state is desperate for my master's love;
> As I am a woman,—now alas the day!—
> What thriftless sighs shall poor Olivia breathe!
> O time, thou must untangle this, not I,
> It is too hard a knot for me t'untie.   (II.ii.37)

She has none of the vehement determination of the Italian heroines[12], and, though nimble-witted, she is less resourceful and high-spirited than Rosalind. She foreshadows Perdita and Miranda in the romantically adolescent quality of her part.

There are stronger colors than this in Viola, admittedly. Before she appears on the stage, Orsino has spoken of the capacity for love inherent in a woman's devoted sorrow for her brother; and in two scenes in the middle of the play Viola herself speaks in more passionate terms. But in both cases her own feeling seems muffled or distorted, since she is acting a part, and in both cases her tone is distinctly theatrical. She tells Olivia how, if she were Orsino, she would

> Write loyal cantons of contemned love,
> And sing them loud even in the dead of night;
> Holla your name to the reverberate hills,
> And make the babbling gossip of the air
> Cry out 'Olivia!;   (I.v.279)

she tells Orsino, on the other hand, that her imaginary sister

> never told her love,
> But let concealment, like a worm i'the bud
> Feed on her damask cheek;—   (II.iv.111)

—in each case, with an overtone of romantic excess. She does not speak out in her own voice, therefore, until the later scenes, when the more vigorous (and more artificial) emotions of the older pair have had full play. Meanwhile, the hints of excess in her two fictitious declarations of love reflect on the others as well as herself: she speaks for Orsino in the spirit of his injunction to "be clamorous, and leap all civil bounds"; while her image of repressed desire could apply to Olivia. Her own development in the comedy is closely attuned to the others'.

Shakespeare begins the play with Orsino. He follows Riche in making the lover in his comedy a duke (not, as with the Italians, a citizen), who has been a warrior but has now "become a scholar in love's school"[13]. Orsino suffers from the melancholy proper to courtly and "heroical" love; and Shakespeare fixes attention on his passion, which is more violent and "fantastical" than in the other versions of the story, by keeping Orsino inactive in his court to dramatize his own feelings like Richard II. Unlike the Italian lovers, he has not been fickle, yet changefulness is the very essence of his condition. He twice calls for music in the play, but there is no harmony in himself. Within a few lines, he countermands the first order, to apostrophize the spirit of love:

> Enough, no more!
> 'Tis not so sweet now as it was before.
> O spirit of love, how quick and fresh art thou,
> That, notwithstanding thy capacity
> Receiveth as the sea, nought enters there,
> Of what validity and pitch soe'er,
> But falls into abatement and low price,
> Even in a minute: so full of shapes is fancy
> That it alone is high fantastical.   (I.i.7)

This apostrophe carries opposing meanings. "Quick" and "fresh", coming after "sicken" a few lines before, imply the vigor of life, but they also prolong the grosser sense of "appetite" and "surfeiting". The sea image glorifies Orsino's "spirit of love" and, in relation to the drama as a whole, it prepares the way for the sea-change that comes to Viola and Sebastian; but it also leads on to the image of Sir Toby "drowned" in drink (I.v.135). And Orsino's most striking metaphors here, those of sinking and "low price", suggest that what the speaker largely feels is chill and dismay. Nothing has any value by comparison with love;

but also, nothing has any lasting, intrinsic value for a lover. Later, referring to the sea-fight, Orsino utters a similar paradox when he describes the "fame and honour" Antonio had won in "a bawbling vessel . . . For shallow draught and bulk unprizable" (V.i.52). But there, the paradox enhances Antonio's courage; here, it is depressing[14]. For Orsino, the only constant feature of love is instability. He tells Viola (II.iv.17) that all true lovers are

> Unstaid and skittish in all motions else
> Save in the constant image of the creature
> That is beloved;

a moment later, it is the "image" that changes—

> For, boy, however we do praise ourselves,
> Our fancies are more giddy and unfirm,
> More longing, wavering, sooner lost and worn
> Than women's are;—

and then, as he thinks of Olivia, it is the woman's "appetite", not the man's, that can "suffer surfeit, cloyment, and revolt" (II.iv.98). Feste sketches the life of such a lover with fitting ambiguity: "I would have men of such constancy put to sea, that their business might be every thing and their intent every where; for that's it that always makes a good voyage of nothing" (II.iv.75); they dissipate their advantages and can be satisfied with illusions. By its very nature, then, Orsino's love for Olivia is self-destructive, subject to time and change. Although, or rather, because, it is "all as hungry as the sea", it is impossible to satisfy. And it seems almost without an object, or incommensurate with any object, a "monstrosity" in the same sense as Troilus' love for Cressida, in its grasping after the infinite.

Moreover, Orsino's "spirit of love" seems something outside the rest of his personality, a tyrant from whom he longs to escape. His desires pursue him "like fell and cruel hounds". He wants music to diminish his passion, to relieve it with the thought of death. And when at last he confronts Olivia, something like hatred bursts through his conventional phrases of love-homage: "yond same sovereign cruelty" (II.iv) is now (V.i) a "perverse", "uncivil lady", "ingrate and unauspicious", "the marble-breasted tyrant". In his jealous rage he feels himself "at point of death":

> Why should I not, had I the heart to do it,
> Like to the Egyptian thief at point of death,
> Kill what I love? a savage jealousy
> That sometime savours nobly.   (V.i.115)

In all this, however, there is as much injured vanity as anything else. His "fancy" is at the point of dying, not his heart; and it is fully consistent with his character that he can swerve almost at once to Viola, gratified and relieved by the surprise of her identity and the full disclosure of her devotion to himself. His emotions, then, give a powerful upsurge to the play, but they are kept within the bounds of comedy. His real "error", in Shakespeare, is that he only imagines himself to be pursuing love. Olivia's, correspondingly, is that she only imagines herself to be flying from it.

With Olivia, even more than with Orsino, Shakespeare diverges from his possible sources, making her a much more prominent and interesting character than her prototypes. In the Italian stories, the second heroine is heiress to a wealthy old dotard, is kept out of sight most of the time, and is treated with ribald irony for her amorous forwardness. In *Apolonius and Silla*, she is a wealthy widow. In all three, she is considered only as rival and pendant to the Viola-heroine. Shakespeare, however, makes her a virgin, psychologically an elder sister to Viola, and better able to sustain the comedy of awakening desire. At the same time, she is the mistress of a noble household, and hence the focus of the sub-plot as well as the main plot[15]. When she first appears, she can rebuke Malvolio with aristocratic courtesy (I.v.94): "To be generous, guiltless, and of free disposition, is to take those things for bird-bolts that you deem cannon-bullets." But Olivia, like Orsino—like Malvolio, even—suffers from ignorance of herself, and must be cured of affectation; as Sebastian says (V.i.262), "nature to her bias drew in that".

Her vow of mourning has a tinge of the same aristocratic extravagance as Orsino's "spirit of love". Orsino compares her to an angry Diana; but then there follows at once the account of her vow, which already begins to disclose the comic, unseasonable side of her assumed coldness:

> The element itself, till seven years' heat,
> Shall not behold her face at ample view;
> But, like a cloistress, she will veiled walk,
> And water once a day her chamber round
> With eye-offending brine: all this to season
> A brother's dead love, which she would keep fresh
> And lasting in her sad remembrance.   (I.i.25)

Olivia is to be rescued from her cloister (like Diana's priestess in *The Comedy of Errors* or Hermia in *A Midsummer Night's Dream*[16]) and exposed to the sunshine. Feste warns her, in gentle mockery, that she is a "fool"; the hood does not make the monk, and "as there is no true cuckold but calamity, so beauty's a flower" (I.v). She is obliged to unveil her beauty, and has natural vanity enough to claim that "'twill endure wind and weather" (I.v.246); and Viola's speech, which stirs her heart, is also a form of comic retribution, hollaing her name to "the reverberate hills" and "the babling gossip of the air"—

> O, you should not rest
> Between the elements of air and earth,
> But you should pity me.   (I.v.281)

"Element" is made one of the comic catchwords of the play[17].

The comic reversal of Olivia's attitude culminates in her declaration of love to Viola, the most delicate and yet impressive speech in the play (III.i.150). It is now Olivia's turn to plead against "scorn", to "unclasp the book of her secret soul" to Viola[18]—and, equally, to herself. After two lines, she turns to the same verse form of impersonal, or extra-personal, "sentences" in rhyme that Shakespeare gives to other heroines at their moment of truth:

> O, what a deal of scorn looks beautiful
> In the contempt and anger of his lip!
> A murd'rous guilt shows not itself more soon
> Than love that would seem hid: love's night is noon.
> Cesario, by the roses of the spring,
> By maidhood, honour, truth, and every thing,
> I love thee so, that, maugre all thy pride,
> Nor wit nor reason can my passion hide.
> Do not extort thy reasons from this clause,
> For that I woo, thou therefore hast no cause;
> But rather reason thus with reason fetter,
> Love sought is good, but given unsought is better.

Having already thrown off her original veil, Olivia now breaks through the concealments of her pride, her modesty, and her feminine "wit". Her speech is mainly a vehement persuasion to love, urged "by the roses of the spring"[19]. Yet she keeps her dignity, and keeps it all the more in view of the secondary meaning latent in her words, her timid fear that Cesario's scorn is not the disdain of rejection at all but the scorn of conquest. Logically, indeed, her first rhyming couplet implies just this, implies that his cruel looks are the signs of a guilty lust rising to the surface; and this implication is carried on as she speaks of his "pride" (with its hint of sexual desire[20]), and into her last lines, with their covert pleading not to "extort" a callous advantage from her confession. But in either case—whatever Cesario's intentions—love now appears to Olivia as a startling paradox: guilty, even murderous, an irruption of misrule; and at the same time irrepressible, fettering reason, and creating its own light out of darkness. And, in either case, the conclusion to her perplexities is a plain one—"Love sought is good, but given unsought is better". This is Shakespeare's departure from the moral argument of his predecessors[21], and it marks the turning-point of *Twelfth Night*.

There is still a trace of irony attaching to Olivia, in that her wooing is addressed to another woman and has been parodied beforehand in Maria's forged love-letter (II.v). And this irony pursues her to the end, even in her marriage, when once again she tries, and fails, "To keep in darkness what occasion now Reveals before 'tis ripe" (V.i.151). But from the point of her declaration to Viola, the way is clear for the resolution of the whole comedy on the plane of sentiment. In terms of sentiment, she has justified her gift of love to a stranger. She is soon completely sure of herself, and in the later scenes she handles Sir Toby, Orsino, and Cesario-Sebastian with brusque decision; while her demon of austerity is cast out through Malvolio. The main action of *Twelfth Night*, then, is planned with a suggestive likeness to a revel, in which Olivia is masked, Orsino's part is "giddy" and "fantastical", Viola-Sebastian is the mysterious stranger—less of a character and more of a poetic symbol than the others—and in the end, as Feste says of his own "interlude" with Malvolio, "the whirligig of time brings in his revenges".

Although Olivia's declaration forms the crisis of the main action, the resolution of the plot has still to be worked out. And here Shakespeare departs in a new way from his predecessors. Shakespeare's Sebastian, by character and adventures, has little in common with the brother in *Gl'Ingannati*, and still less with Silla's brother in Riche; but nearly everything in common—as Manningham presumably noticed—with the visiting brother in Plautus, Menaechmus of Syracuse. And Antonio's part in the plot (though not his character) is largely that of Menaechmus' slave in Plautus, while his emotional role stems from the Aegeon story that Shakespeare himself had already added to *Menaechmi* in *The Comedy of Errors*. These Plautine elements in the brother's story have been altered in *Gl'Ingannati* and dropped from, or camouflaged in, *Apolonius and Silla*. Whichever of the latter Shakespeare used for Viola, therefore, he deliberately reverted to Plautus for Sebastian, sometimes drawing on his own elaborations in *The Comedy of Errors*, but mainly going back directly to the original[22].

Hence the second half of *Twelfth Night* is largely more farcical than its predecessors, whereas the first half had been, in a sense, more romantic. Shakespeare thus provides a telling finale, proper, as Dr. Johnson observes, to the stage. But he does much more than this. His farcical dénouement gives tangible shape to the notion of misrule inherent in his romantic exposition. Faults of judgment in the first part of *Twelfth Night* are answered with mistakes of identity in the second, while the action swirls to a joyful ending through a crescendo of errors. And by the same manoeuvre, Shakespeare charges his romance with a new emotional significance, bringing it nearer to tragedy.

How are Viola and Olivia to be freed? In *Apolonius and Silla*, the widow, pregnant after her welcome to Silla's brother, demands justice of the disguised heroine, thus forcing her to reveal herself and clearing the way for her marriage to the duke. Only when the rumor of this wedding has spread abroad does the wandering brother return to the scene and espouse the widow. In the Italian stories, the heroine reaches an understanding with her master by her own devices and the aid of her nurse, without any kind of help from the arrival of her brother; and this is a logical solution, since the heroine's love-service is the clear center of interest. But Shakespeare has been more broadly concerned with love as a force in life as a whole. He has shifted the emphasis to the two older lovers, keeping Viola's share of passion in reserve. And even after the crisis, he continues to withhold the initiative the Italians had given her. Shakespeare is alone in making the heroine reveal herself *after* her brother's marriage with the second heroine, as a consequence of it. And the whole Plautine sequence in *Twelfth Night* is designed to lead to this conclusion. Hence, while the first half of Shakespeare's comedy dwells on self-deception in love, the second half stresses the benevolent irony of fate.

In the early scenes, fate appears to the speakers as an overriding power which is nevertheless obscurely rooted in their own desires (the obverse, that is, to Orsino's "spirit of love", which springs from himself, yet seems to dominate him from without)[23]. Thus, Viola trusts herself to "time"; Olivia, falling in love, cries, "Fate, show thy force: ourselves we do not owe"; and the letter forged in her name yields an echo to her words: "Thy Fates open their hands; let thy blood and spirit embrace them"[24]. Antonio and Sebastian strengthen this motif and clarify it.

Antonio stands for an absolute devotion that is ultimately grounded on fate; he is the embodiment of Olivia's discovery, and his speeches on this theme are interwoven with hers. Shortly after her first lines about fate—and chiming with them—comes his declaration to Sebastian (II.i.47):

> But, come what may, I do adore thee so,
> That danger shall seem sport, and I will go;

and after her cry that love should be a gift, he tells Sebastian in more positive terms

> I could not stay behind you: my desire,
> More sharp than filed steel, did spur me forth. (III.iii.4)

In the last scene, again, he proclaims to Orsino—

> A witchcraft drew me hither:
> That most ingrateful boy there by your side,

From the rude sea's enrag'd and foamy mouth
Did I redeem. (V.i.74)

The resonant sea-image of destiny here dominates the bewildered tone still appropriate, at this point, to a comedy of errors[25].

Sebastian's part runs parallel with this. When he first appears (II.i), he feels the same melancholy as his sister, and shows a similar vague self-abandonment in his aims: "My determinate voyage is mere extravagancy". But a stronger impression of him has been given already by the Captain, in the outstanding speech of Viola's first scene:

                    I saw your brother,
Most provident in peril, bind himself,
Courage and hope both teaching him the practice,
To a strong mast that lived upon the sea;
Where, like Arion on the dolphin's back,
I saw him hold acquaintance with the waves
So long as I could see.

The Captain has told Viola to "comfort [herself] with chance"; Sebastian is "provident in peril", on friendly terms with destiny. When he bobs up resurrected at the end, accordingly, he does precisely what Malvolio had been advised to do, grasps the hands of the Fates and lets himself float with "the stream", with "this accident and flood of fortune" (IV.i.62, IV.iii.11)[26]. By the same turn of mind, moreover, he imparts to the dénouement a tone as of clarity following illusion, of an awakening like the end of *A Midsummer Night's Dream*:

Or I am mad, or else this is a dream. . . . (IV.i.63)

This is the air; that is the glorious sun;
This pearl she gave me, I do feel't and see't;
And though 'tis wonder that enwraps me thus,
Yet 'tis not madness. . . .   (IV.iii.1)

"Mad" the lady may appear; but Sebastian—like Olivia before him, except that he does it in all coolness—is ready to "wrangle with his reason" and welcome the gift of love. The comedy of errors in which he figures is thus both counterpart and solution to the initial comedy of sentiment. Riche had called his love-story the work of "Dame Error"; Shakespeare, in effect, takes the hint, and goes back to Plautus.

Having planned his dénouement on these lines, moreover, Shakespeare goes further, adding a superb variation on his Plautine theme in the farcical scene leading up to Viola's meeting with Antonio (III.iv). This scene as a whole, with its rapid changes of mood and action, from Olivia to the sub-plot and back towards Sebastian, braces together the whole comic design. It brings to a climax the misrule, farcical humours, and simulated emotions of the play—with Olivia confessing "madness", Sir Toby triumphant, Malvolio *in excelsis* ("Jove, not I, is the doer of this . . . "), Sir Andrew allegedly "bloody as the hunter"[27], and Viola, after her unavoidable coldness to Olivia, submitted for the first time to the laughable consequences of her change of sex. And the duel with its sequel perfect this comic catharsis. This duel, or what Sir Toby and Fabian make of it, bears a strong affinity to the sword dances and Mummers' play combats of a season of misrule; it becomes another encounter between St. George and Captain Slasher, the Turkish Knight. One champion is "a devil in private brawl: souls and bodies hath he divorced three"; the other is "a very devil, . . . a firago. . . . He gives me the stuck-in with such a mortal motion that it is inevitable"—and "they say he has been fencer to the Sophy". Now in one sense the duel and what follows are superfluous to the main action, since it is not strictly necessary for Viola to meet Antonio, or to meet him in this way. But in effect this episode of misrule[28] contains the principal conflict between the serious and the ludicrous forces in the play; it prepares emotionally for the resurrection of Sebastian; and, by a further swerve of constructive irony, the additional, gratuitous comedy of errors involving Antonio gives new force to the main theme of the romance.

As it concerns Viola, the dialogue here restores the balance in favor of her character, in that her generosity and her lines against "ingratitude" prepare the audience for her culminating gesture of self-sacrifice in the last act. But, more than this, Antonio's speeches stress the paradox of love that has been gathering force through the play:

> *Antonio*: Let me speak a little. This youth that you see here
> I snatch'd one half out of the jaws of death,
> Reliev'd him with such sanctity of love,
> And to his image, which methought did promise
> Most venerable worth, did I devotion.
> *Officer*: What's that to us? The time goes by: away!
> *Antonio*: But, O, how vile an idol proves this god.
> Thou hast, Sebastian, done good feature shame.
> In nature there's no blemish but the mind;
> None can be call'd deform'd but the unkind:
> Virtue is beauty, but the beauteous evil
> Are empty trunks o'erflourished by the devil.
> *Officer*: The man grows mad: away with him! . . . (III.iv.372)

It is in keeping with the comedy of errors that Antonio here has mistaken his man, to the point of seeming "mad", that Viola, happy to hear of her brother again, promptly forgets him—as Sir Toby notices (III.iv.400)—and that Antonio, as it turns out, should help Sebastian most effectively by so being forgotten. But this same quirk of fate brings the mood of the play dangerously near the confines of tragedy. The comedy has no answer to his problem of sincere devotion given to a false idol[29].

Antonio stands outside the main sphere of the comedy. He belongs to the world of merchants, law, and sea-battles, not the world of courtly love. His love for Sebastian is irrational, or beyond reason, and his danger in Orsino's domains is due, similarly, to irrational persistence in an old dispute (III.iii.30–37). But he gives himself completely to his principles, more seriously than anyone else in the play, and tries to live them out as rationally as he can. In contrast to the lovers (except possibly Viola), he is not satisfied with truth of feeling, but demands some more objective standard of values; in his world, law and "time" mean something external, and harder than the unfolding of natural instinct. His problems are appropriate to *Troilus* or *Hamlet*. In one way, therefore, he marks a limit to festivity. Nevertheless, precisely because he takes himself so seriously, he helps to keep the comic balance of the play.

The comedy of errors in the main plot, the element of mummery and misrule, implies a comment on the serious follies of love, and bring a corrective to them. In the sub-plot (or -plots)—his addition to the Viola story—Shakespeare makes this corrective explicit and prepares for the festive atmosphere at the end. "What a plague means my niece, to take the death of her brother thus? I am sure care's an enemy to life. . . . " "Does not our lives consist of the four elements?—Faith, so they say; but I think it rather consists of eating and drinking." Sir Toby, Maria, Feste, Fabian stand for conviviality and the enjoyment of life, as opposed to the melancholy of romance.

At the same time, however, the sub-plot action reproduces the main action like a comic mirror-image, and the two of them are joined to form a single symmetrical pattern of errors in criss-cross. Shakespeare had attempted a similar pattern before, in *The Comedy of Errors*, *A Midsummer Night's Dream*, and *Much Ado*, for example, but nowhere else does he bring it off so lightly and ingeniously.

In the main plot there is a lover who pursues love and a lady who tries to hide from it. In the sub-plot there is Malvolio, who pursues love, and Sir Toby, who prefers drinking. Olivia and Sir Toby are "consanguineous" but of opposite tempers; the other two disturb both of them. On their side, Orsino and Malvolio are both self-centred, but one neglects "state" and the other affects it; however, one is a lover who likes solitude, the other a solitary who turns to love. Both imagine they are in love with Olivia, while one is really fired by a forged letter, and the other is blind to the wife in front of his eyes. In the upshot, Orsino unwittingly helps to find a husband for Olivia, and Malvolio, a wife for Sir Toby. At the beginning of the comedy, Olivia had mourned a brother, while Orsino resented it; at the end, she finds a brother again, in Orsino himself.

Between Orsino and Olivia come the twins, Viola-Sebastian, opposite and indistinguishable. Between Malvolio and Sir Toby comes Maria, the "Penthesilia" who forges a false identity. The twins are heirs to fortune, unsuspecting and unambitious; Maria is an intriguer, who signs herself "The Fortunate-Unhappy". In their first scene together, Sir Andrew "accosts", "woos" and "assails" Maria, who drops his hand; Antonio likewise accosts, woos, and assails Viola and Sebastian, who lose or ignore him. The symmetrical pattern is completed at the mid-point of the play, when Sir Andrew and Antonio confront each other with drawn swords. This encounter between the romantic and the comic figures is twice repeated, and on the last occasion it seems to be Viola's double who is the aggressor (V.i.178–180). Hence, although Sir Andrew and Antonio do not know each other or why they are quarrelling, they co-operate to bring about an unexpected result; Sir Andrew, to provide a wife for Sebastian, and Antonio, to provide a husband for Maria.

This dance of changed partners and reversed fortunes is much more complicated than anything in *Gl'Ingannati*. Shakespeare devises it partly by carrying the Plautine themes of twinship and of the lost being found again, or brought back to life, much farther than the Italian had gone; and partly by pursuing his own allied and festive theme of a Twelfth Night mask of misrule. By this means, he laces sub-plot and main plot together in a single intricate design.

The interest of the sub-plot is more varied, moreover, and its links with the main plot are more complex, than a bare summary of the action can indicate. In relation to the main plot, the comic figures are somewhat like scapegoats; they reflect the humours of Orsino and Olivia in caricature and through them these humours are purged away. Secondly, the sub-plot is a Feast of Fools[30], containing its own satire of humours in Malvolio and Sir Andrew. And, from another point of view, Sir Toby's "uncivil rule" is complementary to the problem of "time" in the main plot.

Besides Malvolio, Sir Toby and Sir Andrew are to some extent parodies of Orsino. One will drink Olivia's health till he is "drowned" or "his brains turn o' the toe like a parish-top"; the other is a model of gentlemanly indecision, hopes to woo Olivia without speaking to her, and attacks Viola from jealousy. The strains of unconscious parody in the sub-plot help to amplify the general theme of delusion and error.

On Olivia's side, moreover, the disorder in her household is a direct reaction to her attitude at the beginning of the play[31]. Malvolio affects a grave austerity to please her, but the instincts are in revolt. Sir Toby redoubles the clamor of love for her and personifies her neglect of time and the reproach of the clock (III. i.135). Sir Andrew, a fool, helps to find her a husband. In Malvolio's "madness" she comes to see a reflection of her own (III.iv.15), and at the end he takes her place in cloistered darkness.

In addition, the comic dialogue echoes the thought of the serious characters and twists it into fantastic shapes. To the serious actors, life is a sea-voyage: the comic actors deal with journeys more specific, bizarre, and adventurous than theirs, ranging in time from when "Noah was a sailor" to the publishing of "the new map with the augmentation of the Indies", and from the Barents Sea to the gates of Tartar or the equinoctial of Queubus. The serious actors scrutinize a fate which might be pagan in its religious coloring: the comic speakers, for their part, are orthodox Christians, and their dialogue is peppered with biblical and ecclesiastical references. Sir Toby, for instance, "defies lechery" and counts on "faith"; Sir Andrew plumes himself on having "no more wit than a Christian or an ordinary man has", and would beat Malvolio for no "exquisite reason" save that of thinking him a puritan[32], the duel scene and the madness scenes are full of "devils". In part, these ecclesiastical jokes reinforce the suggestion of Twelfth Night foolery and of mock sermons like Erasmus' sermon of Folly; from this aspect, they lead up to Feste's interlude of Sir Topas. But in part, too, their tone of moral security to the degree of smugness gives a counterweight to the emotions of the serious actors.

Moreover, Sir Andrew and Sir Toby are both alike in feeling very sure of their ideal place in the scheme of things. They are contrasted as shrewd and fatuous, parasite and gull, Carnival and Lent; but they are both, in their differing ways, "sots", and both gentlemen[33]. Their conversation is a handbook to courtesy. And while Sir Andrew is an oafish squire, who will "have but a year in all these ducats", Sir Toby is a degenerate knight, who will not "confine himself within the modest limits of order" and, possessed of the rudiments of good breeding, delights in turning them upside-down. He is repeatedly called "uncivil" (II. iii.125, III.iv.265, IV.i.55), and his merry-making is out of time and season. He tells Malvolio, "We did keep time, sir, in our catches"; but when at the end he leaves the stage with a broken head, driving Sir Andrew off before him, he is abusing the surgeon, on the lines of the same pun, for "a drunken rogue" whose eyes are "set at eight". Despite his resemblance to Falstaff, Sir Toby has a smaller mind, and this shows itself in his complacency with his position in Olivia's household.

Malvolio is a more complex and formidable character. Evidently Maria's "good practise" on this overweening steward was the distinctive attraction of *Twelfth Night* to Stuart audiences; but that does not mean (as some critics would have it, reacting against Lamb[34]) that Malvolio is presented as a contemptible butt. An audience is more likely to enjoy and remember the humiliation of someone who in real life would be feared than the humiliation of a mere impostor like Parolles. Malvolio is neither a puritan nor an upstart, though he has qualities in common with both. Olivia and Viola call him a "gentleman" (V.i.279, 282), as the steward of a countess's household no doubt would be, and in seeking to repress disorders he is simply carrying out the duties of his office:

> Have you no wit, manners, nor honesty, but to gabble like tinkers at this time of night? Do ye make an alehouse of my lady's house, that ye squeak out your coziers' catches without any mitigation or remorse of voice? Is there no respect of place, persons, nor time in you? (II.iii.89)

These early speeches to Sir Toby have a firm ring about them that explains Olivia's confidence in Malvolio, without as yet disclosing the "politic" affectation that Maria sees in him. On the other hand, his principle of degree and order is simply a mask for his pride. He is "sick of self-love", unable to live spontaneously as one of a community, as is hinted from the outset by his recoil from the sociable side of the jester's art—an office that also requires the understanding of place, persons, and time. And even before finding Maria's letter, he shows the self-ignorance of a divided personality in the daydream he weaves about himself and Olivia, indulging his "humour of state". Nevertheless, when his humour has been mocked to the full, Shakespeare still makes him protest that he "thinks nobly of the soul", and he remains a force to be reckoned with right to the end. With his unconscious hypocrisy in the exercise of power and his rankling sense of injustice, he comes midway between Shylock and the Angelo of *Measure for Measure*.

Sir Toby, Sir Andrew and Malvolio—all three—are striving to be something false, whether novel or antiquated, which is out of place in a healthy community; they are a would-be retainer, a would-be gallant, a would-be "politician". But the conflict over revelry between Malvolio and Sir Toby is a conflict of two opposed reactions towards changing social and economic conditions. In Malvolio's eyes, Sir Toby "wastes the treasure of his time". So he does; and so, in their ways, do Olivia and Orsino. A natural way of living, Shakespeare seems to imply, must observe impersonal factors such as time as well as the healthy gratification of instinct—and in the last resort, the two may be incompatible with each other. Hence Malvolio in the end is neither crushed nor pacified. He belongs, like Antonio, to the world of law and business, outside the festive circle of the play. Both are imprisoned for a while by the others. They stand for two extremes of self-sacrifice and self-love, but they share a rigid belief in principle. And neither can be fully assimilated into the comedy.

There are discordant strains, then, in the harmony of *Twelfth Night*—strains of melancholy and of something harsher. As far as any one actor can resolve them, this task falls to Feste.

Feste is not only the most fully portrayed of Shakespeare's clowns, he is also the most agile-minded of them. He has fewer set pieces than Touchstone and fewer proverbs than the Fool in *Lear*. He is proud of his professional skill—"better a witty fool than a foolish wit"—but he wields it lightly, in darting paradoxes; he is a "corrupter of words". Yet, besides being exceptionally imaginative and sophisticated, he is exceptionally given to scrounging for tips. This trait is consistent with the traditional aspect of his role, especially as the fool in a feast of misrule, but it helps to make him more like a real character and less like a stage type.

This money-sense of Feste and his awareness of his social status bring him within the conflict of ideas affecting the other actors. Although he depends for his living on other people's pleasure, and can sing to any tune—"a love-song or a song of good life"—Feste is neither a servile entertainer nor an advocate of go-as-you-please. On the contrary, he is a moralist with a strong bent towards scepticism. "As there is no true cuckold but calamity, so beauty's a flower. . . . Truly, sir, and pleasure will be paid, one time or another. . . The whirligig of time brings in his revenges": one factor will always cancel another. As against Malvolio, he belittles the soul; but he shows hardly any more confidence in the survival-value of folly, and marriage is the only form of it he recommends. For Feste himself could very easily belong to the ship of fools he designates for Orsino, having his business and intent everywhere and making "a good voyage of nothing". (The same thought is present when he tells Viola that foolery "does walk about the orb like the sun; it shines every where".) There is a persistent hint, then, that his enigmas glance at himself as well as others, and that he feels his own position to be insecure. And it is consistent with this that he should be the only character in Shakespeare to take pleasure, or refuge, in fantasies of pure nonsense: "as the old hermit of Prague, that never saw pen and ink, very wittily said to a niece of King Gorboduc, 'That that is is'." It is impossible to go further than a non-existent hermit of Prague.

Feste is not the ringleader in *Twelfth Night*, nor is he exactly the play's philosopher. He is cut off from an independent life of his own by his traditional role in reality and on the stage, and what he sees at the bottom of the well is "nothing". He knows that without festivity he is nothing; and he knows, in his epilogue, that misrule does not last, and that men shut their gates against tosspots, lechers, knaves, and fools. A play is only a play, and no more. Yet it is precisely on this finely-poised balance of his that the whole play comes to rest. Orsino, Olivia, Viola, Sebastian, Sir Toby, Maria, Malvolio, Feste himself—nearly everyone in *Twelfth Night* acts a part in some sense, but Feste is the only one who takes this aspect of life for granted. The others commit errors and have divided emotions; but Feste can have no real emotions of his own, and may only live in his quibbles. Yet by virtue of this very disability, he sees the element of misrule in life more clearly than the rest, appreciating its value because he knows its limitations. A play to Feste may be only a play, but it is also the breath of life.

Feste is the principal link between the other characters in *Twelfth Night*. Unless Puck is counted, he is the only clown for whom Shakespeare provides an epilogue. And as it happens, his is the epilogue to the whole group of Shakespeare's romantic comedies.

APPENDIX

Shakespeare and Plautus (see above): The Plautine motif of confused identities is present in *Gl'Ingannati*, and possibly in Riche. But a comparison of *TN* with *Menaechmi* and *CE* on one side, and with *Gl'Ingannati*, Bandello, and Riche on the other makes it seem certain that Shakespeare was consciously borrowing from Plautus in planning Sebastian's role, at the same time, however, enlarging this borrowed material on the lines of *CE*:

(a) *Background*: In *Men.*, there are twin brothers, long separated and unknown to each other; their father is dead. In *CE*, they have been separated by a tempest; their father is alive. In both, one of the "lost" brothers hopes to find the other in the course of his travels. In *Gl'Ingannati* and Bandello, the twin brother has been lost since the sack of Rome in 1527; he comes expecting to find his father, still alive, and his sister. In Riche, the brother sets off in pursuit of his sister, who has followed the duke and has suffered shipwreck; their father is still alive. So far, *TN* might be a compound of all the others.

(b) *Sebastian*: In *Men.*, Menaechmus of Syracuse, searching for his brother, lands at Epidamnus with his slave. He is hot-tempered (Loeb ed., II.i.269)—a trait only emphasized here and in *TN*. Leaving his slave, he meets in turn a cook, a courtesan, and a parasite, who mistake him for his twin. He thinks them mad, or drunk, or dreaming (II.iii.373, 395), but sleeps with the courtesan, accepts her gifts—a mantle and a bracelet—and makes off "while time and circumstance permit", thanking the gods for his unexpected luck (III.iii.551–3). He misses his slave, and gets involved in a squabble with his sister-in-law and her father, feigning madness to frighten them off. His doings react on his brother. Finally, the brothers meet, compare notes about their father, and recognize each other with the help of the slave.

Sebastian's actions follow exactly the same pattern. He appears in Illyria with a companion, then leaves him; he is going to the court, but has no definite goal since his twin sister has apparently died (II.i). Meeting his companion again, he says he wants to view "the reliques of this town"; they separate a second time, after making an appointment (III.iii). He then meets in turn a clown, a parasite (Sir Toby) and his friend, and a lady, who mistake him for his twin. He thinks they are mad, or that he is mad or else dreaming, fights the parasite and his friend, but accepts the lady's invitation to accompany her (IV.i). He has missed his companion, but accepts the lady's gift of a pearl, welcomes "this accident and flood of fortune", and agrees to marry her (IV.iii). Off-stage, he fights the parasite a second time (V.i.178–80). Meanwhile, his doings have reacted on his twin, partly through the agency of his companion. Finally, the twins meet, compare notes about their father, and recognize each other.

In *Gl'Ingannati*, the brother comes to Modena with a servant and a tutor, a pedant who describes the sights of the town in detail (III.i). He leaves them to go sight-seeing, meets the second heroine's maid, and agrees to visit the mistress, supposing her to be some courtesan (III.v). Then he meets her father and his own father, who take him to be his twin sister, dressed as a man; he calls them mad, and they lock him up with the second heroine (III.vii), whereupon he seduces her. He does not meet his twin sister until she is married.

In Bandello the only characters the brother meets at first are the second heroine and her maid; in Riche, only the second heroine.

With Sebastian, then, Shakespeare ignores *Gl'Ingannati* (except conceivably for the sight-seeing), and follows Plautus in detail. He had used much of this material before, in *CE*. But there he had introduced variations (e.g. the "lost" brother's business affairs and the character of Luciana); here he goes back directly to his source.

(c) *Messaline*. Apparently no editor of *TN* has explained satisfactorily why Shakespeare makes Sebastian come from "Messaline", "a town unknown to geography". Perhaps this is because they have concentrated unduly on the Italian background of *TN*; (cp. Draper, who suggests Manzolino, or "Mensoline", near Modena, pp. 262–263). But reference to Plautus offers a very likely solution. In *Men.*, II.i the slave asks Menaechmus of Syracuse how long he means to go on searching for his twin: "Istrians, Spaniards, *Massilians*, *Illyrians* (*Massiliensis*, *Hilurios*), the entire Adriatic, and foreign Greece and the whole coast of Italy—every section the sea washes—we've visited in our travels . . . " (Loeb ed., pp. 235–238). This scene corresponds to *TN*, II.i, where Sebastian mentions "Messaline", telling Antonio that his "determinate voyage is mere extravagancy" because his sister is drowned. Hence it seems almost certain that Shakespeare invented the name "Messaline", in connexion with Illyria, from a reminiscence of these lines of Plautus (where, in addition, the speaker's name is Messenio); (cp. *Times Lit. Supp.*, June 3, 1955). This suggests that the parallel between Sebastian and Menaechmus was clearly present to Shakespeare's mind from the beginning.

(d) *Antonio*. In *Men.*, the slave is a purse-bearer, warns Menaechmus against the dangers of Epidamnus, intervenes to save his master's twin from danger, is promised his liberty, has the promise withdrawn, and then has it renewed. Antonio's part corresponds to this closely. There is nothing like this in *Gl'Ingannati*, nor much in the Dromio of *CE*. On the other hand, Shakespeare seems to have taken some traits in Antonio from Aegeon in *CE* (cp. note 28, above).

(e) The *Captain* who comes on with Viola in *TN*, I.ii has only a minimal part as her confidant. In this, his only scene, his main speech concerns Sebastian; while the later news of his arrest at Malvolio's suit (V.i.276–278) recalls the legal business in *CE*, like the arrest of Antonio. He therefore belongs to Sebastian's part in the composition of *TN*, rather than Viola's. (There is a captain in *Apolonius and Silla*, but he tries to rape the heroine, and then disappears.)

(f) *Illyria*. The assumption that Shakespeare's knowledge of *Men.* played a large—and not merely an incidental—part in the composition of *TN* throws some further light on Shakespeare's methods of construction. In particular, it suggests why he set the play in "Illyria". On the face of it, there is no special reason for this choice of a setting, unless perhaps Viola's pun on "Elysium" when the place is first mentioned. Although the name has since acquired a romantic aura from the play itself, there is nothing specially Arcadian or Ruritanian about "Illyria" in *TN*, and no strong local color, as there is for Modena in *Gl'Ingannati*, or for Venice in Shakespeare's other plays. What there is, moreover, is slightly inconsistent; for Antonio's warning to Sebastian about the dangers of "these parts", which he says are "rough and inhospitable" (III.iii.8–11), is not exactly borne out by the rest of the play, and is vague in any case, so that it seems to belong to Antonio, not to Illyria. This speech can be traced back, however, to the more specific warning of the slave in *Men.* II.i.258–264, to the effect that Epidamnus is a town of "rakes, drinkers, sycophants and alluring harlots", owing its very name to the tricks it plays on strangers—and this (together with the way the warning is falsified) does correspond very closely to Illyria as Sebastian finds it. Further, Hotson points out that the real Illyria of Shakespeare's day was known for riotous behavior, drinking and piracy (p. 151). These touches account for the sea-fighting in *TN* (but not the tricks of fortune), and otherwise they match with Epidamnus; so that Epidamnus and the real country together furnish the sketchy local color of "Illyria" in *TN*. It looks, therefore, as if Shakespeare, having planned to modify the Viola story with the aid of Plautus, looked for a place-name that would fit the attributes he wanted, and chose "Illyria" accordingly. If so, his memory could have prompted him from the same line of *Men.* that yields the source of "Messaline".

(g) *Olivia's household*. Assuming that Shakespeare founded Illyria from Epidamnus, he would have looked to the mother-town for some of the inhabitants and their customs. There is a good deal of banqueting in Epidamnus, and some talk of lawsuits. And there is one important character whom Shakespeare had not used already in *CE*. This is the parasite, Peniculus or "Brush", a greedy drinker and a schemer. He pushes himself on the courtesan's house, urges his patron to dance at one point (*Men.*, I.iii.197—cp. *TN*, I.iii.143), and elsewhere provokes Menaechmus of Syracuse. And he seems to be reincarnated in the person of Sir Toby.

Secondly, there are the episodes of feigned inspiration, or frenzy, in *Men.*, V, with a comic doctor and a scuffle over the wrong twin. Shakespeare had used these already in *CE*, IV.iv, but there was no reason why he should not use them again. They could well have furnished hints for the duel scene with its "devils" in *TN* and the scene of Malvolio and Sir Topas.

Moreover, anyone approaching the Viola story by way of Plautus would be inclined to give more prominence to the second heroine (the supposed "courtesan" of the Italian tales) and her companions. And in fact, Olivia and her household, in their actions towards Sebastian, reproduce very closely the actions of the courtesan, her servants, and the parasite in *Men.*, without any hint of indebtedness to *Gl'Ingannati*, Riche, or the transformed Plautine incidents of *CE*. These considerations need not imply that Shakespeare imagined Olivia and her household simply as afterthoughts to the Plautine twin; but they do seem to suggest how, once he had begun thinking about the material in Plautus, the whole of his composition could have fallen into shape.

Finally, (h) *Errors and misrule.* The circumstances of the performance of *CE* at the Gray's Inn revels of 1594 could well have suggested to Shakespeare the plan of introducing a Plautine comedy of mistaken identity into a larger framework of misrule. He had done something like this already in *The Shrew*, where the sub-plot is a comedy of changed identities borrowed from Ariosto, and the framework story of Sly as a lord is an episode of misrule.

To sum up, it is plausible to reconstruct the composition of *TN* somewhat as follows. Reading the Viola story, in Riche or elsewhere, Shakespeare was struck by the notion of "error" implicit in "following them that fly from us", and this gave him the hint for Orsino and Olivia. Secondly, "error" suggested the role of Sebastian, with its Plautine farce and its romantic overtones of sea-adventure prolonged from *CE*. And the same notion of "error" also suggested the stage devices of misrule, prominent in the sub-plot of *TN* and latent in the whole play. Though it leaves much of the emotional content of *TN* untouched, this conjecture does seem to account for the way the whole stage design of the play holds so beautifully together.

NOTES

1. Karl F. Thompson, "Shakespeare's Romantic Comedies", *PMLA*, LXVII (1952); E. C. Pettet, *Shakespeare and the Romance Tradition* (1949), 122–132. "Tempests dissolved in music" is the phrase of G. Wilson Knight, *The Shakespearian Tempest* (1953 ed.), pp. 121–127.

2. This is the interpretation of John W. Draper, *The Twelfth Night of Shakespeare's Audience* (Stanford Univ. Press, 1950).

3. "Shakespearian comedy . . . speculates imaginatively on modes, not of preserving a good already reached, but of enlarging and extending the possibilities of this and other kinds of good". H. B. Charlton, *Shakespearian Comedy* (1938), pp. 277–278.

4. Enid Welsford, *The Fool* (1935), p. 251; cp. E. K. Chambers, *Mediaeval Stage* (1903), I, 403 n. Leslie Hotson gives further details connecting the play with the Feast of Mis-rule in *The First Night of Twelfth Night* (1954), ch. vii. To the various possible meanings of Malvolio's yellow stockings (Hotson, p. 113) it is worth adding that, according to Stubbes, yellow or green "or some other light wanton colour" was the livery of "my Lord of Mis-rule" in the parishes (*Anatomy of Abuses*, 1583: ed. Furnivall, p. 147). Stubbes is speaking of summer games, but misrule was not confined to Christmas—cp. *TN* (Arden edn.), III. iv. 148: "More matter for a May morning".

5. P. Mueschke and J. Fleisher, "Jonsonian Elements in the Comic Underplot of *TN*", *PMLA*, XLVIII, (1933).

6. "Ma come si dice che egli era innamorato, subito cessa l'ammirazione, perciò che questa passione amorosa è di troppo gran potere e fa far cose assai piú meravigliose e strabocchevoli di questa. Né crediate che per altro la fabulosa Grecia finga i dèi innamorati aver fatte tante pazzie vituperose . . . , se non per darci ad intendere che come l'uomo si lascia soggiogar ad amore . . . , egli può dir d'aver giocata e perduta la sua libertà, e che miracolo non è se poi fa mille errori!" Bandello, *Le Novelle*, II, xxxvi (ed. G. Brognoligo, Bari, 1911, III, 252).

7. Riche's *Apolonius and Silla* (ed. Morton Luce, The Shakespeare Classics, 1912), p. 53; cp. p. 52: "in all other things, wherein we show ourselves to be most drunken with this poisoned cup [of error], it is in our actions of love; for the lover is so estranged from that is right, and wandereth so wide from the bounds of reason, that he is not able to deem white from black . . . ; but only led by the appetite of his own affections, and grounding them on the foolishness of his own fancies, will so settle his liking on such a one, as either by desert or unworthiness will merit rather to be loathed than loved". Contrasts between love and reason are prominent, again, in Erasmus' *In Praise of Folly* and Sidney's *Arcadia*, two likely sources of the general themes of *TN*. Bacon's essay "Of Love" comes nearer still to the subject-matter of Shakespeare's play, illustrating the tension of ideas there from a point of view almost directly opposite: "The stage is more beholding to love than the life of man; for as to the stage, love is ever matter of comedies, and now and then of tragedies; but in life it doth much mischief, sometimes like a Siren, sometimes like a Fury. . . . Great spirits and great business do keep out this weak passion . . . ; for whosoever esteemeth too much of amorous affection, quitteth both riches and wisdom. This passion hath his floods in the very times of weakness, which are, great prosperity and great adversity . . . ; both which times kindle love, and make it more fervent, and therefore show it to be the child of folly." This essay could almost be a commentary on Malvolio, Orsino, Viola and Sebastian.

8. The idea of representing life as a festival of misrule was already implicit, of course, in the common notion that "all the world's a stage", and in the general Renaissance tradition of Folly, especially in Erasmus (cp. Welsford, pp. 236–242). Robert Armin, who acted Feste, may have helped to give point to the idea; in his *Nest of Ninnies* (1600–08; ed. J. P. Collier, 1842), he represents the World, sick of a surfeit of drink and revelling, being shown a pageant of fools, who are partly endearing and partly symbols of the World's vices (cp. Welsford, pp. 162–165, 284). Armin does not treat of love, but John Heywood's *Play of Love* (–1533) is a Christmas interlude consisting of debates on the "reasons" of love between Lover not Loved, Loved not Loving (the woman), Lover Loved, and Neither Lover nor Loved (the Vice). And much nearer to *TN* comes Jonson's *Cynthia's Revels; or, the*

Fountain of Self-Love (1600). Moreover, Shakespeare himself is very likely to have remembered the suggestive episode of December 28, 1594, when the *Comedy of Errors* was performed in the "disordered" revels of Gray's Inn: "So that Night was begun, and continued to the end, in nothing but Confusion and Errors; whereupon, it was ever afterwards called, *The Night of Errors*. . . . We preferred Judgments . . . against a Sorcerer or Conjuror that was supposed to be the cause of that confused Inconvenience. . . . And Lastly, that he had foisted a Company of base and common Fellows, to make up our Disorders with a Play of Errors and Confusions; and that that Night had gained to us Discredit, and itself a Nickname of Errors" (*Gesta Grayorum*; E. K. Chambers, *Shakespeare*, Appendix, "Performances"). Lastly, Shakespeare uses the metaphor of life as a mask of misrule directly in *Troilus*, a play linked in several ways with *TN*: 'Degree being vizarded, / The unworthiest shows as fairly in the mask' (I.iii.83).

9. This paragraph is based on Morton Luce's Arden ed. of *TN* (1906) and his ed. of Riche. Luce assembles parallels between *TN* and Riche, Bandello, and *Gl'Ingannati*, from which it seems very possible, though not certain, that Shakespeare knew any or all of the latter. Luce mentions, but does not examine, Shakespeare's debt to Plautus.

10. "Due ammaestramenti sopra tutto ne cavarete: quanto possa il caso e la buona fortuna nelle cose d'amore; e quanto, in quella, vaglia una longa pazienzia accompagnata da buon consiglio" (ed. I. Sanesi, *Commedie del Cinquecento*, Bari, 1912, I, 316).

11. "Io credo che questa sia certamente volontá di Dio che abbia avuto pietá di questa virtuosa giovane e dell'anima mia; ch'ella non vada in perdizione. E però, madonna Lelia, . . . io non voglio altra moglie che voi . . . " (V.iii; ed. Sanesi, p. 393). Cp. Bandello, pp. 273–275; Riche, p. 82.

12. Cp. Lelia, in *Gl'Ingannati*: "O what a fate is mine! I love him who hates me. . . . I serve him who knows me not; and, worse still, I help him to love another . . . only in the hope of gratifying these eyes with seeing him, one day, in my own way." About her rival, she says: "I pretend not to want to love her, unless she makes Flamminio withdraw from his love to her; and I have already brought the affair to a conclusion . . . " (I.iii, pp. 322, 328). Bandello's heroine says: "I have done so much that I want to see the end of it, come what may. . . . Then God will help me, who knows my heart and knows I have only taken these pains so as to have Lattanzio for a husband" (p. 262).

13. Riche, p. 64. Draper (ch. vi) argues that Orsino is meant as a wholly admirable or sympathetic character, and that *TN* is "a genial satire on the vulgar love of Malvolio and Sir Andrew in contrast to the refined passion of Orsino, Olivia, and Viola-Sebastian" (p. 131). As regards Orsino, Riche's mildly scoffing attitude to his ducal lover hardly bears this out; nor do the quotations that Draper brings forward from the psychologists, e.g. his apt quotation from Burton: "Love . . . rageth with all sorts and conditions of men, yet is most evident among such as are young and lusty, in the flower of their years, nobly descended, high fed, such as live idly, and at ease; and for that cause (which our Divines call burning lust) . . . this mad and beastly passion . . . is named by our Physicians *Heroical* Love, and a more honorable title put upon it, *amor nobilis*, . . . because Noble men and women make a common practice of it, and are so ordinarily affected with it" (Burton, pt. III. ii. 1. 2; Draper, p. 122). For similar reasons, it is difficult to accept Hotson's conjecture (ch. vi) that Orsino is meant for the visiting Virginio Orsino, Duke of Bracciano,

and Olivia for the Virgin Queen; if Shakespeare intended flattery, it seems unlikely that he would have presented both characters in an ironic light.

14. Cp. Julina's speech in Riche, p. 66: " . . . men be of this condition, rather to desire those things which they cannot come by, than to esteem or value of that which . . . liberally is offered unto them; but if the liberality of my proffer hath made to seem less the value of the thing that I meant to present, it is but in your own conceit. . . . " Shakespeare returns to the problems of value and the self-destruction of desire in *Hamlet* and *Troilus*. Orsino's "shapes" and "fancy" recall Theseus' lines in *MND*, V.i.4–22; and in *Henry IV*, pt. 2, Falstaff connects them with drink: "A good sherris-sack . . . ascends me into the brain; . . . makes it apprehensive, quick, forgetive, full of nimble, fiery, and delectable shapes . . . " (IV.iii.107). These are points of contact between Orsino and Sir Toby.

15. Cp. Draper, pp. 215–219.

16. Cp. *MND*, I.i.65–78 (" . . . For aye to be in shady cloister mew'd"), and Portia, in *MV*, I.ii.112–114. In *The Comedy of Errors*, Shakespeare moves the scene from the Epidamnus of *Menaechmi* to Ephesus so as to make Aemilia the priestess, or "abbess", of Diana's temple there. Possibly he was turning to account the passage in *Miles Gloriosus*, where the courtesan pretends to give thanks to Diana of Ephesus for rescuing her from Neptune's blustering realm (Loeb ed., II.v.411 ff; cp. Aegeon's narrative of the storm in *C.E.*, I.i, which has no equivalent in *Menaechmi*). But in any case, the motif of a woman rescued from imposed celibacy after a sea-adventure is an important part of what could be called Shakespeare's mythology—Wilson Knight's "tempest" theme; cp. Portia again, (*MV*, III.ii.53–57), and, of course, Marina, Perdita and Miranda. (There are satiric references to a convent from which the heroine runs away in Bandello and *Gl'Ingannati*).

17. Cp. II.iii.10, III.i.62, III.iv.130. There are other echoes, mainly comic, of the theme of Olivia-cloister-moon at: I.ii.32 (gossip); I.iii.126–128 (Mistress Mall's curtained picture); I.v.20 (". . . let summer bear it out"); I.v.206 (" 'tis not that time of moon with me"); II.iii. 59, etc. ("rouse the night-owl in a catch"); II.iv.44 ("the knitters in the sun"); II.v.164 ("Daylight and champain discovers not more"); III.i.41 ("Foolry . . . does walk about the orb like the sun"); III.i.89 ("the heavens rain odours on you"); III.iv.58 ("midsummer madness"); IV.ii (Malvolio in darkness); IV.iii.1 ("that is the glorious sun"); IV.iii.28–35 ("conceal it . . . heavens so shine"); V.i.151 ("To keep in darkness . . . "); V.i.295–9 (Feste shouting); V.i.346 ("Kept in a dark house, visited by the priest"); and "the wind and the rain" in Feste's epilogue.

18. Cp. Orsino, I.iv.13–14. For Olivia's use of rhyme here, cp. Beatrice (*Much Ado*, III.i.107), Helena (*All's Well*, I.i.223) and Cressida (*Troilus*, I.ii.307).

19. Cp. I.v.53 (" . . . so beauty's a flower"), II.iv.38 ("For woman are as roses . . . "), II.iv.112 ("concealment, like a worm i' the bud . . . ").

20. Cp. Tarquin, in *Lucrece*, 432, and the setting there. It is worth noting that Olivia's seal is a "Lucrece" (II.v.96).

21. There is no real equivalent to this interview, or Olivia's share of it, in Shakespeare's likely sources, unless partly in Riche, p. 66 (quoted above, note 14. But cp. Pasquella, in *Gl'Ingannati*, II.iii, p. 339; and Luce, *TN*, p. 184, cites verbal parallels from Bandello for III.i.117 and 149). As to the moral argument of the tale, both the Italians and Riche dwell on the justice and reason of exchanging love for love—e.g. *Gl'Ingannati*, I.iii (quoted above, note 12), IV.ii (p. 349), V.ii (p. 390; the lover here decries "ingratitude", as in *TN*, III. iv.367), V.ii (quoted

above, note 11); Bandello, 273–275. Further, Bandello's heroine tells her master that his sufferings in his second love are a just retribution for ingratitude in his first: "you have received the return (*contracambio*) you deserved, because if you had been so much loved by a girl as beautiful as you say, you have done endlessly wrong to leave her for this one, who is avenging her without knowing it. A lover wants to be loved, not to follow someone in flight (*Egli si vuol amar chi ama e non seguir chi se ne fugge*). Who knows if this beautiful girl is not still in love with you and living in the greatest misery for you?" (Bandello, pp. 265–266). As Luce points out (*TN*, p. 184), this dialogue as a whole may have suggested Viola's dialogue with Orsino in II.iv.90–120; but the notion of love is still an exchange, not a gift. Similarly, Riche, p. 53, stresses "desert", or reciprocity, as "the ground of reasonable love", and he echoes Bandello: "for to love them that hate us, to follow them that fly from us, . . . who will not confess this to be an erroneous love, neither grounded upon wit nor reason?" Olivia's speech could almost be a reply to this.

22. See appendix to this article, "Shakespeare and Plautus", below.

23. Cp. Paul Reyher, *Essai sur les Idées dans l'Oeuvre de Shakespeare* (Paris, 1947), pp. 374–378.

24. *TN*, I.ii.42; II.ii.41; I.v.319; II.v.149.

25. Cp. the theme of "witchcraft" (not present in *Menaechmi*) in *CE*, I.ii.100; II.ii.189; III.ii.45–52, 153; IV.iii.11, 66; and IV.iv.146. Antonio's "witchcraft", however, also harks back to the "enchantment" Cesario has worked on Olivia (III.i.117).

26. Cp. the sailors in the storm in *CE*, I.i.75–95; and the speeches of Menaechmus of Syracuse, where, after receiving the courtesan's gifts, he thanks the gods and hurries off "while time and circumstance permit" ("dum datur mi occasio / tempusque"; *Menaechmi*, Loeb ed., III.ii.473–474, 551–553). Bandello's young man, at a similar point in the story, also decides to "try his luck" ("Lasciami andar a provar la mia fortuna", p. 267), but Sebastian comes nearer to Plautus; cp. note 23. The Italians virtually ignore the Plautine motif of resurrection, which Shakespeare develops; cp. note 29.

27. III.iv.231; cp. Orsino's "desires, like fell and cruel hounds" (I.i.21) and Olivia's metaphor at III.i.123–125.

28. Cp. Chambers, *Mediaeval Stage*, I, 190–198 (Christmas sword-dances), 206–227 (Mummers' plays), and *The English Folk-Play* (1933), pp. 3–9, 23–33 (the champions). Besides the rodomontade quoted above and the comic fighting, the following details of contact or resemblance between the duel episode and the Mummers' plays seem worth noting: two of the main actors here are a fool and a woman dressed as a man; there is a lady in the background, like St. George's Sabra (*EFP*, pp. 25, 175), and the duel is a kind of wooing contest (*EFP*, pp. 99–104); "cockatrices" and "firago" suggest the Dragon (*EFP*, pp. 30, 156, 177, 204); the deliberate nonsense and Fabian's "bear" (III.iv.307–308) recall the clowning in *Mucedorus* (which has Mummers' play associations—cp. R. J. E. Tiddy, *The Mummers' Play*, pp. 84–85, 129–133); Sir Andrew's offer of a reward for sparing his life has some resemblance to Jack of Lent's offer in the processional game described by Machyn (Chambers, *EFP*, pp. 155–156), while Antonio's entry corresponds to the entry of a Mummers' play Doctor; and finally, like the Mummers' play combats (*EFP*, p. 194), the duel is followed by a kind of resurrection—the resurrection of one of the fighters' second self.

On the other hand (apart from a desire to satirize the duello), there is a possible source for this episode in the episode of feigned madness and demonic possession in *Menaechmi*, V.ii (which Shakespeare had already used in *CE*, IV.iv). Antonio's part resembles the sequel in *Men.*, V.vii–viii, where the slave rushes in to rescue his master's twin from a scuffle, is promised his liberty, and then loses it again; and there, too, the episode of "devils" leads on to a resurrection. In addition, Antonio's part here recalls the passages in *CE* where Aegeon is arrested on a journey of love (I.i.124–139), and where the Officer arrests Angelo for debt (IV.i); and this indirectly strengthens the case for attributing this part of *TN* to a borrowing from Plautus. It is quite plausible, however, to suppose that Shakespeare noted the likeness between the resurrection motif and the folk-plays and the resurrection motif in Plautus, and decided to exploit it.

29. Antonio's lines about "empty trunks" hark back to Viola's speeches earlier (at I.ii.46–50 and II.ii.28–29) and to speeches in the previous comedies, e.g. Bassanio in the casket scene (*MV*, III.ii.73 ff.). But the tone of his "idolatry" metaphor rather points forward to the debate between Troilus and Hector in *Troilus*, II.ii. Cp. Bacon's comments on love as the worship of an "idol", "and how it braves the nature and value of things", in his essay "Of Love".

30. The first offspring of Folly, according to Erasmus, are Drunkenness, Ignorance and Self-Love.

31. Cp. Morris P. Tilley, "The Organic Unity of *TN*", *PMLA*, XXIX (1914).

32. *TN*, I.v.129–133; I.iii.85 and II.iii.145–150. There are many other instances, e.g.: I.iii.129 ("go to church in a galliard"); I.v.9–15 ("a good lenten answer . . . "); I.v.28 (Maria "as witty a piece of Eve's flesh . . . "); I.v.57 ("cucullus non facit monachum"); I.v.70–3 (Olivia's brother's soul in "hell"); II.iii.119 ("by Saint Anne"; cp. Hotson, p. 101); II.v.43 ("Fie on him, Jezebel!"); III.i.3–7 (Feste lives "by the church"); III.ii.16 ("Noah"); III.ii.31 ("a Brownist"); III.ii.71–74 ("Malvolio is turned heathen, a very renegado; for there is no Christian, that means to be saved by believing rightly, can ever believe such impossible passages of grossness"); III.ii.78; III.iv.89–131 ("all the devils in hell . . . the fiend is rough . . . 'tis not for gravity to play at cherry-pit with Satan . . . Get him to say his prayers", etc.); III.iv.245–306 ("devil", repeated; "souls and bodies hath he divorced three . . . death and sepulchre . . . perdition of souls"); IV.ii.1–63 (Sir Topas, "the old hermit of Prague", "Satan", "the Egyptians in their fog", Pythagoras and the soul, etc.); III.iv.126–137 ("Like to the old Vice . . . Adieu, goodman devil"); V.i.35–38 (Christmas dicing—cp. Hotson, p. 164,—and "the bells of Saint Bennet"); V.i.45 ("the sin of covetousness"); V.i.178–180 ("For the love of God . . . the very devil incardinate"); V.i.286 ("Beelzebub"); V.i.289–299 ("gospels"—cp. J. Dover Wilson, *TN*, Cambridge ed., p. 168); V.i.381 (the whirligig—cp. Hotson, p. 164). In addition, Sir Toby anticipates Sebastian's reference to astrology (I.iii.139, II.i.3). By contrast with these numerous comic references to religion, the serious actors cite mythology; and, apart from Olivia's Priest, also a little comic, they hardly refer to orthodox religion at all (unless Antonio's words at III.iv.327 and 363 contain such a reference implicitly—"I take the fault upon me", and "Do not . . . make me so unsound a man"; cp. Wilson, p. 156). Among the sub-plot actors, however, Malvolio is notable for his references to "Jove" (II.v.177, 183; III.iv.79, 87). Wilson, p. 97, argues that these are a sign of alterations in the text, to satisfy the statute of 1606 against blasphemy; but they seem more likely to be a comic sign that Malvolio is coming within the orbit of romance.

33. Draper, chs. ii–iii, gives much illuminating material on the social background of Sir Toby and Sir Andrew. But he introduces the very questionable assumption that Sir Andrew is meant to be a social climber of nouveau-riche parentage. Draper bases his argument on Sir Andrew's "carpet"-knighthood and his boorishness. But the son of an ambitious self-made man would have been quite likely to be sent to a university (like Yellowhammer junior in *A Chaste Maid in Cheapside*); and, on the other side, a gentleman might buy a knighthood (if that is in fact what "carpet consideration" implies—Draper, p. 48). Sir Andrew's follies are simply those of a wealthy heir. He admires his horse, has no sense of humor, is quarrelsome, frowns or capers without reason, has no languages, dresses absurdly, and gets drunk—and this is the catalogue of follies in Portia's noble suitors in *MV*, I.iii. He is thin, vain, and insignificant, like Justice Shallow in his youth, and has grown up a similar ignoramus (*2 H. IV*, III.ii, V.i.65–80); precisely as Orlando, too, fears to grow up if he, a "gentleman" by birth, is kept "rustically at home" for his education (*AYLI*, I.i). Some of Shakespeare's contemporaries comment scornfully on the English custom of keeping a wealthy heir "like a mome" on his estate, while his younger brother must fend for himself (T. Wilson, *The State of England, 1600*, ed. F. J. Fisher, pp. 23–24; cp. *Cyvile and Uncyvile Life*, 1579, Roxburghe Library ed., p. 24; Fynes Moryson, *Itinerary*, 1617, ed. MacLehose, IV,61). Sir Andrew, with his self-esteem, seems just such an heir, now converting himself into an Improvident Gallant. In short (apart from his ambitions on Olivia, which are really very faint), the point of the satire is not that Sir Andrew is trying to climb above his class, but that he is a gentleman born, adjusting himself foolishly to changing manners and conditions. The same could be said of the comparable characters in Ben Jonson, e.g. Master Stephen or Kastril, the angry boy.

34. E.g. O. J. Campbell, *Shakespeare's Satire* (New York, 1943), pp. 84–88; Draper, ch. v. The Countess's Steward in *All's Well* is apparently a gentleman by rank; Antonio in *The Duchess of Malfi* is certainly one; and the historical characters who have been suggested as possible originals for Malvolio have been of the rank of knights or above (cp. Luce, *Apolonius and Silla*, p. 95; Draper, pp. 110–111; Hotson, ch. v). The argument that Malvolio must be plebeian because he is presumptuous seems to rest on a false assumption about Elizabethan satire.

1959—C. L. Barber. "Testing Courtesy and Humanity in *Twelfth Night*," from *Shakespeare's Festive Comedy*

C. L. Barber was a professor of literature at the University of California, Santa Cruz. He also wrote *The Whole Journey: Shakespeare's Power of Development* and *The Story of Language*.

. . . nature to her bias drew in that.

The title of *Twelfth Night* may well have come from the first occasion when it was performed, whether or not Dr. Leslie Hotson is right in arguing that its first night was the court celebration of the last of the twelve days of Christmas on January 6, 1600–1601.[1] The title tells us that the play is like holiday misrule—though not just like it, for it adds "or what you will." The law student John Manningham, who saw it at the Middle Temple's feast on February 2, 1602, wrote in his diary that it was "much like the Comedy of Errores, or Menechmi in Plautus, but most like and neere to that in Italian called *Inganni*." Actually, Shakespeare used, in addition to Plautine devices with which he was familiar, not *Gl'Inganni* to which Manningham refers, but Rich's tale *Of Apolonius and Silla*, a romance perhaps derived indirectly from that Italian comedy. And he used no written source for the part Manningham specially praised: "A good practise in it to make the Steward beleeve his Lady widdowe was in love with him. . . . "[2] So *Twelfth Night* puts together a tale from a romance, Plautine farce, festivity, and the sort of merry sport or "practice" which Shakespeare customarily added from his own invention.

Shakespeare can be inclusive in his use of traditions because his powers of selection and composition can arrange each element so that only those facets of it show which will serve his expressive purpose. He leaves out the dungeon in which Rich's jealous Orsino shuts up Viola, as well as Sebastian's departure leaving Olivia with child; but he does not hesitate to keep such events as the shipwreck, or Sebastian's amazing marriage to a stranger, or Orsino's threat to kill Viola. It is not the credibility of the event that is decisive, but what can be expressed through it. Thus the shipwreck is made the occasion for Viola to exhibit an undaunted, aristocratic mastery of adversity—she settles what she shall do next almost as though picking out a costume for a masquerade:

> I'll serve this duke,
> Thou shalt present me as an eunuch to him;
> It may be worth thy pains. For I can sing,
> And speak to him in several sorts of music . . .
> (I.ii.55–58)

What matters is not the event, but what the language says as gesture, the aristocratic, free-and-easy way she settles what she will do and what the captain will do to help her. The pathetical complications which are often dwelt on in the romance are not allowed to develop far in the play; instead Viola's spritely language conveys the fun she is having in playing a man's part, with a hidden womanly perspective about it. One cannot quite say that she is playing in a masquerade, because disguising *just* for the fun of it is a different thing. But the same sort of festive pleasure in transvestism is expressed.

It is amazing how little happens in *Twelfth Night*, how much of the time people are merely talking, especially in the first half, before the farcical complications are sprung. Shakespeare is so skillful by now in rendering attitudes by the gestures of easy conversation that when it suits him he can almost do without events. In the first two acts of *Twelfth Night* he holds our interest with a bare minimum of tension while unfolding a pattern of contrasting attitudes and tones in his several persons. Yet Shakespeare's whole handling of romantic story, farce, and practical joke makes a composition which moves in the manner of his earlier festive comedies, through release to clarification.[3]

"A most extracting frenzy"

Olivia's phrase in the last act, when she remembers Malvolio and his "madness," can summarize the way the play moves:

> A most extracting frenzy of mine own
> From my remembrance clearly banish'd his.
> (V.i.288–289)

People are caught up by delusions or misapprehensions which take them out of themselves, bringing out what they would keep hidden or did not know was there. *Madness* is a key word. The outright gull Malvolio is already "a rare turkey-cock" from "contemplation" (II.v.35) before Maria goes to work on him with her forged letter. "I do not now fool myself, to let imagination jade me" (II.v.179), he exclaims when he has read it, having been put "in such a dream that, when the image of it leaves him, he must run mad" (II.v.210–211). He is too self-absorbed actually to run mad, but when he comes at Olivia, smiling and cross-gartered, she can make nothing else of it: "Why, this is very mid-summer madness" (III.iv.61). And so the merrymakers have the chance to put him in a dark room and do everything they can to face him out of his five wits.

What they bring about as a "pastime" (III.iv.151), to "gull him into a nayword, and make him a common recreation" (II.iii.145–146), happens unplanned to others by disguise and mistaken identity. Sir Toby, indeed, "speaks nothing but madman" (I.v.115) without any particular occasion. "My masters, are you mad?" (II.iii.93) Malvolio asks as he comes in to try to stop the midnight singing. Malvolio is sure that he speaks for the countess when he tells Toby that "though she harbors you as her kinsman, she's nothing allied to your disorders" (II.iii.103). But in fact this sober judgment shows that he is not "any more than a steward" (II.iii.122). For his lady, dignified though her bearing is, suddenly finds herself doing "I know not what" (I.v.327) under the spell of Viola in her page's disguise: "how now? / Even so quickly may one catch the plague?" (I.v.313–314) "Poor lady," exclaims Viola, "she were better love a dream!" (II.ii.27) In their first interview, she had told the countess, in urging the count's suit, that "what is yours to bestow is not yours to reserve" (I.v.200–201). By the end of their encounter, Olivia says the same thing in giving way to her passion: "Fate, show thy force! Ourselves we do not owe" (I.v.329). And soon her avowals of love come pouring out, overcoming the effort at control which shows she is a lady:

> O, what a deal of scorn looks beautiful
> In the contempt and anger of his lip!
> A murd'rous guilt shows not itself more soon
> Than love that would seem hid: love's night is noon.
> Cesario, by the roses of the spring,
> By maidhood, honour, truth, and everything,
> I love thee so . . .
>   (III.i.157–163)

A little later, when she hears about Malvolio and his smile, she summarizes the parallel with "I am as mad as he, / If sad and merry madness equal be" (III. iv.15–16).

The farcical challenge and "fight" between Viola and Sir Andrew are another species of frantic action caused by delusion. "More matter for a May morning" (III.iv.156) Fabian calls it as they move from pretending to exorcise Malvolio's devil to pretending to act as solicitous seconds for Sir Andrew. When Antonio enters the fray in manly earnest, there is still another sort of comic error, based not on a psychological distortion but simply on mistaken identity. This Plautine sort of confusion leads Sebastian to exclaim, "Are all the people mad?" (IV. i.29) Just after we have seen "Malvolio the lunatic" (IV.ii.26) baffled in the dark room ("But tell me true, are you not mad indeed? or do you but counterfeit?" IV.ii.121–123), we see Sebastian struggling to understand his wonderful encounter with Olivia:

> This is the air; that is the glorious sun;
> This pearl she gave me, I do feel't and see't;
> And though 'tis wonder that enwraps me thus,
> Yet 'tis not madness.
>   (IV.iii.1–4)

The open-air clarity of this little scene anticipates the approaching moment when delusions and misapprehensions are resolved by the finding of objects appropriate to passions. Shakespeare, with fine stagecraft, spins the misapprehensions out to the last moment. He puts Orsino, in his turn, through an extracting frenzy, the Duke's frustration converting at last to violent impulses toward Olivia and Cesario, before he discovers in the page the woman's love he could not win from the countess.

That it should all depend on there being an indistinguishable twin brother always troubles me when I think about it, though never when I watch the play.

Can it be that we enjoy the play so much simply because it is a wish-fulfillment presented so skillfully that we do not notice that our hearts are duping our heads? Certainly part of our pleasure comes from pleasing make-believe. But I think that what chance determines about particular destinies is justified, as was the case with *The Merchant of Venice*, by the play's realizing dynamically general distinctions and tendencies in life.

"You are betroth'd both to a maid and man"

The most fundamental distinction the play brings home to us is the difference between men and women. To say this may seem to labor the obvious; for what love story does not emphasize this difference? But the disguising of a girl as a boy in *Twelfth Night* is exploited so as to renew in a special way our sense of the difference. Just as a saturnalian reversal of social roles need not threaten the social structure, but can serve instead to consolidate it, so a temporary, playful reversal of sexual roles can renew the meaning of the normal relation. One can add that with sexual as with other relations, it is when the normal is secure that playful aberration is benign. This basic security explains why there is so little that is queazy in all Shakespeare's handling of boy actors playing women, and playing women pretending to be men. This is particularly remarkable in *Twelfth Night*, for Olivia's infatuation with Cesario-Viola is another, more fully developed case of the sort of crush Phebe had on Rosalind. Viola is described as distinctly feminine in her disguise, more so than Rosalind:

> . . . they shall yet belie thy happy years
> That say thou art a man. Diana's lip
> Is not more smooth and rubious; thy small pipe
> Is as the maiden's organ, shrill and sound,
> And all is semblative a woman's part.
>   (I.iv.30–34)

When on her embassy Viola asks to see Olivia's face and exclaims about it, she shows a woman's way of relishing another woman's beauty—and sensing another's vanity: "'Tis beauty truly blent . . . . " "I see you what you are—you are too proud" (I.v.257, 269). Olivia's infatuation with feminine qualities in a youth takes her, doing "I know not what," from one stage of life out into another, from shutting out suitors in mourning for her brother's memory, to ardor for a man, Sebastian, and the clear certainty that calls out to "husband" in the confusion of the last scene.

We might wonder whether this spoiled and dominating young heiress may not have been attracted by what she could hope to dominate in Cesario's youth—but it was not the habit of Shakespeare's age to look for such implications. And besides, Sebastian is not likely to be dominated; we have seen him respond to Andrew when the ninny knight thought he was securely striking Cesario:

> *Andrew.* Now, sir, have I met you again? There's for you!
> *Sebastian.* Why, there's for thee, and there, and there!
> (IV.i.26–27)

To see this manly reflex is delightful—almost a relief—for we have been watching poor Viola absurdly perplexed behind her disguise as Sir Toby urges her to play the man: "Dismount thy tuck, be yare in thy preparation. . . . Therefor on, or strip your sword naked; for meddle you must, that's certain" (III. iv.244–245, 274–276). She is driven to the point where she exclaims in an aside: "Pray God defend me! A little thing would make me tell them how much I lack of a man" (III.iv.331–333). What she lacks, Sebastian has. His entrance in the final scene is preceded by comical testimony of his prowess, Sir Andrew with a broken head and Sir Toby halting. The particular implausibility that there should be an identical man to take Viola's place with Olivia is submerged in the general, beneficent realization that there is such a thing as a man. Sebastian's comment when the confusion of identities is resolved points to the general force which has shaped particular developments:

> So comes it, lady, you have been mistook.
> But nature to her bias drew in that.
> (V.i.266–267)

Over against the Olivia–Cesario relation, there are Orsino–Cesario and Antonio–Sebastian. Antonio's impassioned friendship for Sebastian is one of those ardent attachments between young people of the same sex which Shakespeare frequently presents, with his positive emphasis, as exhibiting the loving and lovable qualities later expressed in love for the other sex.[4] Orsino's fascination with Cesario is more complex. In the opening scene, his restless sensibility can find no object: "naught enters there, . . . / But falls into abatement . . . / Even in a minute" (I.i.11–14). Olivia might be an adequate object; she at least is the Diana the sight of whom has, he thinks, turned him to an Acteon torn by the hounds of desires. When we next see him, and Cesario has been only three days in his court, his entering question is "Who saw Cesario, ho?" (I.iv.10) and already he has unclasped to the youth "the book even of [his] secret soul" (I.iv.14). He has found an object. The delight he takes in Cesario's fresh youth and graceful responsiveness in conversation and in service, is one part of the spectrum of love for a woman, or better, it is a range of feeling that is common to love for a youth and love for a woman. For the audience, the woman who is present there, behind Cesario's disguise, is brought to mind repeatedly by the talk of love and of the differences of men and women in love. "My father had a daughter loved a man . . . " (II.iv.110)

> She never told her love,
> But let concealment, like a worm i' th' bud,
> Feed on her damask cheek.
>   (II.iv.113–115)

This supremely feminine damsel, who "sat like patience on a monument," is not Viola. She is a sort of polarity within Viola, realized all the more fully because the other, active side of Viola does not pine in thought at all, but instead changes the subject: ". . . and yet I know not. / Sir, shall we to this lady?—Ay, that's the theme" (II.iv.124–125). The effect of moving back and forth from woman to sprightly page is to convey how much the sexes differ yet how much they have in common, how everyone who is fully alive has qualities of both. Some such general recognition is obliquely suggested in Sebastian's amused summary of what happened to Olivia:

> You would have been contracted to a maid;
> Nor are you therein, by my life, deceiv'd:
> You are betroth'd both to a maid and man.
>   (V.i.267–270)

The countess marries the man in this composite, and the count marries the maid. He too has done he knows not what while nature drew him to her bias, for he has fallen in love with the maid without knowing it.

Liberty Testing Courtesy

We have seen how each of the festive comedies tends to focus on a particular kind of folly that is released along with love—witty masquerade in *Love's Labour's Lost*, delusive fantasy in A *Midsummer Night's Dream*, romance in *As You Like It*, and, in *The Merchant of Venice*, prodigality balanced against usury. *Twelfth Night* deals with the sort of folly which the title points to, the folly of misrule. But the holiday reference limits its subject too narrowly: the play exhibits the liberties which gentlemen take with decorum in the pursuit of pleasure and love, including the liberty of holiday, but not only that. Such liberty is balanced against time-serving. As Bassanio's folly of prodigality leads in the end to gracious fulfillment, so does Viola's folly of disguise. There is just a suggestion of the risks when she exclaims, not very solemnly,

> Disguise, I see thou art a wickedness
> Wherein the pregnant enemy does much.
>   (II.ii.28–29)

As in *The Merchant of Venice* the story of a prodigal is the occasion for an exploration of the use and abuse of wealth, so here we get an exhibition of the use and abuse of social liberty.

What enables Viola to bring off her role in disguise is her perfect courtesy, in the large, humanistic meaning of that term as the Renaissance used it, the *corteziania* of Castiglione. Her mastery of courtesy goes with her being the daughter of "that Sebastian of Messalina whom I know you have heard of": gentility shows through her disguise as does the fact that she is a woman. The impact on Olivia of Cesario's quality as a gentleman is what is emphasized as the countess, recalling their conversation, discovers that she is falling in love:

> 'What is thy parentage?'
> 'Above my fortunes, yet my state is well.
> I am a gentleman.' I'll be sworn thou art.
> Thy tongue, thy face, thy limbs, actions, and spirit
> Do give thee fivefold blazon. Not too fast! soft, soft!
> Unless the master were the man.
>   (I.v.308–313)

We think of manners as a mere prerequisite of living decently, like cleanliness. For the Renaissance, they could be almost the end of life, as the literature of courtesy testifies. *Twelfth Night* carries further an interest in the fashioning of a courtier which, as Miss Bradbrook points out,[5] appears in several of the early comedies, especially *The Two Gentlemen of Verona*, and which in different keys Shakespeare was pursuing, about the same time as he wrote *Twelfth Night*, in *Hamlet* and *Measure for Measure*. People in *Twelfth Night* talk of courtesy and manners constantly. But the most important expression of courtesy of course is in object lessons. It is their lack of breeding and manners which makes the comic butts ridiculous, along with their lack of the basic, free humanity which, be it virile or feminine, is at the center of courtesy and flowers through it.

Mr. Van Doren, in a fine essay, observes that *Twelfth Night* has a structure like *The Merchant of Venice*. "Once again Shakespeare has built a world out of music and melancholy, and once again this world is threatened by an alien voice. The opposition of Malvolio to Orsino and his class parallels the opposition of Shylock to Antonio and his friends. The parallel is not precise, and the contrast is more subtly contrived; Shakespeare holds the balance in a more delicate hand. . . ."[6] One way in which this more delicate balance appears is that the contest of revellers with intruder does not lead to neglecting ironies about those who are on the side of pleasure. We are all against Malvolio, certainly, in the great moment when the whole opposition comes into focus with Toby's "Dost thou think, because thou art virtuous, there shall be no more cakes and ale?" (II.iii.123–125) The festive spirit shows up the killjoy vanity of Malvolio's decorum. The steward shows his limits when he calls misrule "this uncivil rule." But one of the revellers is Sir Andrew, who reminds us that there is no necessary salvation in being a fellow who delights "in masques and revels sometimes altogether" (I.iii.121). There was no such ninny pleasure-seeker in *The Merchant of Venice*; his role continues Shallow's, the would-be-reveller who is comically inadequate. To put such a leg as his into "a flame-coloured stock" only shows how meager it is. This thin creature's motive is self-improvement: he is a version of the stock type of prodigal who is gulled in trying to learn how to be gallant. As in Restoration comedy the fop confirms the values of the rake, Auguecheek serves as foil to Sir Toby. But he also marks one limit as to what revelry can do for a man: "I would I had bestowed that time in the tongues that I have in fencing, dancing and bear-baiting" (I.iii.97–99).

Sir Toby is gentlemanly liberty incarnate, a specialist in it. He lives at his ease, enjoying heritage, the something-for-nothing which this play celebrates, as *The Merchant of Venice* celebrates wealth—what he has without having to deserve it is his kinsman's place in Olivia's household:

> *Maria.* What a caterwauling do you keep here! If my lady have not call'd up her steward Malvolio and bid him turn you out of doors, never trust me.
> *Sir Toby.* My lady's a Catayan, we are politicians, Malvolio's a Peg-a-Ramsay, and [sings] "Three merry men be we." Am I not consanguineous? Am I not of her blood? Tilly-vally, lady.
> (II.iii.76–83)

Sir Toby has by consanguinity what Falstaff has to presume on and keep by his wits: "Shall I not take mine ease in mine inn but I shall have my pocket pick'd?" (*1 H. IV* III.iii.92–94) So Sir Toby is witty without being as alert as Sir John; he does not need to be:

> *Olivia.* Cousin, cousin, how have you come so early by this lethargy?
> *Toby.* Lechery? I defy lechery. There's one at the gate.
> *Olivia.* Ay, marry, what is he?
> *Toby.* Let him be the devil an he will. I care not!
> Give me faith, say I. Well, it's all one.
> (I.v.131–137)

Stage drunkenness, here expressed by wit that lurches catch-as-catch-can, conveys the security of "good life" in such households as Olivia's, the old-fashioned sort that had not given up "housekeeping." Because Toby has "faith"—the faith that goes with belonging—he does not need to worry when Maria teases him about confining himself "within the modest limits of order." "Confine? I'll confine myself no finer than I am" (I.iii.8–11). In his talk as in his clothes, he has the ease of a gentleman whose place in the world is secure, so that, while he can find words like *consanguineous* at will, he can also say "Sneck up!" to Malvolio's accusation that he shows "no respect of persons, places nor time" (II.iii.99). Sir Toby is the sort of kinsman who would take the lead at such Christmas feasts as Sir Edward Dymoke patronized in Lincolnshire—a Talboys Dymoke.[7] His talk is salted with holiday morals: "I am sure care's an enemy of life" (I.iii.2–3). "Not to be abed before midnight is to be up betimes" (II.iii.1–2). He is like Falstaff in maintaining saturnalian paradox and in playing impromptu the role of lord of misrule. But in his whole relation to the world he is fundamentally different from Prince Hal's great buffoon. Falstaff makes a career of misrule; Sir Toby uses misrule to show up a careerist.

There is little direct invocation by poetry of the values of heritage and housekeeping, such as we get of the beneficence of wealth in *The Merchant of Venice*. But the graciousness of community is conveyed indirectly by the value put on music and song, as Mr. Van Doren observes. The Duke's famous opening lines start the play with music. His hypersensitive estheticism savors strains that have a dying fall and mixes the senses in appreciation: "like the sweet sound / That breathes upon a bank of violets" (I.i.5–6). Toby and his friends are more at ease about "O mistress mine," but equally devoted to music in their way. (Toby makes fun of such strained appreciation as the Duke's when he concludes their praises of the clown's voice with "To hear by the nose, it is dulcet in contagion" II.iii.57–58.) Back at court, in the next scene, the significance of music in relation to community is suggested in the Duke's lines about the "old and antique song":

> Mark it, Cesario; it is old and plain.
> The spinsters and the knitters in the sun,
> And the free maids that weave their thread with bones,
> Do use to chant it. It is silly sooth,
> And dallies with the innocence of love
> Like the old age.
>   (II.iv.44–49)

The wonderful line about the free maids, which throws such firm stress on "free" by the delayed accent, and then slows up in strong, regular monosyllables, crystallizes the play's central feeling for freedom in heritage and community. It is consciously nostalgic; the old age is seen from the vantage of "these most brisk and giddy-paced times" (II.iv.6).

Throughout the play a contrast is maintained between the taut, restless, elegant court, where people speak a nervous verse, and the free-wheeling household of Olivia, where, except for the intense moments in Olivia's amorous interviews with Cesario, people live in an easy-going prose. The contrast is another version of pastoral. The household is more than any one person in it. People keep interrupting each other, changing their minds, letting their talk run out into foolishness—and through it all Shakespeare expresses the day-by-day going on of a shared life:

> *Maria.* Nay, either tell me where thou hast been, or I will not open my
> lips so wide as a bristle may enter in way of thy excuse.
> (I.v.1–3)
> *Fabian.* . . . You know he brought me out o' favour with my lady about
> a bear-baiting here.
> *Toby.* To anger him we'll have the bear again . . .
> (II.v.8–11)
> *Fabian.* Why, we shall make him mad indeed.
> *Maria.* The house will be the quieter.
> (III.iv.146–147)

Maria's character is a function of the life of "the house"; she moves within it with perfectly selfless tact. "She's a beagle true-bred," says Sir Toby: her part in the housekeeping and its pleasures is a homely but valued kind of "courtiership."

All of the merrymakers show a fine sense of the relations of people, including robust Fabian, and Sir Toby, when he has need. The fool, especially, has this courtly awareness. We see in the first scene that he has to have it to live: he goes far enough in the direction of plain speaking to engage Olivia's unwilling attention, then brings off his thesis that *she* is the fool so neatly that he is forgiven. What Viola praises in the fool's function is just what we should expect in a play about courtesy and liberty:

> This fellow is wise enough to play the fool,
> And to do that well craves a kind of wit.
> He must observe their mood on whom he jests.
> The quality of persons and the time . . .
> (III.i.67–70)

It is remarkable how little Feste says that is counterstatement in Touchstone's manner: there is no need for ironic counterstatement, because here the ironies are embodied in the comic butts. Instead what Feste chiefly does is sing and beg—courtly occupations—and radiate in his songs and banter a feeling of liberty based on accepting disillusion. "What's to come is still unsure . . . Youth's a stuff will not endure" (II.iii.50, 53). In *The Merchant of Venice*, it was the gentlefolk who commented "How every fool can play upon the word!" but now it is the fool himself who says, with mock solemnity: "To see this age! A sentence is but a chev'ril glove to a good wit!" (III.i.12–13). He rarely makes the expected move, but conveys by his style how well he knows what moves are expected:

> so that, conclusions to be as kisses, if your four negatives make your two affirmatives, why then, the worse for my friends and the better for my foes.
> *Duke.* Why, this is excellent.
> *Feste. By* my troth, sir, no; though it pleases you to be one of my friends.
>   (V.i.24–29)

His feeling for people and their relations comes out most fully when he plays "Sir Topas the curate, who comes to visit Malvolio the lunatic" (IV.ii.25–26). This is the pastime of "dissembling" in a minister's gown that led to so much trouble for Sir Edward Dymoke's bailiff, John Craddock the elder.[8]

Viola, who as "nuntio" moves from tense court to relaxed household, has much in common with Feste in the way she talks, or better, uses talk; but she also commands effortlessly, when there is occasion, Shakespeare's mature poetic power:

> It gives a very echo to the seat
> Where love is throned.
>   (II.iv.21–22)

"Thou dost speak masterly," the Duke exclaims—as we must too. Part of her mastery is that she lets herself go only rarely, choosing occasions that are worthy. Most of the time she keeps her language reined in, often mocking it as she uses it, in Feste's fashion. Perhaps it is because he finds himself beaten at his own game that he turns on her ungraciously, as on no one else:

> *Viola.* I warrant thou art a merry fellow and car'st for nothing.
> *Clown.* Not so, sir; I do care for something; but in my conscience, sir, I do not care for you. If that be to care for nothing, sir, I would it would make you invisible.
>   (III.i.32–35)

Once when she is mocking the elaborate language of compliment, greeting Olivia with "the heavens rain odors on you," Sir Andrew overhears and is much impressed: "That youth's a rare courtier. 'Rain odors'—well" (III.i.97–98). He plans to get her fancy words by heart. Of course, as a rare courtier, she precisely does *not* commit herself to such high-flown, Osric-style expressions. Her constant shifting of tone in response to the situation goes with her manipulation of her role in disguise, so that instead of simply listening to her speak, we watch her conduct her speech, and through it feel her secure sense of proportion and her easy, alert consciousness: "To one of your receiving," says Olivia, "enough is shown" (III.i.131–132).

Olivia says that "it was never merry world / Since lowly feigning was called compliment" (III.i.109–110). As Sir Toby is the spokesman and guardian of that merry world, Malvolio is its antagonist. He shows his relation to festivity at once by the way he responds to Feste, and Olivia points the moral: he is "sick of self love" and tastes "with a distempered appetite." He is not "generous, guiltless, and of free disposition." Of course, nothing is more helpful, to get revelry to boil up, than somebody trying to keep the lid on— whatever his personal qualities. But the "stubborn and uncourteous parts" in Malvolio's character, to which Fabian refers in justifying the "device," are precisely those qualities which liberty shows up. Malvolio wants "to confine himself finer than he is," to paraphrase Toby in reverse: he practices behavior to his own shadow. His language is full of pompous polysyllables, of elaborate syntax deploying synonyms:

> Do ye make an alehouse of my lady's house, that ye squeak out your coziers' catches without any mitigation or remorse of voice? Is there no respect of place, persons, nor time in you?
>
> (II.iii.96–99)

In "loving" his mistress, as Cesario her master, he is a kind of foil, bringing out her genuine, free impulse by the contrast he furnishes. He does not desire Olivia's person; *that* desire, even in a steward, would be sympathetically regarded, though not of course encouraged, by a Twelfth-Night mood. What he wants is "to be count Malvolio," with "a demure travel of regard—telling them I know my place, as I would they should do theirs" (II.v.59–61). His secret wish is to violate decorum himself, then relish to the full its power over others. No wonder he has not a free disposition when he has such imaginations to keep under! When the sport betrays him into a revelation of them, part of the vengeance taken is to make him try to be festive, in yellow stockings, and cross-gartered, and smiling "his face into more lines than is in the new map with the augmentation of the Indies" (III.ii.91–93). Maria's letter *tells* him to go brave, be gallant, take liberties! And when we see him "acting this in an obedient hope," (as he puts it later) he is anything but free: "This does make some obstruction of the blood, this cross-gartering . . ." (III.iv.21–23).

In his "impossible passages of grossness," he is the profane intruder trying to steal part of the initiates' feast by disguising himself as one of them—only to be caught and tormented for his profanation. As with Shylock, there is potential pathos in his bafflement, especially when Shakespeare uses to the limit the conjuring of devils out of a sane man, a device which he had employed hilariously in *The Comedy of Errors*. There is no way to settle just how much of Malvolio's pathos should be allowed to come through when he is down and out in the dark hole. Most people now agree that Charles Lamb's sympathy for the steward's enterprise and commiseration for his sorrows is a romantic and bourgeois distortion. But he is certainly pathetic, if one thinks about it, because he is so utterly cut off from everyone else by his anxious self-love. He lacks the freedom which makes Viola so perceptive, and is correspondingly oblivious:

> *Olivia.* What kind o' man is he?
> *Malvolio.* Why, of mankind.
> (I.v.159–160)

He is too busy carrying out his mistress' instructions about privacy to notice that she is bored with it, as later he is too busy doing her errand with the ring to notice that it is a love-token. He is imprisoned in his own virtues, so that there is sense as well as nonsense in the fool's "I say there is no darkness but ignorance, in which thou art more puzzled than the Egyptians in their fog" (IV.ii.46–49). The dark house is, without any straining, a symbol: when Malvolio protests about Pythagoras, "I think nobly of the soul and no way approve his opinion," the clown's response is "Remain thou still in darkness." The pack of them are wanton and unreasonable in tormenting him; but his reasonableness will never let him out into "the air; . . . the glorious sun" (IV.iii.1) which they enjoy together. To play the dark-house scene for pathos, instead of making fun out of the pathos, or at any rate out of most of the pathos, is to ignore the dry comic light which shows up Malvolio's virtuousness as a self-limiting automatism.

Malvolio has been called a satirical portrait of the Puritan spirit, and there is some truth in the notion. But he is not hostile to holiday because he is a Puritan; he is like a Puritan because he is hostile to holiday. Shakespeare even mocks, in passing, the thoughtless, fashionable antipathy to Puritans current among gallants. Sir Andrew responds to Maria's "sometimes he is a kind of Puritan," with "if I thought that, I'd beat him like a dog" (II.iii.151–153). "The devil a Puritan he is, or anything constantly," Maria observes candidly, "but a time-pleaser" (II.iii.159–160). Shakespeare's two greatest comic butts, Malvolio and Shylock, express basic human attitudes which were at work in the commercial revolution, the new values whose development R. H. Tawney described in *Religion and the Rise of Capitalism*. But both figures are conceived at a level of esthetic abstraction which makes it inappropriate to identify them with specific social groups in the mingled actualities of history: Shylock, embodying ruthless money power, is no more to be equated with actual bankers than Malvolio, who has something of the Puritan ethic, is to be thought of as a portrait of actual Puritans. Yet, seen in the perspective of literary and social history, there is a curious appropriateness in Malvolio's presence, as a kind of foreign body to be expelled by laughter, in Shakespeare's last free-and-easy festive comedy. He is a man of business, and, it is passingly suggested, a hard one; he is or would like to be a rising man, and to rise he *uses* sobriety and morality. One could moralize the spectacle by observing that, in the long run, in the 1640's, Malvolio *was* revenged on the whole pack of them.

But Shakespeare's comedy remains, long after 1640, to move audiences through release to clarification, making distinctions between false care and true freedom and realizing anew, for successive generations, powers in human nature and society which make good the risks of courtesy and liberty. And this without blinking the fact that "the rain it raineth every day."

Outside the Garden Gate

Twelfth Night is usually placed just before *Hamlet* and the problem plays to make neat groupings according to mood, but it may well have been written after some of these works. In thinking about its relation to the other work of the period from 1600 to 1602 or 1603, it is important to recognize the independent artistic logic by which each play has its own unity. There are features of *Twelfth Night* that connect it with all the productions of this period. There is the side of Orsino's sensibility, for example, which suggests Troilus' hypersensitivity:

Enough, no more!
'Tis not so sweet now as it was before.
                              (I.i.7–8)

How will she love when the rich golden shaft
Hath kill'd the flock of all affections else
That live in her; when liver, brain, and heart,
Those sovereign thrones, are all supplied and fill'd,
Her sweet perfections, with one self king!
Away before me to sweet beds of flow'rs!
                              (I.i.35–40)

Troilus carries this sort of verse and feeling farther:

                    What will it be
When that the wat'ry palates taste indeed
Love's thrice-repured nectar? Death, I fear me;
Sounding destruction; or some joy too fine,
Too subtile-potent, tun'd too sharp in sweetness
For the capacity of my ruder powers.
                              (*Troi.* III.ii.21–26)

Troilus' lines are a much more physical and more anxious development of the exquisite, uncentered sort of amorousness expressed by Orsino. But in *Twelfth Night* there is no occasion to explore the harsh anti-climax to which such intensity is vulnerable, for instead of meeting a trivial Cressida in the midst of war and lechery, Orsino meets poised Viola in a world of revelry. The comparison with *Troilus and Cressida* makes one notice how little direct sexual reference there is in *Twelfth Night*—much less than in most of the festive comedies. It may be that free-hearted mirth, at this stage of Shakespeare's development, required more shamefastness than it had earlier, because to dwell on the physical was to encounter the "monstruosity in love" which troubled Troilus: "that the desire is boundless and the act a slave to limit" (*Troi.* III.ii.89–90).

It is quite possible that *Measure for Measure* and *All's Well That Ends Well* did not seem to Shakespeare and his audiences so different from *Twelfth Night* as they seem to us. Both of them use comic butts not unlike Andrew and Malvolio: Lucio and Parolles are, each his way, pretenders to community who are shown up ludicrously by their own compulsions, and so expelled. Our difficulty with these plays, what makes them problem plays, is that they do not feel festive; they are not merry in a deep enough way. Part of our response may well be the result of changes in standards and sentiments about sexual behavior, and of alterations in theatrical convention. But the fact remains that in both plays, release often leads, not simply to folly, but to the vicious or contemptible; and the manipulations of happy accidents which make all well in the end are not made acceptable by the achievement of distinctions about values or by a convincing expression of general beneficent forces in life. Shakespeare's imagination tends to dwell on situations and motives where the energies of life lead to degradation or destruction:

> Our natures do pursue
> Like rats that ravin down their proper bane,
> A thirsty evil, and when we drink, we die.
> (*Meas.* I.ii.132–134)

There's not a soldier of us all that, in the thanksgiving before meat, do relish the petition well that prays for peace.
(*Meas.* I.ii.14–17)

Pompey, you are partly a bawd, Pompey, howsoever you colour it in being a tapster, are you not? . . .
Pompey. Truly, sir, I am a poor fellow that would live.
(*Meas.* II.i.230–235)

This sort of paradox is not brought home to us in *Twelfth Night*. In the problem comedies, vicious or perverse release leads to developments of absorbing interest, if not always to a satisfying movement of feeling in relation to awareness. But that is beyond our compass here.

We can notice here that the fool in *Twelfth Night* has been over the garden wall into some such world as the Vienna of *Measure for Measure*. He never tells where he has been, gives no details. But he has an air of knowing more of life than anyone else—too much, in fact; and he makes general observations like

> Anything that's mended is but patch'd; virtue that transgresses is but
> patch'd with sin, and sin that amends is but patch'd with virtue. If that
> this simple syllogism will serve, so; if it will not, what remedy?
> (I.v.52–56)

His part does not darken the bright colors of the play; but it gives them a dark outline, suggesting that the whole bright revel emerges from shadow. In the wonderful final song which he is left alone on stage to sing, the mind turns to contemplate the limitations of revelry: "By swaggering could I never thrive. . . . " The morning after, the weather when the sky changes, come into the song:

> With tosspots still had drunken heads
> For the rain it raineth every day.
> (V.i.412–413)

It goes outside the garden gate:

> But when I come to man's estate,
> With hey, ho, the wind and the rain,
> 'Gainst knaves and thieves men shut their gate,
> For the rain it raineth every day.
> (V.i.402–405)

Yet the poise of mirth, achieved by accepting disillusion, although it is now precarious, is not lost:

> A great while ago the world begun,
> With hey, ho, the wind and the rain;
> But that's all one, our play is done,
> And we'll strive to please you everyday.
> (V.i.414–417)

There is a certain calculated let-down in coming back to the play in this fashion; but it is the play which is keeping out the wind and the rain.

The festive comic form which Shakespeare had worked out was a way of selecting and organizing experience which had it own logic, its own autonomy: there is no necessary reason to think that he did not play on that instrument in *Twelfth Night* after making even such different music as *Hamlet*. Indeed, across the difference in forms, the comedy has much in common with the tragedy: interest in courtesy and free-hearted manners; consciousness of language and play with it as though a sentence were but a chev'ril glove; the use of nonsequitur and nonsense. Malvolio absurdly dreams of such a usurpation of heritage, "having come from a day bed, where I have left Olivia sleeping," as Claudius actually accomplishes. The tragedy moves into regions where the distinction between madness and sanity begins to break down, to be recovered only through violence; the fooling with madness in the comedy is an enjoyment of the control which knows what is mad and what is not. The relation between the two plays, though not so close, is not unlike that which we have noticed between *Romeo and Juliet* and *A Midsummer Night's Dream*.

But there is a great deal in *Hamlet* which the festive comic form cannot handle. The form can only deal with follies where nature to her bias draws; the unnatural can appear only in outsiders, intruders who are mocked and expelled. But in *Hamlet*, it is insiders who are unnatural. There is a great deal of wonderful fooling in the tragedy: Hamlet's playing the all-licensed fool in Claudius' court and making tormented fun out of his shocking realization of the horror of life. For sheer power of wit and reach of comic vision, there are moments in *Hamlet* beyond anything in the comedies we have considered. But to control the expression of the motives he is presenting, Shakespeare requires different movement, within which comic release is only one phase. After *Twelfth Night*, comedy is always used in this subordinate way: saturnalian moments, comic counterstatements, continue to be important resources of his art, but their meaning is determined by their place in a larger movement. So it is with the heroic revels in *Antony and Cleopatra*, or with the renewal of life, after tragedy, at the festival in *The Winter's Tale*.

NOTES

1. In *The First Night of "Twelfth Night"* (New York, 1954), Dr. Hotson has recovered, once again, documents that are astonishingly *à propos*. The most exciting is a long letter home written by a real nobleman named Orsino, who was Elizabeth's honored guest when she witnessed a play "in the Hall, which was richly hanged and degrees placed round about it." Don Virginio Orsino's account to his Duchess of the way he was honored gives a vivid picture of the Twelfth Day occasion at court, which Mr. Hotson skillfully supplements with

other evidence, much of it also new, so as to give us the most complete and graphic description we have of the circumstances of a dramatic performance at a court holiday. The Duke's candid letter reports that "there was acted a mingled comedy, with pieces of music and dances" (*una commedia mescolata, con musiche e balli*). But then it adds "and this too I am keeping to tell by word of mouth." What maddening bad luck! Here, and everywhere else, the clinching proof eludes Dr. Hotson, despite his skill and persistence. He himself cannot resist regarding it as a fact that *Twelfth Night* was the play in question on January 6, 1600–1601. But a sceptic can begin by asking where, in *Twelfth Night*, are those *balli* which Don Virginio witnessed—the play is notable, among Shakespeare's gay comedies, for its *lack* of dances. One could go on to ask whether it would not be more likely that the name Orsino would be used sometime *after* the great man's visit, when the elegant ring of it would still sound in people's ears but no offense be done. A devil's advocate could go on and on, so rich, and so conjectural, is Dr. Hotson's book.

But it makes a real contribution, even if one is not convinced that the play on that night must have been *Twelfth Night*, and even if one rejects many of its sweeping conclusions about such matters as staging. Dr. Hotson is a "literalist of the historical imagination," to use Marianne Moore's phrase. He has produced something equivalent to an "imaginary garden with real toads in" it—real circumstances and actions of Elizabethan life. He makes us aware of what the high day at court was like. And he describes and exemplifies many features of Twelfth Night custom in a fresh way, and so defines for us the *sort* of thing that Shakespeare refers to by his title. He also provides, from his remarkable knowledge of the period, a wealth of useful incidental glosses to hard places in the play.

But useful as his book can be, whether literally right or not, it is very misleading in one respect. For he writes as though the festive quality of *Twelfth Night* were wholly derived, on a one-to-one sort of basis, from its being commissioned for a court revel. He neglects the fact that, whatever its first night, the play was designed to work, also, on the public stage, so that it had to project the spirit of holiday into forms that would be effective everyday. He also ignores the fact that by the time Shakespeare came to write *Twelfth Night*, festive comedy was an established specialty with him.

2. E. K. Chambers, *William Shakespeare*, II, 327–328.

3. I hope that a reader who is concerned only with *Twelfth Night* will nevertheless take the time to read the generalized account of festive comedy in Ch. 1, for that introduction is assumed in the discussion here.

4. The latest treatment of this motif, in *The Two Noble Kinsmen* (especially Act I, Scene iii), is as generously beautiful as the exquisite handling of it which we have examined in *A Midsummer Night's Dream* (above, pp. 129–130).

5. *Shakespeare and Elizabethan Poetry*, Ch. IX.

6. *Shakespeare*, p. 161.

7. The whole encounter between Talboys Dymoke's revellers and the Earl of Lincoln is remarkably like that between Sir Toby's group and Malvolio. See Ch. 3, pp. 37–51. The parallels are all the more impressive because no influence or "source" relationship is involved; there must have been many such encounters.

8. See above, pp. 46–48.

1966—Jan Kott. From "Shakespeare's Bitter Arcadia," from *Shakespeare Our Contemporary*

Jan Kott (1914–2001), a critic, translator, and professor, was born in Poland and taught at the University of Warsaw. In 1969, he came to the United States and taught at the State University of New York at Stonybrook. Among his books are *The Bottom Translation: Marlowe and Shakespeare and the Carnival Tradition* and *The Eating of the Gods: An Interpretation of Greek Tragedy.*

Twelfth Night opens with a lyrical fugue accompanied by an orchestra:

> If music be the food of love, play on,
> Give me excess of it, that, surfeiting,
> The appetite may sicken, and so die.
> That strain again! It had a dying fall. (I, 1)

The exposition gives one the impression of a broken string; broken by itself, or by someone. It is like an overture in which the instruments got mixed up. From the first scene, music and lyrical elements sound in disharmony. The orchestra has stopped, then begins again. In vain:

> . . . Enough, no more!
> 'Tis not so sweet now as it was before. (I, 1)

The passions are hungry, but choke with their own appetite. The Duke's monologue is spoken in the style and poetic diction we know from the Sonnets. The style is refined, the diction authentic. There is tension and anxiety in it. Love is an entry into the sphere of risk and uncertainty; everything in it is possible.

> O spirit of love, how quick and fresh art thou!
> . . . .
> . . . So full of shapes is fancy
> That it alone is high fantastical. (I, 1)

This hurrying of images we also know from the Sonnets. The lyrical fugue breaks just as suddenly as the music. The dialogue becomes brutal and quick:

> *Curio.* Will you go hunt, my lord?
> *Duke.* What, Curio?
> *Curio.* The hart. (I, 1)

From the very first lines everything in *Twelfth Night* is ambiguous. The hunt is for Olivia. But the hunter has been hunted down himself. The Duke himself is both Actaeon and stag. Again the phrasing reminds one of the Sonnets:

And my desires, like fell and cruel hounds,
E'er since pursue me. (I, 1)

Viola with the Captain will presently be shipwrecked ashore the very same country of Illyria. Shakespeare deals with the plot of a sister losing her twin brother in a sea storm, in just a couple of lines. The plot is a pretext. The theme of the play is disguise. Viola, in order to serve the Duke, has to pretend she is a boy. Girls have dressed up as boys in fairy tales, stories, and legends, in the folklore of all peoples, in lyric and epic poetry from Homer to the present time.[16] They hide their sex under armour in order to fight in war; or under a monk's hood to enter a monastery; they put on students' clothes to enter an Alma Mater. The Middle Ages knew heroic disguise and hagiographic disguise. The Renaissance took a liking to amorous disguise. We find it in Italian comedy, as well as in the volumes of tales from which Shakespeare derived the plots and ideas for his comedies. Disguise had its justification in prevailing customs. Girls could not travel alone; they were not even supposed to walk alone in the evenings in the streets of Italian cities. Disguise had its theatrical justification, too: it created at the outset a *quid pro quo*, facilitated the development of the plot, was a ready-made farcical situation.

        . . . I'll serve this duke,
Thou shalt present me as an eunuch to him. (I, 2)

Disguise was not anything out of the ordinary. But in this first scene between Viola and the Captain we observe the striking brutality of the dialogue. In the first version of the comedy, say the experts, Viola was to sing the songs later given to the Clown, and that is why the Captain introduces her to the Duke as an Italian *castrato*. But even with this correction there is something shocking in the proposition. A young girl is to turn into a eunuch. It is as if a chill went down our spines. As with everything in Shakespeare, this is intended. The same words will be repeated, only more strongly:

Be you his eunuch, and your mute I'll be.
When my tongue blabs, then let mine eyes not see. (I, 2)

Disguise was nothing out of the ordinary, but in *Twelfth Night* there is something disturbing in it. A girl disguised herself as boy, but first a boy had disguised himself as girl. On the Elizabethan stage female parts were acted by boy actors. That was a limitation, as theatre historians well know. Female parts in Shakespeare are decidedly shorter than male parts. Shakespeare was well aware of the limitations of boy actors. They could play girls; with some difficulty they could play old women. But how could a boy act a mature woman? In all Shakespeare's plays, in the whole of Elizabethan drama even, there are very few such parts. Lady Macbeth and Cleopatra are sexually mature. Their parts, however, are curtailed to suit a boy actor's scope. This is a fact known to all actresses who have played Cleopatra or Lady Macbeth. There is little substance in those parts; as if whole pages had been torn out of them, they are full of gaps. Shakespeare was afraid to show Cleopatra in love scenes, he preferred to relate them. He described her physical charms, but did not want to show them. Between Macbeth and his wife matters of sex are never clearly explained. Either the conjugal bed was burnt-out land for them, or in this marriage the woman had the role of the man. In *Macbeth*, or in *Antony and Cleopatra* one can see how Shakespeare grappled with the limitations of his actors. But on at least two occasions Shakespeare used this limitation as the theme and theatrical instrument of comedy. *Twelfth Night* and *As You Like It* were written for a stage on which boys played the parts of girls. The disguise is a double one; played on two levels as it were: a boy dresses up as girl who disguises herself as boy.

> 'Tis beauty truly blent, whose red and white
> Nature's own sweet and cunning hand laid on.
> Lady, you are the cruell'st she alive
> If you will lead these graces to the grave,
> And leave the world no copy. (I, 5)

This passage has been compared with the Sonnets. Even the actual words are similar:

> She carv'd thee for her seal, and meant thereby
> Thou shouldst print more, not let that copy die. (XI)

That appeal was addressed by a man to a youth who was his lover and patron at the same time. In *Twelfth Night* the lines are spoken by the Duke's page to Countess Olivia; by a girl disguised as boy, to a boy disguised as girl. But the girl disguised as boy is a boy disguised as girl.

> What country, friends, is this?
> This is Illyria, lady. (I, 2)

We are still in Illyria. In that country ambiguity is the principle of love as well as of comedy. For, in fact, Viola is neither a boy nor a girl. Viola-Cesario is the "master mistress" of the Sonnets. The music of *Twelfth Night* has been written for that particular instrument. Viola is an ephebe and an androgyny.

> Dear lad, believe it;
> For they shall yet belie thy happy years
> That say thou art a man. Diana's lip
> Is not more smooth and rubious; thy small pipe
> Is as the maiden's organ, shrill and sound,
> And all is semblative a woman's part. (I, 4)

Duke Orsino, Viola, Olivia are not fully drawn characters. They are blank, and the only element that fills them is love. They cannot be dissociated from one another. They have no independent being. They exist only in and through mutual relationships. They are infected, and they infect, with love. Orsino is in love with Olivia, Olivia is in love with Cesario, Cesario is in love with Orsino. That is how things look on the surface of the dialogue, on the upper level of Shakespearean disguise. A man, a youth, a woman: love has three faces, as in the Sonnets. This is the Illyria theme. Duke Orsino is the First Person here. He personifies the *Eros socraticus*:

> There is no woman's sides
> Can bide the beating of so strong a passion
> As love doth give my heart; no woman's heart
> So big to hold so much; they lack retention.
> Alas, their love may be call'd appetite—
> No motion of the liver, but the palate. (II, 4)

And a little later, in the same outburst:

> . . . Make no compare
> Between that love a woman can bear me
> And that I owe Olivia. (II, 4)

Everyone in Illyria speaks about love in verse. It is a refined, occasionally too contrived verse. Authentic drama takes place under the surface of that court rhetoric. Only sometimes the rhythm is broken and a cry reaches out to the surface. So Olivia cries after Cesario's first departure:

Even so quickly may one catch the plague? (I, 5)

This cry might have been uttered by Orsino or by Viola. Every character here has something of the fair youth and the Dark Lady. Every character has been endowed with a bitter knowledge about love. Love in Illyria is violent and impatient; it cannot be gratified or reciprocated.

> . . . As I am man,
> My state is desperate for my master's love.
> As I am woman (now alas the day!),
> What thriftless sighs shall poor Olivia breathe! (II. 2)

As in the Sonnets, the three characters exhaust all forms of love. Olivia loves Cesario, Cesario loves Orsino, Orsino loves Olivia. But Cesario is Viola. On the middle level of Shakespearean disguise Olivia loves Viola, Viola loves Orsino, Orsino loves Olivia. Shakespeare's triangle has been modified: there are now two women and one man, or rather a man, a girl, and a woman.

> How will this fadge? My master loves her dearly;
> And I (poor monster) fond as much on him;
> And she (mistaken) seems to dote on me. (II, 2)

Viola seems to Olivia a girlish youth and to Orsino a boyish girl. A Shakespearean androgyne acts a youth for Olivia and a girl for Orsino. This triangle is now commuted for the third time. Olivia and Orsino are now simultaneously in love with Cesario-Viola, with the youth-girl. Illyria is a country of erotic madness. Shakespearean names and places often have hidden associations. The circle has been closed, but it is a *circulus vitiosus*. In all metamorphoses, on all levels of Shakespearean disguise, these three—Olivia, Viola, and Orsino—chase one another, unable to join. Like wooden horses on a merry-go-round, to use Sartre's expression. Viola-Cesario incessantly circles between Olivia and Orsino.

The appearance of Sebastian does not really make any difference. Sebastian is a character in the plot of the play, but does not participate in the real love drama. He was taken over by Shakespeare lock, stock, and barrel from the Italian story to provide the solution proper for a comedy. But even in the adventures of this conventional character Shakespeare does not abandon ambiguity. In Illyria the aura of inversion embraces everybody:

> I could not stay behind you. My desire,
> More sharp than filed steel, did spur me forth. (III, 3)

Antonio, the other captain of the ship, is in love with Sebastian. He has saved him from shipwreck and now accompanies him on his adventures, following him round Illyria. He is faithful and brave, but also ridiculous and common. He should be big and fat, very ugly, should have an uncouth beard and look amazingly like the first Captain who accompanied Viola. Shakespeare frequently repeats in the *buffo* tone a theme previously dealt with seriously or lyrically. Sebastian is Viola's twin and double. If Viola is boyish, Sebastian must be girlish. A bearded giant now chases a girlish youth round Illyria. This is the last but one of *Twelfth Night*'s metamorphoses.

The appearance of Sebastian does not dispel the basic ambiguity of erotic situations in Illyria, but, on the contrary, seems to aggravate it even more. Who has been deceived? Olivia or Orsino? Who has been deluded by appearance? Is desire part of the order of nature, or of love? Love is mad. But what about nature? Can nature be mad and irrational? Olivia fell in love with Cesario; Cesario turned out to be Viola. But Viola changed again into Sebastian:

> . . . you have been mistook.
> But nature to her bias drew in that. (V, 1)
> A youth fell in love with the Duke; the youth was a disguised girl.

Nothing stands in the way of another marriage to be concluded:

> Your master quits you; and for your service done him,
> So much against the mettle of your sex,
> . . . .
> . . . you shall from this time be
> Your master's mistress. (V, 1)

The comedy is over. *Twelfth Night; or, What You Will.* What will you have: a boy, or a girl? The actors take off their costumes: first the Duke, then Viola and Olivia. The last metamorphosis of the amorous triangle has been accomplished. What remains is a man and two youths. "But nature to her bias drew in that." A boy acted girl who acted boy; then the boy changed again into a girl who again turned into a boy. Viola transformed herself into Cesario, then Cesario became Viola, who turned into Sebastian. Ultimately then, in this comedy of errors, what was just an appearance? There is only one answer: sex. Love and desire pass from a youth to a girl and from a girl to a youth. Cesario is Viola, Viola is Sebastian. The court model of ideal love has been ironically analysed to the end. Or rather, presented more realistically.

> . . . So full of shapes is fancy
> That it alone is high fantastical. (I, 1)

Genet's play *The Maids* begins with a scene in which the mistress punishes the maid, scolding and slapping her on the face. After a dozen lines or so we begin to realize that this is a game, that on the stage there is no mistress or maid, but two sisters, one of whom pretends to be the mistress and the other—her own sister. They play a comedy of rebellion and humiliation. In *The Maids* there are three female parts: the mistress and two sisters, but in a commentary to the play Genet asks that all parts be acted by men. Passion is one; it only has different faces: of man and woman; of revulsion and adoration; of hate and desire.

There have been productions of *Twelfth Night* in which Sebastian and Viola were acted by one and the same person. This seems the only solution, even if its consistent treatment requires the epilogue to be dealt with in a thoroughly conventional manner. But it is not enough for Cesario-Viola-Sebastian to be acted by one person. That person must be a man. Only then will the real theme of Illyria, erotic delirium or the metamorphoses of sex, be shown in the theatre.

NOTE

16. The motif of the "change of sexes" is listed (ATh 514) in the international catalogue of popular fairy tales. On this motif in legends, stories and fairy tales, cf. J. Krzyzanowski, *Dziewczyna chlopcem* (Girl turned boy), *Slavia Orientalis*, vol. XII (1963), no. 2.

—◇◇◇—   —◇◇◇—   —◇◇◇—

1987—Harold Bloom. "Introduction," from *Twelfth Night* (Chelsea House)

Harold Bloom is Sterling Professor of the Humanities at Yale University. He has edited many anthologies of literature and literary criticism and is the author of more than 30 books, including *The Western Canon* and *Shakespeare: The Invention of the Human.*

Clearly a kind of farewell to unmixed comedy, *Twelfth Night* nevertheless seems to me much the funniest of Shakespeare's plays, though I have yet to see it staged in a way consonant with its full humor. As some critics have noted, only Feste the clown among all its characters is essentially sane, and even he allows himself to be dragged into the tormenting of the wretched Malvolio, whose only culpability is that he finds himself in the wrong play, as little at home there as Shylock is in Venice.

Everything about *Twelfth Night* is unsettling, except for Feste again, and even he might be happier in a different play. Perhaps *Twelfth Night* was Shakespeare's practical joke upon his audience, turning all of them into Malvolios. Like *Measure for Measure*, the play would be perfectly rancid if it took itself seriously, which it wisely refuses to do. *Twelfth Night*, I would suggest, is a highly deliberate outrage, and should be played as such. Except for Feste, yet once more, none of its characters ought to be portrayed wholly sympathetically, not even Viola, who is herself a kind of passive zany, since who else would fall in love with the self-intoxicated Orsino?

What is most outrageous about *Twelfth Night* is Shakespeare's deliberate self-parody, which mocks his own originality at representation and thus savages representation or aesthetic imitation itself. Nothing happens in *Twelfth Night*, so there is no action to imitate anyway; *The Tempest* at least represents its opening storm, but *Twelfth Night* shrugs off its own, as if to say perfunctorily: let's get started. The shrug is palpable enough when we first meet Viola, at the start of scene 2:

> VIOLA. What country, friends, is this?
> CAPTAIN. This is Illyria, lady.
> VIOLA. And what should I do in Illyria?
> My brother he is in Elysium.
> Perchance he is not drown'd—what think you, sailors?

Illyria is a kind of madcap elysium, as we have discovered already, if we have listened intently to the superbly eloquent and quite crazy opening speech of its duke:

> If music be the food of love, play on,
> Give me excess of it; that surfeiting,
> The appetite may sicken, and so die.
> That strain again, it had a dying fall;
> O, it came o'er my ear like the sweet sound
> That breathes upon a bank of violets,
> Stealing and giving odor. Enough, no more,
> 'Tis not so sweet now as it was before.
> O spirit of love, how quick and fresh art thou,
> That notwithstanding thy capacity
> Receiveth as the sea, nought enters there,
> Of what validity and pitch soe'er,
> But falls into abatement and low price
> Even in a minute. So full of shapes is fancy
> That it alone is high fantastical.

Shakespeare himself so liked Orsino's opening conceit that he returned to it five years later in *Antony and Cleopatra* where Cleopatra, missing Antony, commands: "Give me some music; music, moody food / Of us that trade in love." Orsino, not a trader in love but a glutton for the idea of it, is rather more like John Keats than he is like Cleopatra, and his beautiful opening speech is inevitably echoed in Keats's "Ode on Melancholy." We can call Orsino a Keats gone bad, or even a little mad, returning us again to the mad behavior of nearly everyone in *Twelfth Night*. Dr. Samuel Johnson, who feared madness, liked to attribute rational design even where it seems unlikely:

> Viola seems to have formed a very deep design with very little
> premeditation: she is thrown by shipwreck on an unknown coast, hears
> that the prince is a batchelor, and resolves to supplant the lady whom he
> courts.

Anne Barton more accurately gives us a very different Viola, whose "boy's disguise operates not as a liberation but merely as a way of going underground in a difficult situation." Even that seems to me rather more rational than the play's Viola, who never does come up from underground, but, then, except for Feste, who does? Feste surely speaks the play's only wisdom: "And thus the whirligig of time brings in his revenges." "Time is a child playing draughts; the lordship is to the child" is the dark wisdom of Heracleitus. Nietzsche, with some desperation, had his Zarathustra proclaim the will's revenge against time, and in particular against time's assertion, "It was." Shakespeare's time plays with a spinning top, so that time's revenges presumably have a circular aspect. Yet Feste sings that when he was a young fool, he was taken as a toy, certainly not the way we take him now. He knows what most critics of Shakespeare will not learn, which is that *Twelfth Night* does not come to any true resolution, in which anyone has learned anything. Malvolio might be an exemplary figure if we could smuggle him into a play by Ben Jonson, but *Twelfth Night*, as John Hollander long ago noted, appears to be a deliberately anti-Jonsonian drama. No one could or should be made better by viewing or reading it.

If it has no moral coherence, where then shall its coherence be found? Orsino, baffled by the first joint appearance of the twins Viola and Sebastian, is driven to a famous outburst:

> One face, one voice, one habit, and two persons,
> A natural perspective, that is and is not!

Anne Barton glosses this as an optical illusion naturally produced, rather than given by a distorting perspective glass. Dr. Johnson gives the same reading rather more severely: "that nature has here exhibited such a show, where shadows seem realities; where that which 'is not' appears like that which 'is.'" A natural perspective is in this sense oxymoronic, unless time and nature are taken as identical, so that time's whirligig then would become the same toy as the distorting glass. If we could imagine a distorting mirror whirling in circles like a top, we would have the compound toy that *Twelfth Night* constituted for Shakespeare. Reflections in that mirror are the representations in *Twelfth Night*:

Viola, Olivia, Sir Toby and Sir Andrew, Orsino, Sebastian, and all the rest
except for Malvolio and Feste.

It is difficult for me to see Malvolio as an anti-Puritan satire, because
Sir Toby, Sir Andrew, and Maria are figures even more unattractive, by any
imaginative standards. Sir Toby is not a Falstaffian personage, no matter
what critics have said. Falstaff without preternatural wit is not Falstaff, and
Belch is just that: belch, rather than cakes and ale. Malvolio is an instance of
a character who gets away even from Shakespeare, another hobgoblin run off
with the garland of Apollo, like Shylock or like both Angelo and Barnardine in
Measure for Measure. The relations between Ben Jonson and Shakespeare must
have been lively, complex, and mutually ambivalent, and Malvolio seems to me
Shakespeare's slyest thrust at Jonsonian dramatic morality. But even as we laugh
at Malvolio's fall, a laughter akin to the savage merriment doubtless provoked
in the Elizabethan audience by the fall of Shylock, so we are made uneasy at
the fate of Malvolio and Shylock alike. Something in us rightly shudders when
we are confronted by the vision of poor Malvolio bound in the dark room. An
uncanny cognitive music emerges in the dialogue between Feste, playing Sir
Topas the curate, and "Malvolio the lunatic":

> MALVOLIO. Sir Topas, Sir Topas, good Sir Topas, go to my lady.
> CLOWN. Out, hyperbolical fiend! how vexest thou this man!
> Talkest thou nothing but of ladies?
> SIR TOBY. Well said, Master Parson.
> MALVOLIO. Sir Topas, never was man thus wrong'd. Good Sir
> Topas, do not think I am mad; they have laid me here in hideous
> darkness.
> CLOWN. Fie, thou dishonest Sathan! I call thee by the most modest
> terms, for I am one of those gentle ones that will use the devil himself
> with courtesy. Say'st thou that house is dark?
> MALVOLIO. As hell, Sir Topas.
> CLOWN. Why, it hath bay windows transparent as barricadoes, and
> the [clerestories] toward the south north are as lustrous as ebony; and
> yet complainest thou of obstruction?
> MALVOLIO. I am not mad, Sir Topas, I say to you this house is dark.
> CLOWN. Madman, thou errest. I say there is no darkness but
> ignorance, in which thou art more puzzled than the Egyptians in their
> fog.
> MALVOLIO. I say this house is as dark as ignorance, though
> ignorance were as dark as hell; and I say there was never man thus
> abus'd. I am no more mad than you are; make the trial of it in any
> constant question.
> CLOWN. What is the opinion of Pythagoras concerning wild-fowl?

MALVOLIO. That the soul of our grandam might happily inhabit a bird.

CLOWN. What think'st thou of his opinion?

MALVOLIO. I think nobly of the soul, and no way approve his opinion.

CLOWN. Fare thee well. Remain thou still in darkness. Thou shalt hold th' opinion of Pythagoras ere I will allow of thy wits, and fear to kill a woodcock lest thou dispossess the soul of thy grandam. Fare thee well.

MALVOLIO. Sir Topas, Sir Topas!

We are almost in the cosmos of *King Lear*, in Lear's wild dialogues with Edgar and Gloucester. Feste is sublimely wise, warning Malvolio against the ignorance of his Jonsonian moral pugnacity, which can make one as stupid as a woodcock. But there is a weirder cognitive warning in Feste's Pythagorean wisdom. Metempsychosis or the instability of identity is the essence of *Twelfth Night*, the lesson that none of its characters are capable of learning, except for Feste, who learns it better all the time, even as the whirligig of time brings in his revenges:

A great while ago the world begun,
With hey ho, the wind and the rain,
But that's all one, our play is done,
And we'll strive to please you every day.

TWELFTH NIGHT
IN THE TWENTY-FIRST CENTURY
ॐ

In the late twentieth and early twenty-first centuries, critics have been increasingly occupied with gender roles in *Twelfth Night*. At the same time, others have continued to examine traditional concerns, such as the roles of Malvolio and of disguise in the play.

David Bevington, in exploring how *Twelfth Night*, like many of Shakespeare's plays, "takes pains to remind us that we are in the theatre," pointed out that the Malvolio subplot mirrors the experience of watching a play. Here, as Malvolio reads the supposed letter from Olivia, the other comic characters observe, enjoy, make satiric stabs, and later report on how they appreciated the performance. Although Malvolio chastises the others for their behavior, he secretly wishes he could partake in their worldly pleasures as well.

R. W. Maslen focused on disguise, female roles, and comedy. Maslen wrote that women disguising themselves was not uncommon on the stage of Shakespeare's day. He noted that, in addition to Viola, the other females in the play also defy the usual female conventions and are "articulate" and "active." Maslen compared the powerful and determined Olivia to Queen Elizabeth. The character Maria also refuses the usual submissive female role, for she plays the part of the female prankster in carrying out the trick on Malvolio; she is smart, witty, and realistic. Even Sir Toby, who seems concerned only with how to have more fun, can appreciate her. Maslen also examined the other male characters in terms of how they see women and one another. It can be argued that violence is needed for men to prove their commitment to each other, although male friendships also seem the most open and reciprocal.

2002—David Bevington. From "Last Scene of All: Retirement from the Theatre," from *Shakespeare: An Introduction*

David Bevington (1931–) is a professor at the University of Chicago. He has written or edited more than 30 volumes on Shakespeare and his contemporaries, including *Action Is Eloquence: Shakespeare's Language of Gesture.*

Twelfth Night gives us another perspective on theatre as mimetic illusion. This play, like so many of Shakespeare's, takes pains to remind us that we are in the theatre, especially as we watch the subplot of Malvolio, Sir Toby, Sir Andrew, Maria, Fabian, and Feste. Sir Toby and his friends serve as a mirthful audience for the spectacle of Malvolio 'practising behaviour to his own shadow' with his affected mannerisms and then finding the ambiguous letter seemingly written for his benefit by the Countess Olivia but really authored by Maria. The clowns punctuate his reading of the letter, and his teasing out of it a meaning suited to his own self-love, with their satirical barbs, much like the onstage audience of 'Pyramus and Thisbe'. Afterwards, they savour the experience like an appreciative theatre audience. 'I will not give my part of this sport for a pension of thousands to be paid from the Sophy,' Fabian declares. And when they have confronted Malvolio and have heard him persist in his imagined new role as Olivia's favoured wooer, the comedians are sure they have never seen a more delicious dramatic performance. 'If this were played upon a stage, now', comments Fabian, 'I could condemn it as an improbable fiction.' The very unbelievability of Malvolio's infatuation is part of what makes it so richly enjoyable.

Malvolio is a well-suited target for satire—indeed, just about the most pointed satire that Shakespeare ever wrote, other than in *Troilus and Cressida*—because he is an enemy of merriment and hence a foe of the kind of theatre that *Twelfth Night* represents. Malvolio believes in sobriety. That is presumably why the Countess Olivia retains him as her chief steward; he helps maintain the decorum that belongs to a house in mourning for the death of the Countess's brother. He tries to suppress the noisy merrymaking of Toby, Andrew, and Feste by inquiring in acid tones if they intend to make 'an alehouse of my lady's house' with their catches and their quaffing of much liquor. He has a point, surely, for the party has lasted into the wee hours of the morning; at the end of the scene (2.3), Toby concludes that ''Tis too late to go to bed now', and so he and Andrew resolve to warm up some more imported Spanish wine. Even Maria, no friend of Malvolio's and quite devoted to Toby, tries to warn them that their caterwauling is sure to awaken Olivia and prompt her to commission Malvolio to turn them all out of doors. Toby is an impecunious relative of Olivia's and a kind of Falstaffian moocher whose continued presence in the house is a drain on Olivia's patience and her pocketbook.

Malvolio's sober-sided performance of duty would be acceptable as a counterweight to Toby and Andrew's excessive merriment were it not for the fact that Malvolio is a hypocrite. Secretly he longs for the pleasures of this world and for the authority to control others, both of which can be best attained by his becoming 'Count Malvolio'. He fantasizes about sharing Olivia's daybed and, even more than that, about putting Toby and Andrew in their place. He is vulnerable to Maria's scheme of the planted letter, supposedly written by Olivia, because Malvolio has long dreamed of being her favourite. What might otherwise be entrapment is justified, according to the satirical code governing this part of the play, by the fact that Malvolio is drawn into a 'crime' of social aspiration in which he is an active participant. Malvolio brings his downfall on himself, albeit with the eager assistance of those who hate him for being a killjoy.

Maria describes Malvolio as sometimes 'a kind of puritan'. Nowhere else does Shakespeare use this term (though Angelo's being 'precise' in *Measure for Measure* hints at a similar inclination), and seldom if ever does Shakespeare take such potent aim at a topical target. When challenged for her reasons in saying 'puritan', Maria backs off and settles for declaring that Malvolio is a 'time-pleaser' and 'affectioned ass' who is far too well 'persuaded of himself'. Still, the word 'puritan' has been thrown up for consideration. Is Malvolio a puritan? Only, it seems, to the extent that puritans too are likely to be hypocrites of this sort. Maria draws back from labelling puritans generally in this way, but issues an implicit warning: if any puritans are like Malvolio, they deserve to be outwitted and humiliated. Puritanism was a hot-button issue when Shakespeare wrote *Twelfth Night* around 1600–2. Some reformers were vociferous in their opposition to the theatre, so much so that the authorities in London (where the longing for religious reform was particularly strong) took every excuse they could find to close down the playhouses. Playwrights like Ben Jonson and Thomas Dekker were soon to spice up their plays with openly satirical sketches of puritan hypocrites, anticipating some of the points that Molière would caricature later in seventeenth-century France in his *Tartuffe*. Shakespeare, with characteristic tact, avoids any wholesale indictment of puritanism. At the same time, he sounds a warning that has a direct bearing on the world of the theatre. If Malvolio is hostile to the liberation of the human spirit that theatre can help celebrate and enhance, then there is no room for him in the concluding harmonies of this play.

Feste, as Malvolio's nemesis and opposite number, is the apostle of merriment. Olivia's presumed reason for keeping Feste around as her fool is that she wishes to be cheered up from time to time, just as she also prefers at other times to be watched over by the melancholy Malvolio. Feste's gnomic advice to Olivia, when it is his turn, is that she give up her self-willed mourning for a dead brother in favour of a full participation in life's joys; her brother is in heaven, and she is still on earth, where she has an obligation to be happy. Feste's songs celebrate the age-old notion of seizing the moment of pleasure while one is still young:

What is love? 'Tis not hereafter;
Present love hath present laughter;
    What's to come is still unsure.
In delay there lies no plenty.

Then come and kiss me, sweet and twenty;
    Youth's a stuff will not endure. (2.3.47–52)

This is the gospel of innocent hedonism that often takes the name of
Epicureanism, though Epicurus' thought is much more complex than a simple
urging to seize the moment of pleasure.

At any rate, the battle is joined between Lent and Carnival in this play,
and Carnival consistently wins the contest for our hearts. Toby's riposte
to Malvolio, when he is attempting to break up their late-night party, has
become famous, if only through the title of Somerset Maugham's novel, *Cakes
and Ale*: 'Dost thou think, because thou art virtuous, there shall be no more
cakes and ale?' The point is well taken. Malvolio has a right to be 'virtuous'
(translate here as self-righteous) himself, but he has no right to impose his
sense of moral propriety on others. If he is a moral censor, then he is too
like those who keep trying to close down the London theatres, and were also
hostile to maypoles, village fairs, and the church-ales or festive gatherings
at churches that Toby may be referring to. The only way to respond to such
would-be arbiters of personal behaviour is to lay a trap for them made out of
their own vulnerability to self-regard and a secret, hypocritical longing for the
very pleasures they would deny to others.

Malvolio is harshly handled in this unusually satirical play, so much so
that he is able to cry, with understandable feeling, 'Madam, you have done
me wrong, / Notorious wrong'. He is blaming the wrong person, mainly,
but Olivia has countenanced the imprisonment of her steward because she
has feared for his sanity. Her response to his outburst is properly gracious
and generous; using his very words, she allows that Malvolio 'hath been
most notoriously abused', and no doubt agrees with Orsino that Malvolio
should be pursued and entreated 'to a peace'. Whether Malvolio can be
placated, however, remains doubtful. His warning shot as he stalks away
is that 'I'll be revenged on the whole pack of you'. He cannot have known,
of course, that puritan reformers would close all English theatres in 1640,
at the outbreak of war between militant reformers and supporters of the
monarch and the Established Church. Still, Malvolio certainly did know that
the opponents of revelry had means at their disposal to close the theatres in
the 1600s when plague or other extraordinary conditions prevailed. *Twelfth
Night* comes close to being militant in its defence of merrymaking.
Shakespeare's theatre could not afford to let the killjoy challenge go
unanswered.

———⟨ν/ν⟩— —⟨ν/ν⟩— —⟨ν/ν⟩—

2006—R. W. Maslen. *"Twelfth Night*, Gender, and Comedy," from *Early Modern English Drama: A Critical Companion*

R. W. Maslen is a senior lecturer at the University of Glasgow. He is the author of *Shakespeare and Comedy* and *Elizabethan Fictions.*

Shakespeare's *Twelfth Night*[1] dedicates itself to discovering the sheer strangeness of attitudes to gender and sexuality in the early modern period. Many of these attitudes seem odd to us now, but Shakespeare seems to go out of his way to suggest that theater audiences in his own time should have found them equally puzzling. Characters in the play wander round in astonishment, bemused by the contradictions in the rules that are supposed to govern relationships between men and women or between persons of the same sex. Everyone is doubtful of the identities of others, doubtful of her own identity, doubtful of the path she should take in order to recover her self-assurance, and sure of only one thing: that she is in a state of heightened sexual arousal. The term "madness" haunts the play, but where this word usually connotes behavior or a state of mind that fails to conform with the social expectations of a dominant culture, in Shakespeare's imaginary city of Illyria the condition is so prevalent that it suggests a world that has lost its balance altogether, deprived of any agreed technique for measuring its conflicting cultural values.

In this comedy, women are mistaken for men, men mistaken for women disguised as men, and definitions of manhood and womanhood themselves called into question. Confusions over identity have been the staple fare of comedy since classical times, when the plays of Plautus and Terence were improbably crowded with twins, doppelgängers, and lost family members (Plautus's comedy *Menaechmi*, in particular, has obvious affinities with *Twelfth Night*). Sixteenth-century Italian comedies by Ariosto and others took up the theme of confusion where the classical comedy-writers left off. But it was in Elizabethan England, and especially in Shakespearean comedy, that comic confusion really began to focus on issues of gender. No body of dramatic work before or since Shakespeare's has lent itself to a more thorough investigation of the uncertainties that surround cultural constructions of masculinity, femininity, and erotic attraction of all kinds. This is one reason why his comedies continue to hold the stage today, in another age when gender and sexuality have come under obsessive scrutiny.

It's hardly surprising that Shakespeare took gender as the subject of his comedies, since comedy itself was linked with sexual and social transgression in the early modern period. With the construction of the first purpose-built

playhouses in London during the 1570s, polemical attacks on the theater—
which had occurred sporadically since ancient times—reached unprecedented
levels; and these attacks repeatedly characterized comedy as a seed-bed for
sexual depravity, capable of feminizing men, turning women into voracious
sexual predators, and precipitating the breakdown of the entire social hierarchy
in the process.[2] As the antitheatrical polemicist Stephen Gosson puts it, "The
grounde worke of Commedies, is love, cosenedge, flatterie, bawderie, [and] slye
conveighance of whordome."[3] The devil let them loose in London, says Gosson,
as a follow-up to the "wanton Italian bookes" with which he planned to corrupt
the plain minds of ordinary English people (Kinney 153). Like these books,
comedies assail their recipients with an overwhelming excess of sensory stimuli:
"straunge consortes of melody, to tickle the eare; costly apparel, to flatter the
sight; effeminate gesture, to ravish the sence; and wanton speache, to whet desire
to inordinate lust" (Kinney 89). And the efficacy of this method of corruption
is evident from the behavior of playhouse audiences, which constitutes a "right
Comedie" in itself (Kinney 92): "such wanton gestures, such bawdie speaches,
such laughing and fleering, such kissing and bussing, such clipping and culling,
Suche winckinge and glancinge of wanton eyes, and the like [. . .] as is wonderfull
to beholde."[4] Language like this, in which playhouses become brothels and
comedies degenerate into orgies, occurs repeatedly in sermons, tracts, and official
documents throughout Shakespeare's lifetime, and may well have cast its shadow
over his comic explorations of relations between the sexes, helping to render
them as complex and troubling as they are witty. Putting pen to paper to write a
comedy was to stir up a hornet's nest of controversial connections in Elizabethan
England; indeed, from one point of view, it was to make a pact with the devil
himself. And the most controversial connections of all related to gender.

   Twelfth Night isn't directly based on a "wanton Italian booke," as many of
Shakespeare's comedies are. Its plot comes from a short story, "Apolonius and
Silla" (1581), by the English writer Barnaby Rich—though the story derives
ultimately from *Gl'ingannati*, one of the "baudie Comedies in [. . .] Italian"
that Gosson tells us have been "throughly ransackt to furnish the Playe houses
in London" (Kinney 169). But whatever its sources, *Twelfth Night* certainly
demonstrates Shakespeare's intense awareness of the anticomic sentiment
prevalent among some Londoners. When the heroine Viola disguises herself
as a boy and attracts the amorous attentions of a noblewoman, she remarks,
using a misogynistic vocabulary that might have been drawn from one of the
antitheatrical pamphlets: "Disguise, I see thou art a wickedness / Wherein
the pregnant enemy does much" (2.2.25–26). Later she bandies words with
Feste the clown and goes on to meditate on the tact required by a professional
comedian like Feste if he is to avoid getting into trouble for his witticisms: "He
must observe their mood on whom he jests, / The quality of persons, and the
time [. . .] This is a practice / As full of labor as a wise man's art" (3.1.55–59).

And in the final act of the play both jesting and disguise turn sour. The victim of a practical joke in which the disguised Feste takes part, a would-be lover and social climber called Malvolio, finds himself in prison, suspected of being possessed by "the pregnant enemy"—that is, the devil—and accused of heresy. In an age when doctors prescribed whipping as a treatment for madness, and when heresy was punishable by burning, a prank with an outcome like this was more painful than amusing. Malvolio's fate may have invoked in the audience's minds the link between theater and devilry that had been consolidated by polemicists like Gosson, whose texts were associated with the radical Protestant movement known as Puritanism. Malvolio himself is described as "a kind of puritan" (2.3.125), and his punishment could be seen as comedy's symbolic revenge on its enemies. But the revenge serves also to confirm the polemicists' view that playing with the fire of sexual passions, as Feste and his fellow pranksters do, may have profoundly serious consequences, for the players as well as their victims.

All the same, without some bending of the social and literary conventions that governed gender there could have been no comedies in Shakespeare's time—and certainly no romantic comedies. Contemporary custom dictated that the only virtues women could manifest were passive ones such as sexual self-restraint and verbal and behavioral submissiveness. Women below a certain class who failed to manifest these qualities were given cruel labels—shrew, quean, drab, scold, whore—and ruthlessly punished, with such aggressive forms of torture and public humiliation as the bridle and the ducking stool. At the same time, England had been ruled by women since 1553, and submissiveness was hardly a quality suited to a ruler. Moreover, self-restraint and submissiveness were hardly the most scintillating ingredients out of which to build a good story, let alone a drama. If a woman is supposed to be passive and tongue-tied, what becomes of the processes of courtship that are fundamental to romance? Nobody wanted silent women in a story or a play; even Ben Jonson's comedy *Epicene, or The Silent Woman* has a boy as its heroine, who is only masquerading as the mute wife of the title. So dramatists had to find ingenious ways of having women speak without making them look immodest.

Disguise was an obvious technique: in stories as well as plays women are always donning male disguises to pursue the men they fancy. Barnaby Rich's "Apolonius and Silla" is one such story; and Viola forms part of a line of young girls disguised as boys who populate Shakespeare's plays, from Julia in *The Two Gentlemen of Verona* to Imogen in *Cymbeline*. But in *Twelfth Night* there are also two women who don't feel the need to dress up as men in order to be articulate or active. One is the Countess Olivia, an Elizabeth figure who insists on getting what she wants regardless of custom and who freely exploits all the verbal resources available to women of the ruling classes. The other is Olivia's waiting woman Maria, who represents a third class of active and articulate women: the female trickster, whose exploits were celebrated in the so-called jest-books or collections of comic anecdotes that remained hugely popular from the beginning of the sixteenth century until the time of the modern novel. Maria's wit is of the kind described by John Lyly in his proto-novel *Euphues and His England* (1580): "It is wit that allureth, when every word shall have his weight, when nothing shall proceed but it shall either savour of a sharp conceit or a secret conclusion."[5] Olivia's kinsman Sir Toby Belch clearly agrees with Lyly, since he marries Maria for her wit at the end of the play.

The trio of articulate women who dominate *Twelfth Night* transform the conventional Elizabethan ideal of a woman—Penelope the wife of Odysseus, Virginia the murdered virgin, Patient Griselda, and the rest—into an elusive fantasy that is freely exploited by women for their own ends. Olivia, for instance, plays the part of a chaste, noncommunicative woman in her efforts to avoid the unwelcome attentions of Orsino, duke of Illyria. Since she has sworn, we learn, to marry no man "above her degree, neither in estate, years, nor wit" (1.3.90–91), she chooses to pose as a virginal recluse at the beginning of the play, mourning the death of her brother in solitude for seven years—time enough, one would have thought, to deter even an obsessive admirer like the duke. Viola, too, invokes the ideal chaste and silent woman, after she has disguised herself as the boy Cesario. Cesario enters the service of Duke Orsino, then falls in love with him; and at one point the disguised page tells his master the story of a wordless woman, as a means of hinting at the nature of his own love for the duke. Cesario had a sister, he explains, who fell in love, but who followed the prescriptions of contemporary conduct manuals that enjoined absolute modesty on women:

> She never told her love,
> But let concealment, like a worm i' th' bud,
> Feed on her damask cheek. She pined in thought,
> And with a green and yellow melancholy
> She sat like patience on a monument,
> Smiling at grief. (2.4.109–14)

The "history" or story of this girl, Cesario explains, is nothing but a "blank" (2.4.109). She was constrained, by the restrictive nature of the ideal she imitated, to waste away to nothing without taking part in any kind of narrative. Olivia and Viola, by contrast, are perfectly aware that the ideal is only one of the many fantasies that throng the play. Their confidence that time will resolve their difficulties—Olivia's imposition of a deadline on her mourning, Viola's famous observation, when she learns that Olivia loves her, that "time [. . .] must untangle this, not I" (2.2.38)—may perhaps spring from the fact that they have written themselves into a very different kind of narrative than the blank history of Cesario's sister. Elizabethan fiction—on the page or on the stage—was rich in alternative plots involving women, and most women in Shakespeare's comedies are thoroughly familiar with these plots, choosing between them at will as occasion demands.

The men in this play have their own fantastic versions of the ideal woman, and she too has little in common with the "real" women of flesh and blood we see on stage. (The exception is Sir Toby, who has little patience for the ideal invoked by his niece Olivia and who frankly admires the boldness and wit of her maid, Maria.) The greatest fantasist of them all is the most powerful figure in the play, Duke Orsino. In the first scene, Orsino imagines Olivia's grief as a guarantee of her devotion to him at some fancied future time when she will accept him as her lover:

> O, she that hath a heart of that fine frame
> To pay this debt of love but to a brother,
> How will she love when the rich golden shaft
> Hath killed the flock of all affections else
> That live in her—when liver, brain, and heart,
> These sovereign thrones, are all supplied, and filled,
> Her sweet perfections with one self king! (1.1.32–38)

Clearly the duke has no interest in Olivia's actual thoughts and feelings; his celebrated opening speech is all about his own experience of desire, and Olivia is not even mentioned in it. Instead he is obsessed with a vision of the absolute monarchic power he will wield over the countess when he has won her "liver, brain, and heart," transforming her into an animate receptacle for his own image. In this he resembles Olivia's steward Malvolio, whose fantasies of marrying his mistress focus exclusively on the pleasure he will take in ruling her household while Olivia lies asleep in postcoital exhaustion (2.5.39ff.). The heterosexual fantasies of Shakespeare's men consistently consign women to marginality; so we should hardly be surprised that it's a woman, Viola—disguised as the boy Cesario and sent by Orsino to woo Olivia for him—who delivers the most convincing courtship speech in the play. Asked by Olivia what he would do if he were her lover, Cesario replies that he would set up camp at her gate and fix the world's attention on her by repeatedly calling her name (1.5.235–37). This famous picture of determined wooing may be just another far-fetched fantasy, but at least it's one with *both* Olivia *and* her suitor at the heart of it.

Orsino's view of women, by contrast, is both generalized and inconsistent. In conversation with Cesario, he begins by saying that men are more fickle than women ("Our fancies are more giddy and unfirm, / More longing, wavering, sooner lost and worn, / Than women's are," 2.4.32–34) and ends by claiming precisely the opposite—that women are incapable of loving with equal force to men:

> There is no woman's sides
> Can bide the beating of so strong a passion
> As love doth give my heart; no woman's heart
> So big to hold so much. They lack retention.
> Alas, their love may be called appetite,
> No motion of the liver, but the palate,
> That suffer surfeit, cloyment, and revolt.
> But mine is all as hungry as the sea,
> And can digest as much. Make no compare
> Between that love a woman can bear me
> And that I owe a woman. (2.4.91–101)

Orsino has clearly based this view of women on himself—in other words, it serves only to confirm his narcissism. He started the play, after all, by describing his own love as an "appetite" capable of devouring endless quantities (of sex or of women? He doesn't say which) without being satisfied (1.1.1–15). In that opening speech, his appetite suffers "cloyment, and revolt" after he has listened to romantic music for too long; and this sense of "cloyment" anticipates, one presumes, the devaluation Olivia would suffer in his eyes if once she gave him unrestricted access to her body. Orsino's view of women suggests, in fact, that there is little hope of his achieving a satisfactory long-term relationship with any woman at all. It's in response to his fantastic account of women's inability to love that Viola/Cesario tells him the story of his/her imaginary sister who sat "like Patience on a monument / Smiling at grief." The sister's selflessness is as extreme as Orsino's self-obsession, and her immobility anticipates the likely outcome of any encounter between conventional male and female versions of femininity. Clearly, interaction between the genders depends on the discovery of a third way, to which the boy/girl Viola/Cesario offers a beguiling key.

In the meantime, however, Viola has the unpleasant experience of learning firsthand about men's fantasies of ideal manhood. Throughout Shakespeare's works men define their masculinity through violence, as they often seem to have done in the streets of Elizabethan London (few men did not carry a weapon, and many had no compunction about using these weapons on the slightest provocation).[6] One need only think of Shakespeare's three plays with lovers in their titles—*Romeo and Juliet*, *Troilus and Cressida*, *Antony and Cleopatra*—to see how this association of masculinity with violence can damage men's relationships with women. In *Twelfth Night*, as in these three plays, aggressive manliness is the subject of sometimes painful parody. One of Olivia's would-be suitors, Sir Andrew Aguecheek, is the comic antithesis of a man's man: as Maria points out, "he's a great quarreller, and but that he hath the gift of a coward to allay the gust he hath in quarrelling, 'tis thought among the prudent he would quickly have the gift of a grave" (1.3.25–27). One of the pranks planned by Sir Toby Belch is to expose Sir Andrew's lack of manhood by pitting him in battle against an equally "unmanly" foe, the boy Cesario, whom Sir Toby identifies as failing to conform with the ideal of aggressive masculinity. This prank, like the trick played on Malvolio, turns sour when Sir Andrew confronts first the "Notable pirate" Antonio (5.1.63) and later Viola's brother Sebastian, both of whom are thoroughly "manly" in their willingness to dish out violence. As a result, Sir Andrew and Sir Toby end the play with broken heads. But before this, Cesario/Viola discovers the terrifying pressure exerted on young men by their elders, either to comply with the masculine ideal themselves or else to serve as the guarantor of its embodiment in other men. On being told of Sir Andrew's determination to fight with him, Cesario says: "I have heard of some kind of men that put quarrels purposely on others, to taste their valour. Belike this is a man of that quirk" (3.4.216–18). Sir Toby insists this is not the case, and that Sir Andrew has a genuine grievance against him; but the knight then belies his own words by telling Cesario to strip his phallic sword "quite naked" (3.4.223). Clearly, the abortive combat Sir Toby sets up between the unmanly man Sir Andrew and the womanly boy Cesario is no more than an elaborate comparison of penises. And his own eager participation in the fight that *does* break out— though neither Sir Andrew nor Cesario is involved in it—confirms that the real point of the competition is to prove Sir Toby's own superior manhood rather than to derogate from theirs.

Besides a willingness to resort to violence, the male ideal of masculinity includes an unwavering loyalty to male friends. In *Twelfth Night*, as in many of Shakespeare's plays, this loyalty between men seems inextricably linked with male aggression. Antonio shows his love for Sebastian by twice putting his own life at risk: first following him into Illyria despite the fact that he has "many enemies in Orsino's court" (2.1.39); then substituting himself for the boy in a sword-fight, just as Mercutio substitutes himself for Romeo, with fatal consequences, in Shakespeare's early tragedy. It would seem that loyalty to other men is as much a test of manliness as the intensity of one's passion for combat. When Antonio thinks Sebastian has betrayed him, he stops calling him "sir" and "young gentleman" (3.4.277) and brands him instead an "idol" (3.4.330), an "empty trunk" (3.4.335), a "thing" (5.1.83), a source of "witchcraft" (5.1.70)—terms that strip Sebastian of his gender. Conversely, Sir Andrew's lack of manliness fully justifies Sir Toby in the contempt he shows for his friendship—or so the bibulous knight believes. When Fabian observes to Sir Toby that Andrew is "a dear manikin to you," Sir Toby replies that "I have been dear to him, lad, some two thousand strong or so," converting friendship into exploitation with a flippant pun (3.2.45–47). Sir Toby dupes Sir Andrew of his cash as freely as he tricks him into exposing his cowardice; and in the final act he annuls their friendship with a single vitriolic outburst: "Will *you* help—an ass-head, and a coxcomb, and a knave; a thin-faced knave, a gull?" (5.1.198–99). By virtue of his physical and intellectual frailty, Sir Andrew is a manikin—a little man or a puppet—to be played with and discarded at will by "manly" men like Sir Toby. Male relationships with men, it would seem, are as fragile and fraught with fantasies as are male relationships with women.

Nevertheless, at its best, friendship with other men seems to be the most open, intimate, and reciprocal form of relationship available to men in *Twelfth Night*. Antonio's love for Sebastian is as selfless as the love of Cesario's imaginary sister for an unknown man, and a good deal more active. And in her male disguise as Cesario, Viola gets closer to Orsino than she could ever have done as a woman. After only three days together Orsino is able to tell his new servant, "Thou know'st no less but all. I have unclasped / To thee the book even of my secret soul" (1.4.12–13). This free disclosure of secrets demonstrates that despite their social disparity, in Orsino's eyes Cesario has become what Elizabethan manuals on male friendship describe as a "second self," "another I," a kind of twin of the duke's, as closely bound to him as Viola is to her twin brother. That Orsino sees Cesario in this way is confirmed by his willingness to employ the boy as his substitute in the courtship of Olivia. The mutuality of their affection reveals itself most strikingly in the final act, when Cesario gets the chance to sacrifice his life for his master just as Antonio sacrificed his safety for Sebastian's. On learning that Olivia has fallen in love with Cesario, Orsino promptly resorts to the usual male solution of violence: "I'll sacrifice the lamb that I do love," he declares (5.1.126)—that is, he will kill Cesario to spite Olivia. And the boy at once professes himself willing to die "a thousand deaths" to satisfy Orsino (5.1.129). This is the high point of his/her relationship with the duke. No woman but Viola in Shakespeare's plays gets such an opportunity to achieve, as a man, the ultimate consummation of an Elizabethan man's love for another man, which is to lay down his life for his friend. And no other character, male or female, goes to her death more "jocund, apt, and willingly" than she does here (5.1.128), following him off stage as eagerly as if to a marriage bed.

In Elizabethan culture there was theoretically no place for an erotic relationship between men. The sin of sodomy—which encompassed a range of forbidden sexual activities, among them the penetration of an underaged boy by an older man[7]—was punishable by death, like heresy. Yet there is ample evidence that many of these activities went on, undeterred by the draconian measures taken against them. The boy Cesario's declaration of his willingness to die for Orsino is on one level a public announcement of his willingness to sleep with him: for the Elizabethans, the verb "to die" could also mean "to achieve orgasm." But in Shakespeare's Illyria, unlike Elizabethan London, his wish may legitimately be granted because, of course, Cesario is a woman in disguise. His situation as neither man nor woman, but a hybrid "monster" composed of both (2.2.32), exempts him from the restrictions imposed on men and women, either by law or by the ideal forms of behavior expected of either sex.

The advantages of Cesario/Viola's double gender become obvious soon after Orsino threatens to kill him. Olivia intervenes to save the boy's life, announcing that she has married him (in fact she has married Viola's brother Sebastian), which places him under the protection of Illyrian law. At once the duke turns on Cesario with a verbal attack that seems hardly less vicious than his earlier threat to murder him: "O thou dissembling cub" (5.1.160). But dissembling is not really the issue here; it is distrust. Orsino thinks that the boy has betrayed his trust in him, thus compromising their bond of mutual friendship, which like marriage may be described as "A contract of eternal bond of love" (5.1.152). The misunderstanding is resolved when Sebastian turns up and Cesario/Viola reveals her "true" sex, thus finally unclasping to Orsino the "book" of her "secret soul." At this point the duke discovers that Viola has been dissembling not her love for him but her gender; and *this* kind of deceit he seems to find wholly admirable. He marries her, he says, for "your service done [. . .] So much against the mettle of your sex" (5.1.310–11)—as if it's her ability *not* to be the ideal passive woman he has so far imagined for himself that most delights him about her. In token of this delight, he continues to call her "Cesario" long after he has learned her identity (5.1.372–73), thus preserving our sense of their relationship as a love affair between men as well as between man and woman. And it's in male clothing that Viola leaves the stage with Orsino to begin married life at the end of the play. Her clothes seem to promise that their marriage will be an egalitarian one, based not on mastery and control—as are men's fantasies about women—but on mutual confidence and respect, like the Elizabethan ideal of same-sex friendship. When Orsino discharges Cesario from his service ("Your master quits you"), he installs Viola as "Your master's mistress," his "fancy's queen"—phrases that may be taken to imply that authority will be shared more or less equally between them after marriage (5.1.310–14, 375). ("Master" and "mistress" are terms used throughout the play for men and women in positions of authority: Feste, for instance, tells Viola "I would be sorry, sir, but the fool should be as oft with your master as with my mistress," 3.1.34–35.) In view of the ideals of femininity that have prevailed up to this point, it's hard to imagine Orsino saying these things with such conviction to a woman dressed in ordinary clothes.

The phrase "Your master's mistress" recalls the most explicitly homoerotic poem written by Shakespeare, Sonnet 20. The poem celebrates the beauty of a boy loved by the sonneteer, whose face combines the best qualities conventionally assigned to both sexes: "A woman's face with nature's own hand painted, / Hast thou, the master-mistress of my passion." This suggests, among other things, that Shakespeare could imagine a space where the "masculine" and the "feminine" are fused, and that for him the mind and body of an adolescent boy could constitute such a space. Oscar Wilde supposed that the boy addressed in Shakespeare's sonnets could have been an actor,[8] and there's something profoundly satisfying about the supposition. Boy actors represented a way out of an artistic dilemma created by Elizabethan views on women. Since women were not allowed to perform on the public stage, boys took the female roles in plays. And in doing so they drew attention to the possibility that gender itself might be a matter of performance. As the antitheatrical polemicists pointed out, men could be, or could become, effeminate, and the boy actor's craft showed just how easy it was to accomplish this particular form of gender-bending. Shakespeare's "master-mistress" in the sonnets, and Viola/Cesario in *Twelfth Night*, are bodies in transit through time, altering as they move and attracting men and women alike. In them fantasies of maleness and femaleness intersect and mingle, making possible all sorts of relationships—sexual and nonsexual—that were not officially sanctioned within Elizabethan culture. Hence the polemicists' profound unease about the effect of comedy on its audiences. Hence, too, Wilde's vision of the sonnets as commemorating a boy who gave life to Shakespeare's lines on stage: a vision that itself gave life to new ways of thinking about literature and sexuality in the twentieth century, though not before Wilde himself had been destroyed by late Victorian homophobia.

It is Duke Orsino who first comments on the fusion of gender attributes in Cesario, the page who is also both a woman and a boy actor:

> For they shall yet belie thy happy years
> That say thou art a man. Diana's lip
> Is not more smooth and rubious; thy small pipe
> Is as the maiden's organ, shrill and sound,
> And all is semblative a woman's part. (1.4.29–33)

Malvolio notices it, too, when he says that Cesario stands at a cusp between two stages of male development: "Not yet old enough for a man, nor young enough for a boy [. . .] 'tis with him in standing water, between boy and man [. . .] one would think his mother's milk were scarce out of him" (1.5.139–44). As Malvolio observes, a boy is closer to his mother than most grown men are. And at the end of the play this particular boy is revealed to be a woman, whose performance as the opposite gender has fooled everyone she met in the course of the action. What Viola's achievement as an actor suggests—however improbably—is that nobody need be fixed or trapped in a single mode of being. The comedy begins in stalemate, with Olivia and Orsino locked in the behavior prescribed by their culture for lovers of their class and gender, and with no immediate prospect of escape from their entrapment. When Viola first resolves to enter Orsino's service she plans to present herself to him as a eunuch (1.2.52)—a boy whose sexual development has been artificially arrested by castration, a suitable servant for a man in a state of terminal sexual frustration. But Orsino's and Malvolio's descriptions of Cesario indicate their recognition that he is no eunuch, but an adolescent in the process of growing to sexual maturity, whose mere presence serves as an awakening call to desire for the transfixed characters in the play. Neither male nor female, neither man nor boy, and in the end neither servant nor master, he is a kind of riddle, a pun or double entendre in human form, testifying to the power of comedy as a means of disrupting settled notions and complicating illusory certainties.

The play as a whole is a paean to change, as its full title suggests. The phrase *Twelfth Night* pays homage to a crucial moment of transition in the Elizabethan calendar: the last day of the Christmas festivities, when the celebrations are at their most hilarious as they draw to a close, and when anyone can be "What You Will." *Twelfth Night* extends this moment of transition over many days, and Viola is its presiding spirit, embodying the transitions that are always in process in the human body and mind. At various points in the play, the changes undergone by Viola and her companions look set to be terrible ones, bringing entrapment and death instead of the new life promised by Viola's youth. Melancholy intervenes on many occasions, especially in the songs of the aging clown Feste, which testify to the sorrow that terminates so many transactions between men and women and to the onset of old age and death as the necessary counterweight for the onset of sexual maturity. Even the end of the play is suffused with melancholy, as Malvolio runs off threatening revenge "on the whole pack of you" (5.1.365) and Feste sings his final song alone on stage. But the action as a whole takes place in what Orsino calls a "golden time" (5.1.369)—a time of hope and laughter, like the festival of Christmas. And it's a continuation of this golden time that's predicted in the final scene, when three sets of male/female couples prepare to make a "solemn combination [. . .] Of our dear souls" (5.1.370–71). The play's unsettling emphasis on time, change, and confusion ensures that these final weddings are by no means a return to the "normality" of Elizabethan England, as critics have often described them. Instead, the play makes it possible to believe that there is no such thing as a stable normality where gender is concerned, either in Elizabethan times or in our own.

NOTES

1. All quotations from the play are taken from *The Norton Shakespeare*, ed. Stephen Greenblatt et al. (New York: Norton, 1997).

2. For an account of Elizabethan attacks on the theater, see Jonas A. Barish, *The Antitheatrical Prejudice* (Berkeley: U of California P, 1981). The principal attacks and defenses of the theater are reproduced in E. K. Chambers, *The Elizabethan Stage*, 4 vols. (Oxford: Clarendon P, 1923) esp. vol. 4, Appendix C ("Documents of Criticism") 184ff., and Appendix D ("Documents of Control") 259ff.

3. See Arthur F. Kinney, ed., *Markets of Bawdrie: The Dramatic Criticism of Stephen Gosson* (Salzburg: Universität Salzburg, 1974) 160.

4. Philip Stubbes, *The Anatomie of Abuses* (1583, reprinted 1595), cited in Chambers 4.223.

5. See John Lyly, *Euphues: The Anatomy of Wit* and *Euphues and His England*, ed. Leah Scragg (Manchester: Manchester UP, 2003) 207.

6. See William Harrison, *The Description of England*, ed. Georges Edelen (New York: Dover Publications, 1994) 237–38.

7. See Bruce R. Smith, *Shakespeare and Masculinity* (Oxford: Oxford UP, 2000) 122–26.

8. See Oscar Wilde, "The Portrait of Mr. W.H.," *The Works of Oscar Wilde*, ed. G. F. Maine (London: Magpie Books, 1992) 1089–112.

BIBLIOGRAPHY

&

Archer, William. "'Twelfth Night' at the Lyceum," from *Macmillan's Magazine* 50, no. 298 (August 1884): pp. 271–279.

Berry, Ralph. "The Season of *Twelfth Night*," from *New York Literary Forum* 1 (1978): pp. 139–149.

———. "*Twelfth Night*: The Experience of the Audience," from *Shakespeare Survey* 34 (1981): pp. 121–130.

Bradbrook, M. C. *The Growth and Structure of Elizabethan Comedy* (London: Chatto and Windus, 1962).

Brown, John R. *Shakespeare and His Comedies* (London: Methuen, 1957).

Charlton, H. B. *Shakespearian Comedy* (London: Methuen, 1949).

Charney, Maurice. "Comic Premises of *Twelfth Night*," from *New York Literary Forum* 1 (1978): pp. 151–165.

Clayton, Tom, Susan Brock, and Vincente Forès, eds. *Shakespeare and the Mediterranean* (Newark, Del.: University of Delaware Press, 2004).

Crane, Milton. "*Twelfth Night* and Shakespearian Comedy," from *Shakespeare Quarterly* 6 (1955): pp. 1–8.

Dean, Paul. "'Nothing That Is So Is So': *Twelfth Night* and Transubstantiation," from *Literature and Theology* 17, no. 3 (September 2003): pp. 281–297.

Draper, John W. *The* Twelfth Night *of Shakespeare's Audience* (Stanford, Calif.: Stanford University Press, 1950).

Eagleton, Terence. "Language and Reality in *Twelfth Night*," from *Critical Quarterly* 9 (1967): pp. 217–228.

Evans, Bertrand. *Shakespeare's Comedies* (Oxford: Clarendon, 1960).

Frye, Northrop. "Characterization in Shakespearian Comedy," from *Shakespeare Quarterly* 4 (1953): pp. 271–277.

Giese, Loreen L. "Malvolio's Yellow Stockings: Coding Illicit Sexuality in Early Modern London," from *Medieval and Renaissance Drama in England: An Annual Gathering of Research, Criticism and Reviews* 19 (2006): pp. 235–246.

Gregson, J. M. *Shakespeare:* Twelfth Night (London: Edward Arnold, 1980).

Hardy, Barbara. *Notes on English Literature:* Twelfth Night (Oxford, England: Basil Blackwell and Mott, 1962).

Hobgood, Allison. *"Twelfth Night*'s 'Notorious Abuse' of Malvolio: Shame, Humorality, and Early Modern Spectatorship," from *Shakespeare Bulletin* 24, no. 3 (Fall 2006): pp. 1–22.

Hotson, Leslie. *The First Night of* Twelfth Night (New York: Macmillan, 1954).

Jenkins, Harold. "Shakespeare's *Twelfth Night*," from *Rice Institute Pamphlet* 45 (1959): pp. 19–42.

Jones, G. P. "Malvolio Flouted and Abused," from *English Language Notes* 42, no. 1 (September 2004): pp. 20–26.

Kelsey, Lin. "'Many Sorts of Music': Musical Genre in *Twelfth Night* and *The Tempest*," from *John Donne Journal* 25 (2006): pp. 129–181.

King, Walter, ed. *Twentieth-Century Interpretations of* Twelfth Night: *A Collection of Critical Essays* (Englewood Cliffs, N.J.: Prentice-Hall, 1968).

Leech, Clifford. Twelfth Night *and Shakespearean Comedy* (Toronto: University of Toronto Press, 1965).

Leggatt, Alexander. *Shakespeare's Comedy of Love* (London: Methuen, 1974).

Mahood, Molly Maureen, ed. *Twelfth Night* (Harmondsworth, England: Penguin Books, 1968).

Marciano, Lisa. "The Serious Comedy of *Twelfth Night*: Dark Didacticism in Illyria," from *Renascence* 56, no. 1 (Fall 2003): pp. 3–19.

McDonald, Russ. *Shakespeare and the Arts of Language* (New York: Oxford University Press, 2001).

Muir, Kenneth, ed. *Shakespeare: The Comedies* (Englewood Cliffs, N.J.: Prentice-Hall, 1965).

Palmer, D. J. Twelfth Night: *A Casebook* (New York: Macmillan, 1972).

Palmer, D., and M. Bradbury, eds. *Shakespearean Comedy* (London: Edward Arnold, 1972).

Pettet, E. C. *Shakespeare and the Romance Tradition* (London: Staples Press, 1950).

Potter, Lois. Twelfth Night: *Text and Performance* (Houndmills, England: Macmillan, 1985).

Schalkwyk, David. "Love and Service in *Twelfth Night* and the Sonnets," from *Shakespeare Quarterly* 56, no. 1 (Spring 2005): pp. 76–100.

Siegel, Paul N. "Malvolio: Comic Puritan Automaton," from *New York Literary Forum* 5–6 (1980): pp. 217–230.

Stoll, E. E. *Shakespeare and Other Masters* (Cambridge: Harvard University Press, 1940).

Styan, J. I. *The Shakespeare Revolution: Criticism and Performance in the Twentieth Century* (Cambridge: Cambridge University Press, 1977).

Swinden, Patrick. *An Introduction to Shakespeare's Comedies* (London: Macmillan, 1973).

Wells, Stanley, ed. Twelfth Night: *Critical Essays* (New York: Garland, 1986).

Wilson, John Dover. *Shakespeare's Happy Comedies* (Evanston, Ill.: Northwestern University Press, 1962).

Woodbridge, Linda. "'Fire in Your Heart and Brimstone in Your Liver': Towards an Unsaturnalian *Twelfth Night*," from *The Southern Review* 17 (1984): pp. 270–291.

ACKNOWLEDGMENTS

Twentieth Century

Maurice Hewlett, "Introduction to *Twelfth Night*," from *The Complete Works of William Shakespeare*, edited by Sidney Lee, vol. 4 (Boston and New York: Jefferson Press, 1907), pp. ix–xxiv. © 1907 by the University Press.

Morris P. Tilley, "The Organic Unity of *Twelfth Night*," from *PMLA* 29, no. 4 (1914), pp. 550–566. © 1914 by the Modern Language Association.

William Winter, "Character of Viola," from *Shakespeare on the Stage*, second series (New York: Moffat, Yard, and Company, 1915), pp. 35–39. © 1915 by William Winter.

A. C. Bradley, "Feste the Jester," from *A Book of Homage to Shakespeare*, edited by Israel Gollancz (London: Oxford University Press, 1916), pp. 164–169.

J. B. Priestley, "The Illyrians," from *The English Comic Characters* (New York: Dodd, Mead, and Company, 1925), pp. 43–68.

G. Wilson Knight, "The Romantic Comedies," from *The Shakespearian Tempest* (Oxford: Oxford University Press, 1932). Reprinted in *G. Wilson Knight Collected Works*, vol. 2, *The Shakespearian Tempest* (London and New York: Routledge, 2002), pp. 121–127.

Harold C. Goddard, "*Twelfth Night*," from *The Meaning of Shakespeare* (Chicago and London: University of Chicago Press, 1951), pp. 294–306. © 1951 by the University of Chicago.

Leo Salingar, "The Design of *Twelfth Night*," from *Shakespeare Quarterly* 9, no. 2 (Spring 1958): pp. 117–139. © Folger Shakespeare Library. Reprinted with permission of The Johns Hopkins University Press.

C. L. Barber, "Testing Courtesy and Humanity in *Twelfth Night*," from *Shakespeare's Festive Comedy* (Princeton, N.J.: Princeton University Press, 1959), pp. 240–261. © 1959 Princeton University Press, 1987 renewed PUP. Reprinted by permission of Princeton University Press.

Jan Kott, "Shakespeare's Bitter Arcadia (part III)," from *Shakespeare Our Contemporary*, translated by Boleslaw Taborski, copyright © 1964 by Panstwowe Wydawnictwo Naukowe and Doubleday, a division of Random

Twenty-first Century

David Bevington, "Last Scene of All: Retirement from the Theatre," from *Shakespeare: An Introduction* (Oxford: Blackwell Publishing, 2002), pp. 226–230. © 2002 by David Bevington.

R. W. Maslen, "*Twelfth Night*, Gender, and Comedy," from *Early Modern English Drama: A Critical Companion,* edited by Garrett A. Sullivan, Jr.; Patrick Cheney; and Andrew Hadfield (New York and Oxford: Oxford University Press, 2006), pp. 130–139. © 2006 by Oxford University Press. By permission of Oxford University Press, Inc.

INDEX

❧